Designing for Democracy

Oxford Studies in Digital Politics

Series Editor: Andrew Chadwick, Professor of Political Communication in the Centre for Research in Communication and Culture and the Department of Social Sciences, Loughborough University

Apostles of Certainty: Data Journalism and the Politics of Doubt
C.W. Anderson

Using Technology, Building Democracy: Digital Campaigning and the Construction of Citizenship
Jessica Baldwin-Philippi

Expect Us: Online Communities and Political Mobilization
Jessica L. Beyer

If . . . Then: Algorithmic Power and Politics
Taina Bucher

The Hybrid Media System: Politics and Power
Andrew Chadwick

The Only Constant Is Change: Technology, Political Communication, and Innovation Over Time
Ben Epstein

Tweeting to Power: The Social Media Revolution in American Politics
Jason Gainous and Kevin M. Wagner

When the Nerds Go Marching In: How Digital Technology Moved from the Margins to the Mainstream of Political Campaigns
Rachel K. Gibson

Risk and Hyperconnectivity: Media and Memories of Neoliberalism
Andrew Hoskins and John Tulloch

Democracy's Fourth Wave?: Digital Media and the Arab Spring
Philip N. Howard and Muzammil M. Hussain

The Digital Origins of Dictatorship and Democracy: Information Technology and Political Islam
Philip N. Howard

Analytic Activism: Digital Listening and the New Political Strategy
David Karpf

The MoveOn Effect: The Unexpected Transformation of American Political Advocacy
David Karpf

Prototype Politics: Technology-Intensive Campaigning and the Data of Democracy
Daniel Kreiss

Taking Our Country Back: The Crafting of Networked Politics from Howard Dean to Barack Obama
Daniel Kreiss

Media and Protest Logics in the Digital Era: The Umbrella Movement in Hong Kong
Francis L.F. Lee and Joseph M. Chan

Bits and Atoms: Information and Communication Technology in Areas of Limited Statehood
Steven Livingston and Gregor Walter-Drop

Digital Feminist Activism: Girls and Women Fight Back Against Rape Culture
Kaitlynn Mendes, Jessica Ringrose, and Jessalynn Keller

Digital Cities: The Internet and the Geography of Opportunity
Karen Mossberger, Caroline J. Tolbert, and William W. Franko

Revolution Stalled: The Political Limits of the Internet in the Post-Soviet Sphere
Sarah Oates

Disruptive Power: The Crisis of the State in the Digital Age
Taylor Owen

Affective Publics: Sentiment, Technology, and Politics
Zizi Papacharissi

Money Code Space: Hidden Power in Bitcoin, Blockchain, and Decentralisation
Jack Parkin

The Citizen Marketer: Promoting Political Opinion in the Social Media Age
Joel Penney

Tweeting is Leading: How Senators Communicate and Represent in the Age of Twitter
Annelise Russell

The Ubiquitous Presidency: Presidential Communication and Digital Democracy in Tumultuous Times
Joshua M. Scacco and Kevin Coe

China's Digital Nationalism
Florian Schneider

Credible Threat: Attacks Against Women Online and the Future of Democracy
Sarah Sobieraj

Presidential Campaigning in the Internet Age
Jennifer Stromer-Galley

News on the Internet: Information and Citizenship in the 21st Century
David Tewksbury and Jason Rittenberg

Outside the Bubble: Social Media and Political Participation in Western Democracies
Cristian Vaccari and Augusto Valeriani

The Internet and Political Protest in Autocracies
Nils B. Weidmann and Espen Geelmuyden Rød

The Civic Organization and the Digital Citizen: Communicating Engagement in a Networked Age
Chris Wells

Computational Propaganda: Political Parties, Politicians, and Political Manipulation on Social Media
Samuel Woolley and Philip N. Howard

Networked Publics and Digital Contention: The Politics of Everyday Life in Tunisia
Mohamed Zayani

Designing for Democracy

HOW TO BUILD COMMUNITY IN DIGITAL ENVIRONMENTS

JENNIFER FORESTAL

Oxford University Press is a department of the University of Oxford. It furthers the University's objective of excellence in research, scholarship, and education by publishing worldwide. Oxford is a registered trade mark of Oxford University Press in the UK and certain other countries.

Published in the United States of America by Oxford University Press
198 Madison Avenue, New York, NY 10016, United States of America.

Library of Congress Cataloging-in-Publication Data
Names: Forestal, Jennifer, author.
Title: Designing for democracy : how to build community in digital
environments / Jennifer Forestal.
Description: New York : Oxford University Press, 2022. |
Series: Oxford studies in digital politics series |
Includes bibliographical references and index.
Identifiers: LCCN 2021022693 (print) | LCCN 2021022694 (ebook) |
ISBN 9780197568767 (paperback) | ISBN 9780197568750 (hardback) |
ISBN 9780197568798 | ISBN 9780197568774 | ISBN 9780197568781 (epub)
Subjects: LCSH: Information society—Political aspects. |
Political participation—Technological innovations. | Democracy.
Classification: LCC HM851 .F6746 2021 (print) | LCC HM851 (ebook) |
DDC 303.48/33—dc23
LC record available at https://lccn.loc.gov/2021022693
LC ebook record available at https://lccn.loc.gov/2021022694

DOI: 10.1093/oso/9780197568750.001.0001

9 8 7 6 5 4 3 2 1

Paperback printed by Sheridan Books, Inc., United States of America
Hardback printed by Bridgeport National Bindery, Inc., United States of America

Contents

Acknowledgments

This book, like all products of intellectual labor, was not crafted in isolation. And, as a book about building communities, it seems only appropriate to start off by acknowledging some of the many (*many*) people in mine who made it possible.

My "meet-cute" with political theory happened at *The* Ohio State University. Clarissa Hayward's course, "Power and Resistance" (my first exposure to political theory!) introduced me to the power of the built environment. Mike Neblo and, especially, Eric MacGilvray taught me how to read closely and craft arguments carefully; they also introduced me to democratic theory and pragmatism. Looking back now, the combination of Dewey, democracy, and architecture that forms the theoretical heart of this book—and my thinking, more generally—has its roots in Columbus.

I began working through the book's main premise—that we should think of digital technologies architecturally—while at Northwestern. I am grateful to Jim Farr, Mary Dietz, and Ben Page for pushing me beyond my early and uncritical optimism regarding the democratic promises of digital technologies; their incisive questions and gentle skepticism have made the resulting argument much more compelling. Thanks also to my amazing grad student colleagues, who made each of my six years at Northwestern more enjoyable than the year before. Ross Carroll and Doug Thompson, as organizers of the graduate student Political Theory Workshop—and, crucially, the post-workshop drinks!—created a vibrant, friendly, and fun intellectual environment. Our Friday afternoon meetings were more than just a venue to share works-in-progress; ultimately, the Workshop was a space where I learned to think with others. I am indebted to the friends and fellow theorists who made those meetings my favorite part of grad school and who have continued to think with me even after we left: Doug, Ross, Nick Dorzweiler, Boris Litvin, Lexi Neame, Menaka Philips, Alison Rane, Chris Sardo, Anna Terwiel, and Désirée Weber—thanks to you all. At Northwestern, I was also fortunate to take advantage of the Northwestern Center for Civic

Engagement's Graduate Engagement Opportunities (GEO) Community Practicum. This program—which, IMHO, all grad programs should emulate—is one in which grad students are able to take a (funded!) quarter-long internship and connected seminar focused on Chicago, community organizing, and public scholarship. GEO provided space for me to explore the city in a way I otherwise would not have. And it is no exaggeration to say that this book owes its existence to my experiences with Chicago; the city's unparalleled architectural achievements and rich history of democratic activism ultimately inspired the research agenda I'm still pursuing today.

The bulk of this book was written while at Stockton University. I will forever be grateful to the Stockton POLS program for taking a chance on a young ABD and to the Stockton faculty, generally, for teaching me so much about good pedagogy, great colleagues, and the irreplaceable value—politically, economically, and socially—of a strong union. But a special thanks goes to my fellow junior POLS comrades: Dan Mallinson, Lauren Balasco, and, especially, Claire Abernathy, who made my first four years on the tenure track not just bearable but a true joy.

An additional highlight of my time in New Jersey was the Tri-Co Theory Workshop, organized by Joel Schlosser and Paulina Ochoa Espejo. Joel and Paulina went out of their way to welcome me into their community of theorists; watching the Tri-Co regulars—among them, Joel, Paulina, Craig Borowiak, Tom Donahue, Jeremy Elkins, and Danielle Hanley—engage with new works-in-progress as generous interlocutors, helping to sharpen arguments and land publications, has improved both my thinking and my writing.

The book was finished at Loyola University Chicago, which is in many ways my dream job. Back in Chicago(!), I've found a department full of gracious and supportive colleagues who have been nothing but encouraging in what was, truly, a very strange first couple years (thanks, COVID). I am especially grateful to Claudio Katz and Rob Mayer, who together have reminded me how wonderful it is to have theory colleagues. And it has been a delight to collaborate (scheme?) with Abe Singer on all sorts of endeavors. Conversations with my students in PLSC 300b: "Social Media & Democracy" during Fall 2019 shaped the book's fifth chapter; more generally, being in the classroom with my Loyola students (like their Stockton peers before them) is one of my favorite parts of this job.

Thanks also to those people and institutions who provided material resources and support to write and improve the project. I spent the summer of 2018 as a scholar-in-residence at New York University, sponsored by the Faculty Resource Network; during that time, I drafted an early version of chapter 3. The book was made possible in part by a grant from the National Endowment for the Humanities; Stockton University and Loyola University Chicago also provided material support as I drafted various chapters. A version of chapter 2 was presented at APT, while versions of chapter 4 were presented at APT, APSA,

John McGuire's "Doing Democracy Differently" conference at McMaster, and Northwestern's "Up the Street" workshop; I benefited greatly from all of the feedback from discussants, audiences, and fellow panelists. I presented the book's main argument at the "Structural Transformations of the Public Sphere" colloquium at Princeton's University Center for Human Values; the resulting conversation informed the book's conclusion.

I am grateful especially to Melissa Schwartzberg for her generosity of time and resources, both in convening a book manuscript workshop for me in May 2019, as well as in her advice and mentorship at key career decision-points afterward. A huge thanks also to Elizabeth Cohen, Henry Farrell, and Jack Knight for their close reading, thoughtful comments, and lively conversation during the workshop—hopefully they will see their feedback reflected in this final product. Thank you to Paul Apostolias for comments on how to improve the book proposal (as part of APT's Book Proposal Workshop), which in turn clarified my thinking about the book's argument and how to frame it. Thank you also to Meghan Condon, Danielle Hanley, Boris Litvin, and Lexi Neame, who have each read chapters in their various incarnations; Menaka Philips has, I believe, read them all at multiple stages. Any remaining errors are, of course, all mine.

Angela Chnapko at Oxford has been an excellent guide and sound advice-giver at the various stages of publication, from finishing the manuscript and responding to reviewers, to sourcing images and securing permissions. Thanks also to Timothy DeWerff for thorough copyediting and to Derek Gottlieb for indexing. Emily Davidson (talented painter and good friend!) helped me to find the perfect cover art; thank you to Melissa Brown for granting permission to use her painting *Bridge* (2020) in that capacity.

I owe an enormous debt of gratitude to my friends—both within academia and outside of it. I met Jennie Ikuta at APT in 2016 and have enjoyed talking political theory, binge-worthy TV, and Twitter drama with her ever since. Befriending Danielle Hanley was one of the best things I did while living in Philly. Rachel Moskowitz has been my favorite officemate to date; I miss our Jersey "work sessions." Thanks also to those who make Chicago home (even if you no longer live here): Tyler and Scott, Mike and Sarah, Lauren and Patrick, Stacy and Erik, Erin, Schraedly, Kate and Lauren (and Tim), Alison and Max, Christophe, Emily and John, Josh and Emily, Khairunnisa, Menaka, and Thomas. I will forever sing Ohio's praise with Laura, Kelly, JJ, Lauren, Schraedly, and Joe; you are all a testament to the ways in which clearly bounded shared space—in this case, the Nosker halls—helps cultivate enduring ties of friendship (*how firm,* indeed). "The Herd" have been with me even longer—since high school—and though we are spread coast-to-coast these days, I would not be where I am without A, D, Dawn, Kyle, Mike, Sarah, and especially Tyler. Whatever "place attachment" I have to our hometown, I have because of you all.

Menaka Philips deserves her own special thanks for being the kind of friend-slash-writing-partner that everyone should wish for. The title "co-author" does not do her justice; who else both improves your thinking and writing and also brings your missing shoe to happy hour? We are so constantly in conversation (via WhatsApp, of course) about all things, both work-related and decidedly not, that at times it seems our brains have simply melded together. I think these acknowledgments are my only published work that she hasn't read in advance.

But it is family, as Aristotle tells us, that is the foundation of community life. I am deeply thankful to have been born into families that are large, chaotic, generous, supportive, and tightly knit—and whose members thoroughly enjoy one another's company. To the Dodds and Forestals, thank you for filling my life, from the very beginning, with love and community. And to my first "household"—my parents, Greg and Joyce, and my brother, Rick—I owe many thanks for your unconditional love, for teaching me how to be curious, and for so much else. Rick is the best "little" brother anyone could ask for; I continually try (and fail) to channel his Dude-like chill. It is thanks to Dad that I grew up as a "digital native" with an enthusiasm for deconstructing things, figuring out how they work, and thinking of how to improve them. Conversations with Mom taught me how to appreciate life's difficult questions, even when you don't like the answers. It's been over a decade since I last talked with her, and I miss her more with every day that passes. For all that she gave me and all that she gives still, this book is dedicated to her.

Finally, I will forever thank my lucky stars—or, more accurately, Toni Greenslade-Smith, who until 2011 made all of OSU's housing assignments by herself and *by hand*—for placing Craig just down the hall from my freshman dorm room on Nosker's first floor. For the past sixteen years, he's been my constant companion, closest confidant, best friend, and true life partner. With our dependents, Tonks and (the new addition!) Oliver, I could not imagine any life better than the one we've built together.

1

Digital Technologies and the Problem of Democracy

In December 2019, *Buzzfeed News* published an article reflecting on the "Digital Revolution" of the 2010s. Its conclusions were bleak. Creating or exacerbating "feelings of powerlessness, estrangement, loneliness, and anger," wrote reporter Joseph Bernstein, the growing dominance of digital technologies in our daily lives "incentivizes forms of engagement that make Americans feel less empowered and more alone than ever, to the benefit of very few."[1] Contrary to the cheery predictions of techno-optimists from the late 1990s and early 2000s, argued Bernstein, now-ubiquitous technologies like smartphones and social media had turned out to be tools of control rather than liberation. The "digital revolution," he concluded, "hadn't tamed politics. It set them berserk. And it hadn't brought people closer together. It had alienated them."[2]

In highlighting the disastrous effects of digital technologies in our social and political lives, the *Buzzfeed* article echoed a number of prevalent arguments forwarded by scholars and practitioners over the previous decade. Noting how digital technologies exacerbate racial biases,[3] spread misinformation,[4] amplify hate,[5] and radicalize ideological thinking,[6] scholars have been quick to point out the

[1] Joseph Bernstein, "Alienated, Alone and Angry: What the Digital Revolution Really Did to Us," *BuzzFeed News*, December 17, 2019.

[2] Bernstein, "Alienated, Alone and Angry."

[3] Safiya Umoja Noble, *Algorithms of Oppression: How Search Engines Reinforce Racism* (New York: NYU Press, 2018).

[4] Chris J. Vargo, Lei Guo, and Michelle A. Amazeen, "The Agenda-Setting Power of Fake News: A Big Data Analysis of the Online Media Landscape from 2014 to 2016," *New Media and Society* 20, no. 5 (2018): 2028–49.

[5] Siva Vaidhyanathan, *Antisocial Media: How Facebook Disconnects Us and Undermines Democracy* (New York: Oxford University Press, 2018).

[6] Zeynep Tufekci, "YouTube, the Great Radicalizer," *New York Times*, March 10, 2018.

Designing for Democracy. Jennifer Forestal, Oxford University Press. © Oxford University Press 2022.
DOI: 10.1093/oso/9780197568750.003.0001

myriad ways digital technologies are "undermining democracy."[7] In seeking to "move fast and break things," it seems that digital technologies (and the companies that control them) have broken something important in our collective lives as democratic citizens.

Solutions to the problems posed by digital technologies have varied depending on scholars' specific focus. Citing platforms' unprecedented levels of data collection and surveillance, some, like Zeynep Tufekci, have argued in favor of regulating the companies that create and manage these technologies. A "genuine legislative remedy" to counteract the negative effects of these platforms for democracy, Tufekci persuasively argued in a *New York Times* opinion piece, would involve regulations like opt-in data collection, increased transparency, and oversight around data use.[8] By holding accountable the companies that manage digital platforms, so this argument goes, we can ensure they work for the public good.

Others trace the source of the problem to users themselves. Pointing to bots, trolls, and other "bad actors," as well as the unsuspecting publics they prey upon, scholars, practitioners, and activists have introduced digital literacy programs and called for stricter moderation policies in order to curb the spread of, for example, disinformation, hate speech, and harassment by way of digital media. These efforts, evident in offline workshops,[9] digital organizations like HeartMob (which works to "assist victims, educate communities, and stop harassment online"[10]), and campaigns that pressure platforms like Facebook to alter their moderation policies,[11] all seek to train users in how to engage in "productive" exchanges in digital spaces.

Finally, there are calls to give up on digital technologies' democratic potential altogether. Pointing to the ways that these technologies incentivize undemocratic behavior—such as aggression, polarization, and extremism—scholars like

[7] Matthew Hindman, *The Internet Trap: How the Digital Economy Builds Monopolies and Undermines Democracy* (Princeton, NJ: Princeton University Press, 2018); Vaidhyanathan, *Antisocial Media*; Jonathan Taplin, *Move Fast and Break Things: How Facebook, Google, and Amazon Cornered Culture and Undermined Democracy* (New York: Back Bay Books, 2018).

[8] Zeynep Tufekci, "We Already Know How to Protect Ourselves from Facebook," *New York Times*, April 9, 2018.

[9] Sam Gringlas, "With an Election on the Horizon, Older Adults Get Help Spotting Fake News," *NPR*, February 26, 2020.

[10] Sarah Kessler, "Meet HeartMob: A Tool for Fighting Online Harassment Designed by People Who Have Been Harassed," *Fast Company*, May 14, 2015. See wwww.iheartmob.org for more.

[11] Paris Martineau, "Facebook's New Content Moderation Tools Put Posts in Context," *WIRED*, July 3, 2019; Lauren Dudley, "Year in Review: Content Moderation on Social Media Platforms in 2019," *Council on Foreign Relations: Digital and Cyberspace Policy Program*, December 19, 2019.

Siva Vaidhyanathan argue that we should "put Facebook in its proper place . . . as a source of social and familial contact."[12] A similar logic underlies calls to delete one's accounts, to boycott platforms like Facebook, and to go offline entirely.[13] Despite their variance in both diagnoses and proposed remedies, however, what all of these approaches—regulation, training, and walking away—do is to use formal laws and education, as well as informal social norms, to (re)shape the ways that citizens interact with digital technologies, with the goal of making those interactions more supportive of democratic politics.

These are all important strategies for making digital technologies work for democracy. They may also be quite effective at achieving their stated goals. But they are not my focus in this book, and for two reasons. First, in conceptualizing the democratic effects of digital technologies, these strategies all tend to emphasize the impact of digital tools on existing (offline) political institutions, communities, and forms of participation. But democratic politics, as I will argue, is not confined to the boundaries of states or the formal institutions of governments. Instead, as a form of collective decision-making, democracy is an activity that can, and should, extend to all areas of our lives. And while digital platforms no doubt influence traditional modes of political activity (like social movements or political campaigns), they are also sites where *new* communities—those with no clear offline counterpart—are mobilizing and thriving. The global fan communities on Tumblr, for example, do not have a direct connection to national bodies politic, legislative agendas, or election results.[14] Yet as groups of people gathering together and making decisions that shape their behaviors—both individual and collective—these are nevertheless communities that deserve our attention as potential sites of democratic politics.

Second, framing discussions of digital technologies and democracy in terms of laws and norms cannot fully account for the differences *between* these new digital communities and the platforms that house them. Facebook, for example, looks and feels quite different from Twitter, which is unlike Reddit, which is

[12] Vaidhyanathan, *Antisocial Media*.

[13] David Nield, "Social Media Is Making You Miserable. Here's How to Delete Your Accounts," *Popular Science*, January 20, 2018; Nicola Slawson, "Faceblock Campaign Urges Users to Boycott Facebook for a Day," *The Guardian*, April 7, 2018.

[14] This is not to say that the two never intersect. There is a rich history of fan communities—including online fandoms—engaging in traditional "offline" political activities. The Harry Potter Alliance, for example, famously mobilizes fans of J. K. Rowling's *Harry Potter* series to participate in campaigns around issues like human rights, literacy, and immigration (among others). See Henry Jenkins, "'Cultural Acupuncture': Fan Activism and the Harry Potter Alliance," *Transformative Works and Culture* 10 (2012).

distinct from Wikipedia.[15] Each of these platforms hosts a distinctive community, characterized by unique patterns of user behavior and interpersonal relations. And while these patterns are, of course, influenced by laws and norms, these cannot fully explain the rich variety found among them: users living in the same legal and (offline) social context, for example, will nevertheless act differently on Facebook than they will on Wikipedia. This is because users' experiences as part of these online communities are also profoundly shaped by the *design* of the platforms in question. Platform design, in other words, works alongside laws and norms to help structure user behaviors in ways that can facilitate the formation of digital democratic communities—or else fail to do so.

In this book, then, I make the case that we should tackle the problems posed by digital technologies by studying the role of the *built environment* in structuring our activity, shaping our attitudes, and thus supporting—or not—the kinds of relationships and behaviors that democracy requires of citizens, whether online or offline. There are good reasons for my emphasis on the built environment—on questions of design—instead of the laws and norms that (of course) also influence our behavior. For one, the importance of design on user behavior is a common denominator in much of the empirical literature on the effects of digital technologies; it is also a widely recognized relationship in physical environments, as evident from decades of research in urban design, architecture, environmental psychology, and, yes, political theory. In connecting the built environment, digital technologies, and democratic theory, then, I am building on these existing bodies of work to argue that we should evaluate the democratic potential of digital technologies by focusing on how they are designed—whether they are built in ways that facilitate essential democratic practices.

Ultimately, I argue that "democratic spaces"—built environments that support democratic politics—must provide three requisite *democratic affordances*. These are three fundamental civic practices, or activities necessary for democratic politics: citizens must (1) recognize themselves as members of communities, (2) form attachments to those communities, and (3) work collaboratively to experiment with and improve them. In order to provide these affordances—of recognition, attachment, and experimentalism—democratic spaces must have three characteristics: they must be *clearly bounded*, *durable*, and *flexible*.

Happily, when we examine digital platforms through the lens of democratic space, with its attendant democratic affordances, we find evidence that these technologies are perhaps not as ruinous for democracy as the 2019 *Buzzfeed* article

[15] Interestingly, there has been a shift in recent years toward greater convergence in platform design and user experience as major companies attempt to mimic their competitors' successes. Recently, for example, Twitter introduced "Fleets"—tweets that disappear after 24 hours, set apart from users' normal feeds and located at the top of their screens—which function much like Instagram's successful "Stories" function (which itself is modeled after Snapchat). See Nick Statt, "Twitter's Disappearing Tweets, Called Fleets, Are Now Available for Everyone," *The Verge*, November 17, 2020.

may have us believe. Wikipedia, for example, is a two-decade-long success story of collective decision-making and collaborative experimentation.[16] Likewise, video game platforms like *World of Warcraft* regularly host community gatherings and collective action.[17] Even Facebook, though its cumulative effects for democracy may be troubling, nevertheless hosts robust communities (discussed in chapter 2) that engage in cooperative activity—including mutual aid, emotional support, and information exchange. Using the theoretical framework of democratic space, in other words, we can more clearly identify what we are already doing "right." More specifically, the concept of democratic space can help us tease out the *why* and *how* of these success stories; it can explain, as I demonstrate in chapter 4, why Reddit's subreddits host thriving communities of interest, whose members often demonstrate long-standing attachments and habits of experimentation, when we do not see similar dynamics on sites like Facebook and Twitter.

But the vocabulary of democratic affordances that I outline in this book can do more than simply help us "think what we are doing."[18] It also highlights what we are *not* doing—what is *missing* from our current efforts. While much ink has (rightly) been spilled unpacking the ways that algorithms powering Twitter and Facebook have contributed to the spread of disinformation, hate speech, and extremism, for example, the framework of democratic space reveals additional—and perhaps more fundamental—challenges posed by these platforms. As I discuss in chapters 2 and 3, Facebook largely fails to facilitate the democratic affordance of recognition, while Twitter fails to afford attachment. In both cases, the threat to democratic politics is not simply in the content users disseminate on these platforms. It is, rather, in the ways these spaces facilitate (or not, as the case may be) the community ties upon which democracy depends.

Finally, and perhaps most important, the framework of democratic space can help us identify potentially negative (and unintended) consequences caused by common interventions intended to "fix" digital technologies for democracy. These efforts often work by first identifying discrete problems with digital

[16] Susan Bryant, Andrea Forte, and Amy Bruckman, "Becoming Wikipedian: Transformation of Participation in a Collaborative Online Encyclopedia," in *Proceedings of the 2005 International ACM SIGGROUP Conference on Supporting Group Work— GROUP '05*, (New York: Association for Computing Machinery, 2005), 1–10; Howard T. Welser, et al. "Finding Social Roles in Wikipedia," in *Proceedings of the 2011 iConference* (Seattle, WA: ACM, 2011), 122–29.

[17] Thomas W. Brignall III and Thomas L. Van Valey, "An Online Community as a New Tribalism: The World of Warcraft," in *Proceedings of the 40th Hawaii International Conference on System Sciences* (Los Alamitos, CA: IEEE, 2007), 179b–179b; Bonnie Nardi and Justin Harris, "Strangers and Friends: Collaborative Play in World of Warcraft," in *CSCW 2006: Proceedings of the ACM Conference on Computer-Supported Cooperative Work* (New York: Association for Computing Machinery, 2006), 149–58.

[18] Hannah Arendt, *The Human Condition*, 2nd ed. (Chicago: University of Chicago Press, 1998), 5.

technologies—like filter bubbles, hate speech, and privacy concerns—trying to address them in isolation from one another, and assuming the cumulative results will benefit democracy. This is an understandable approach, and certainly a laudable goal. But, as I show in chapter 5, it can often "backfire" as these piecemeal changes end up canceling each other out—or, worse, exacerbating the undemocratic effects of the platforms they are trying to fix, thereby undermining their stated goals.

Instead of starting with individual problems associated with digital technologies, then, the approach I outline in this book—the framework of democratic space—begins with the question of *what democracy requires* and evaluates digital technologies accordingly. As a result, it gives us a more comprehensive account of not just the challenges digital technologies pose for democratic politics, but also their promise and possibilities. As digital platforms continue to (re)structure our interpersonal relationships and patterns of collective behavior—not just in traditional offline political arenas, but in online communities as well—it becomes ever more critical for us to ensure they are designed and built to support the work of democratic politics and the affordances it requires. The theoretical framework of democratic space I provide in this book is intended to help us do just that.

Democratic Foundations

What kind of built environment does democracy require? That is the question I take up in this book. Democracy, as I understand it, is the collective management of common affairs. As opposed to other forms of decision-making—the use of force, say, or reliance on experts—democratic politics seeks to involve all the members of a community in the collaborative work of identifying, discussing, and making decisions about the things they hold in common. Democracy is, in other words, more than a system of government. Instead, we should understand democracy as a method of collective problem-solving. It is, as twentieth-century American philosopher John Dewey wrote, a set of practices through which we share information, test ideas, discuss results, and work cooperatively and intelligently toward our collective goals.[19] In short, democratic politics is the process through which community members are directly involved in making the decisions that affect their communities—communities that range from the

[19] For more on Dewey's democratic theory, see John Dewey, *The Public and Its Problems: An Essay in Political Inquiry* (Chicago: Gateway Books, 1946); John Dewey, "Creative Democracy—The Task Before Us," in *John Dewey: The Later Works, Vol. 14, 1939–1941*, ed. Jo Ann Boydston (Carbondale: Southern Illinois University Press, 2008), 224–30. See also chapter 4 of this book.

small and intimate, like families, all the way up to larger and more impersonal associations like the state. In all of these communities, despite their differences in structure and aims, members have an equal claim to participate in decision-making because the resulting decisions will ultimately shape their lives and behavior, both individual and collective.

This is, of course, not the only way to understand democracy. But "participatory democracy," as this model is sometimes called, is particularly well suited to help us understand the collective engagements that accompany digital technologies. "[F]or a democratic polity to exist," argues Carol Pateman, "it is necessary for a participatory society to exist, i.e. a society where all political systems have been democratized and socialization through participation can take place in all areas."[20] Taking a participatory approach to democracy, in other words, compels us to apply the same level of scrutiny to all the other spheres of our lives as we traditionally do to the institutions of the state and the formal arenas of governing. Because it expands the scope of democratic politics beyond these traditional formal institutions, participatory democracy underscores the stakes of designing everyday spaces in ways that support maximum participation in the work of collective problem-solving for the communities they host.

It is for this reason that I use the term "citizen" throughout this book to refer not to a specific formal legal status, but instead as a generic term for a member of a given community. A "citizen," in this sense, is one who inhabits a space, shares the consequences of conjoint activity, and therefore has a part in the work of managing them. The term "citizen," as I use it here, thus includes a normative claim: that all denizens of a space, if they are affected by the consequences of a decision, *should* be treated as full members of the community with an equal role in the decision-making process—even if they currently are not. Taking a participatory approach to democracy, then, means that we are tasked with the work of "democratizing" the spaces in which citizens find themselves. We must work to provide, as Pateman puts it, "opportunities for individuals to participate in decision-making in their everyday lives as well as in the wider political system"[21]—and we must create those opportunities if they do not currently exist.

As sites where billions of users gather daily, it is clear that the spaces and communities created by digital technologies should be subject to this project of democratization. Digital technologies are, as we will soon see, designed to induce their users to act in ways they otherwise might not. And because digital technologies have such a wide-ranging influence on both our individual

[20] Carole Pateman, *Participation and Democratic Theory* (Cambridge, UK: Cambridge University Press, 1970), 43.

[21] Carole Pateman, "Participatory Democracy Revisited," *Perspectives on Politics* 10, no. 1 (2012): 10.

and our collective lives, users of digital technologies—as citizens of digital communities—rightly have a claim to participate in the processes of decision-making about those technologies and their effects on the communities they host. In order to democratize digital technologies, then, we must design them in ways that facilitate opportunities for collective decision-making by the communities that exist within the new spaces they create.[22]

In order to make possible the kind of participation in collective decision-making that characterizes participatory democratic politics, however, there are three core conditions that must be met. As a collective enterprise, democracy requires the existence of communities; communities must therefore *form* before democratic politics can take place. And because democracy is a forward-looking activity, it also presumes these communities are not temporary; thus, communities must also *sustain* themselves over time in order to support the long-term work of collective decision-making. Finally, because democracy is the work of collective problem-solving—and because this work will never be finished (there will always be new problems, after all)—these communities must strive to be self-correcting, to *improve* their decisions and decision-making capacities in order to best meet the ever-changing needs of their members.

Certainly, laws and norms can help communities form, sustain, and improve themselves over time. But so, too, can the built environment—which often, as we will see, works in subtle and even invisible ways to thwart or support these democratic goals of forming, sustaining, and improving communities. As I argue in this book, if we are to construct a built environment that facilitates democratic politics—what I call here a "democratic space"—it must have three characteristics: it must be *clearly bounded, durable,* and *flexible.* Clearly bounded spaces facilitate the recognition of what we share and with whom we share it; they help us *form* communities. Durable spaces facilitate our attachments to the communities they house and other members within them; they help us *sustain*

[22] In making this claim, I am arguing in this book that digital technologies (can) host democratic communities and that, as such, they are themselves sites of democratic politics. For many participatory democrats, however, the benefits of participation extend beyond one's immediate involvement in collective decision-making within a single community; democratic participation in, say, workplaces can also be a way for citizens to practice skills that they can then carry over to participation in more formal arenas of politics like the state. The same logic holds true for digital spaces: while members of digital communities have a claim to participate in decision-making around these spaces and the technologies that create them, this participation likely also builds important political skills and invites experimentation with democratic processes that can be imported to other (non-digital) spaces. These experiential and pedagogical effects of digital democratic participation fall outside the scope of my discussion here. But for more on how digital spaces not only host democratic engagements themselves, but also act as "schools" and "labs" for democracy elsewhere, see Cathy J. Cohen et al., "Participatory Politics: New Media and Youth Political Action" (Oakland, CA: Youth and Participatory Research Network, 2012).

communities. And flexible spaces facilitate the experimental habit required for democratic politics; they help us *improve* our communities. This is, as I will show, as true in digital environments like Facebook or Twitter as it is for physical spaces like streets, parks, and town halls.

Over the next three chapters, I explain each of these characteristics in more detail. In the remainder of this chapter, I articulate why I take the particular methodological approach of exploring the democratic potential of digital technologies through the lens of the built environment. Ultimately, the reason is one of power—the built environment exerts considerable power over us, though it does so in often-invisible ways. Insofar as democracy requires citizen participation in the decisions that shape their lives, it is clear that citizens should be as involved in decisions over the built environment as they are with any other shared object or exercise of power. In order to effectively do this work, however, we need a shared vocabulary with which to explain, evaluate, and improve the built environment for democracy. Providing that vocabulary, and thus suggesting ways we might begin to democratize the design of digital environments, is the project of this book.

Democracy, Affordances, and the Power of the Built Environment

While digital technologies introduce new spaces and new dynamics to the practice of democratic politics, the anxieties often expressed over their destructive potential are, in fact, not unique. Indeed, democratic theorists, particularly those working in the participatory mode, have long been concerned with the question of how to ensure that citizens engage in the civic practices required for democratic politics—and the consequences for democracy if they fail to do so. Some argue that the most effective way to shape citizens' behaviors is through formal institutions, like laws and local governments.[23] Others invest more significance in education—and particularly public education—as a mechanism that would help train citizens to regularly engage in the requisite civic practices of recognition, attachment, and experimentalism.[24] Still others turn to informal social norms, like those of friendship or neighborliness, to inculcate the proper

[23] Aristotle, *Aristotle's Politics*, trans. Carnes Lord, 2nd ed. (Chicago: University of Chicago Press, 2013); Alexis de Tocqueville, *Democracy in America*, ed. J. P. Mayer, trans. George Lawrence (New York: HarperPerennial Modern Classics, 1969).

[24] John Dewey, "Democracy and Education," in *John Dewey: The Middle Works, Vol. 9, 1899–1924*, ed. Jo Ann Boydston (Carbondale: Southern Illinois University Press, 1916).

practices in democratic citizens.[25] And, as is also the case with the contemporary iterations we see at play in discussions around digital technologies, these turns to formal and informal institutions as strategies of civic improvement can be effective. In this book, however, I take a different approach to the problem of cultivating democratic practices by focusing instead on the role of the built environment.

In turning to the built environment, I am drawing from much existing, multidisciplinary work. For one, there is a long, though often overlooked, tradition in the history of political thought that recognizes the power of the physical environment in shaping political behavior.[26] Classic thinkers like Aristotle and Machiavelli, for example, note the importance of a city's physical placement and layout for its long-term success;[27] Rousseau and Montesquieu both discuss how geography might influence the internal dynamics of a political community.[28] Likewise, Tocqueville connects the "pronounced physiognomy" of the American township with the feelings of affection and obligation between neighbors,[29] just as Dewey argues that the spaces of the American frontier and local neighborhood were crucial in developing democratic habits in their residents.[30]

More recently, scholars have turned in more detail to chronicle the ways the built environment, as Margaret Kohn puts it, "orchestrate[s] social behavior by providing scripts for encounters and assembly."[31] Drawing on his "spatial obsessions,"[32] for example, Michel Foucault famously showed how the physical spaces of the prison, school, and hospital were sites of disciplinary power that scripted and trained individuals into socially desirable behaviors.[33] And decades of

[25] Danielle S. Allen, *Talking to Strangers: Anxieties of Citizenship since "Brown v. Board of Education"* (Chicago: University of Chicago Press, 2004); Nancy L. Rosenblum, *Good Neighbors: The Democracy of Everyday Life in America* (Princeton, NJ: Princeton University Press, 2016).

[26] For another discussion of this "Topian tradition," and in particular its connection to one's ethical and political obligations, see Paulina Ochoa Espejo, *On Borders: Territories, Legitimacy, and the Rights of Place* (New York: Oxford University Press, 2020).

[27] Aristotle, *Aristotle's Politics*; Niccolò Machiavelli, *Discourses on Livy*, trans. Harvey C. Mansfield and Nathan Tarcov (Chicago: University of Chicago Press, 1995).

[28] Jean-Jacques Rousseau, *The Social Contract and Other Later Political Writings*, ed. and trans. Victor Gourevitch (Cambridge, UK: Cambridge University Press, 1997); Baron de Montesquieu, *The Spirit of the Laws*, ed. Thomas Nugent (New York: Hafner Press, 1994).

[29] Tocqueville, *Democracy in America*.

[30] Jennifer Forestal, "The Architecture of Political Spaces: Trolls, Digital Media, and Deweyan Democracy," *American Political Science Review* 111, no. 1 (2017): 149–61.

[31] Margaret Kohn, *Radical Space: Building the House of the People* (Ithaca, NY: Cornell University Press, 2003), 3.

[32] Michel Foucault, *Power/Knowledge: Selected Interviews and Other Writings 1972–1977*, ed. Colin Gordon, trans. Colin Gordon et al. (New York: Pantheon Books, 1980), 69.

[33] Michel Foucault, *Discipline and Punish: The Birth of the Prison*, 2nd ed. (New York: Vintage Books, 1995).

research in environmental psychology supports his observations, showing how the design of the built environment influences not only our behaviors, but also our attitudes and perceptions as well. The spaces in which we live, work, and play, it turns out, profoundly shape the ways we develop our friendships, our feelings of trust and safety, our perceptions of different identity groups, and our sense of civic efficacy.[34]

And this disciplining effect of the built environment is often wielded consciously by those in power to achieve certain ends. As James C. Scott notes, it was through "modernizing schemes," like Haussmann's redevelopment of Paris in the nineteenth century and Le Corbusier and the Congrès Internationaux d'Architecture Moderne (CIAM)'s high modernism of the twentieth, that states utilized the built environment in order to render their populations more legible and their cities "more governable, prosperous, healthy, and architecturally imposing."[35] Likewise, as Susan Bickford argues, the design of suburbs and, especially, gated communities "enact[s] deep forms of *segregation*" and surveillance, fostering (unrealistic) goals of safety and purity in residents.[36] By "reinforcing relatively stable cues about correct behavior,"[37] in other words, the built environment has often been used intentionally as a powerful disciplinary force—a way to impose order on a disorderly world, clarify and regulate human relationships, and implement principles of beauty and harmony that would (supposedly) take the "mess" out of political life.

[34] Michelle A. Payton, David C. Fulton, and Dorothy H. Anderson, "Influence of Place Attachment and Trust on Civic Action: A Study at Sherburne National Wildlife Refuge," *Society and Natural Resources* 18, no. 6 (2005): 511–28; Ryan D. Enos, *The Space between Us: Social Geography and Politics* (New York: Cambridge University Press, 2017); Lisa Wood et al., "The Anatomy of the Safe and Social Suburb: An Exploratory Study of the Built Environment, Social Capital and Residents' Perceptions of Safety," *Health and Place* 14 (2008): 15–31; R. Robert Huckfeldt, "Social Contexts, Social Networks, and Urban Neighborhoods: Environmental Constraints on Friendship Choice," *American Journal of Sociology* 89, no. 3 (1983): 651–69.

[35] James C. Scott, *Seeing Like a State: How Certain Schemes to Improve the Human Condition Have Failed* (New Haven: Yale University Press, 1998), 59. Haussmann and Le Corbusier were not alone in their attempts to wholly redesign cities to achieve utopian dreams. Many of the most famous architects, including Hippodamus, Vitruvius, Daniel Burnham, and Frank Lloyd Wright, all unveiled grand designs for their ideal cities. And while the actual designs differed—in some cases quite dramatically—they all shared the underlying assumption that designing the "proper" city was the secret to political peace and prosperity. See Vitruvius, *The Ten Books on Architecture*, trans. Morris Hicky Morgan (Cambridge, MA: Harvard University Press, 1914); Charles Moore, *Daniel H. Burnham, Architect, Planner of Cities, Volume 2* (Boston: Houghton Mifflin, 1921); Frank Lloyd Wright, *The Living City* (New York: Horizon Press, 1958); Le Corbusier, *The Radiant City: Elements of a Doctrine of Urbanism to Be Used as the Basis of Our Machine-Age Civilization* (New York: Orion Press, 1967).

[36] Susan Bickford, "Constructing Inequality: City Spaces and the Architecture of Citizenship," *Political Theory* 28, no. 3 (2000): 356.

[37] Kohn, *Radical Space*, 3.

But the "scripts" provided by the built environment do not only constrain our behavior; they can also empower us. The "public things" of the physical environment, argues Bonnie Honig, are vital for constructing and maintaining democratic publics. "Public things," she writes, "press us into relations with others. They are sites of attachment and meaning that occasion the inaugurations, conflicts, and contestations that underwrite everyday citizenships and democratic sovereignties."[38] The physical objects of the built environment help to shape our perceptions of one another; they "bind citizens into the complicated affective circuitries"[39] that help to form the democratic "we." In other words, as Kohn writes, the built environment "can incite democratic effects when it positions both subject and object together in a shared and contestable world."[40] Moreover, the relative permanence of the built environment can extend these democratic relationships into the future, as its spaces serve as the sites of public memory and remembrance that help democratic communities endure.[41]

The built environment shapes our individual attitudes and behaviors as well as our perceptions of interpersonal relationships. But it also, as many political theorists have noted, plays an integral role as a physical location for the *performance* of democratic politics.[42] Politics, Hannah Arendt reminds us, requires "spaces of appearances" to manifest.[43] Indeed, as John Parkinson argues, "democracy depends to a surprising extent on the availability of physical, public space";[44] the physical environment is both the location of democratic activity as well as, in many cases, its subject.[45] It is the importance of publicly accessible spaces for democratic performance, moreover, that has led theorists in the past few decades to lament the privatization of the built environment's public spaces.[46]

[38] Bonnie Honig, *Public Things: Democracy in Disrepair* (New York: Fordham University Press, 2017), 6.

[39] Honig, *Public Things*, 7.

[40] Margaret Kohn, *Brave New Neighborhoods: The Privatization of Public Space* (New York: Routledge, 2004), 12.

[41] Uri Jacob Matatyaou, "Memory-Space-Politics: Public Memorial and the Problem of Political Judgement" (PhD diss., Northwestern University, 2008); Maurice Halbwachs, *On Collective Memory*, trans. Lewis A. Coser (Chicago: University of Chicago Press, 1992).

[42] Ali Aslam, "Building the Good Life: Architecture and Politics" (PhD diss., Duke University, 2010); Alexandra Kogl, *Strange Places: The Political Potentials and Perils of Everyday Spaces* (Lanham, MD: Lexington Books, 2008).

[43] Arendt, *The Human Condition*; Jennifer Forestal, "Constructing Digital Democracies: Facebook, Arendt, and the Politics of Design," *Political Studies* 69, no. 1 (2020): 26–44.

[44] John Parkinson, *Democracy and Public Space* (Oxford: Oxford University Press, 2012), 2.

[45] Parkinson, *Democracy and Public Space*, chap. 2.

[46] Kohn, *Brave New Neighborhoods*; Benjamin Barber, "Malled, Mauled, and Overhauled: Arresting Suburban Sprawl by Transforming Suburban Malls into Usable Civic Space," in *Public Space and Democracy*, ed. Marcel Hénaff and Tracy B. Strong (Minneapolis: University of Minnesota Press, 2001), 201–20.

At stake in this shift, they argue, is the loss of "the people's" control over their environment—and the accompanying concern is that this loss of control will foreclose the democratic possibilities of the spaces in which we live, encounter, and act with others.[47]

There is no question, then, that the built environment influences our behavior and that it does so in ways that have effects for the possibilities of democratic politics. As all of this scholarship recognizes, the design of the built environment can profoundly reshape our patterns of thought and action. And because it can be used to change our behavior in these noticeable ways, the built environment is, in the parlance of political science, a manifestation of power. Moreover, the design choices that underlie the built environment can be just as effective at reshaping "user behavior" as more traditional manifestations of power, like laws and social norms. And, as we will see, this remains just as true in digital environments as it is for the more traditional physical ones. As a result, any effort to "fix" digital technologies—to make them more supportive of democratic politics—must account for the design of the built environment, just as much as the formal and informal institutions that currently dominate our imagination.

THE POWER OF THE BUILT ENVIRONMENT

Though we may not think of it in these terms, the built environment is an expression of power because it shapes our behavior in important—often invisible—ways. Power, in twentieth-century political scientist Robert A. Dahl's famous formulation, is the ability to get someone to do something they would not otherwise do.[48] Because it influences our behavior by enabling certain actions and constraining others, the effects of the built environment are therefore best understood in terms of power. And one way to explain the power of the built environment is by using the language of "affordances."

Originally developed by the ecological psychologist James J. Gibson, "affordances" refer to the "action possibilities," or opportunities for action, that exist due to the specific configuration of one's environment. "The *affordances* of the environment," wrote Gibson, "are what it *offers* the animal, what it *provides* or *furnishes*, either for good or ill."[49] A chair, for example, affords a place to sit; it also

[47] Marcel Hénaff and Tracy B. Strong, eds., *Public Space and Democracy* (Minneapolis: University of Minnesota Press, 2001).

[48] Robert A. Dahl, "The Concept of Power," *Behavioral Science* 2 (1957): 201–15.

[49] James J. Gibson, *The Ecological Approach to Visual Perception* (Hillsdale, NJ: Lawrence Erlbaum Associates, Inc., 1986), 127. Italics in original.

affords something to throw, kick, or bump into. What Gibson highlights with the language of affordances are the ways that the characteristics of certain physical spaces—like a classroom or restaurant—work to shape our actions; they afford certain behaviors, like sitting, over others like swimming or basketball. And this is true in digital environments as well; just as a kitchen stove affords the ability to cook hot meals, so too does Microsoft Excel afford the ability to quickly calculate large sums. Whether physical or digital, the affordances of an environment structure the field of possibilities for our actions.[50]

Crucially, the affordances of the built environment, unlike other manifestations of power like laws or social norms, can place hard restrictions on our activity. A brick wall, for example, makes it physically impossible to pass through or see who is on the other side, while the addition of doors or windows to that wall would make it more permeable. The presence of doorways and windows, then, adds affordances to that environment. And even the distinction between the affordances of a window and those of a doorway—though both might afford sight—is an important one, as anyone who has walked into a sliding glass door can attest.[51]

And while some affordances are naturally occurring—air, for example, affords us the ability to breathe and to move freely—many more, like the doorways and windows of the previous example, are not. They are instead the result of deliberate design choices made by specific actors. The placement of windows,

[50] Importantly, for Gibson, affordances are not themselves agentive; they "do not cause behavior but constrain or control it" (1982, 411). Affordances, in other words, cannot *make* us take the actions they allow; rather, affordances merely structure the field of possibility for action. Thus, affordances alone—and the physical characteristics of the environment, which create those affordances—cannot entirely explain why individuals take the actions they do. Instead, "concepts like motivation and intention seem needed to explain why animals utilize certain affordances and not others at a certain moment in time" (Withagen et al. 2012, 252). Affordances, while important for constraining or enabling our behavior, are not deterministic. For more, see James J. Gibson, "Notes on Affordances," in *Reasons for Realism: Selected Essays of James J. Gibson*, ed. Edward Reed and Rebecca Jones (Hillsdale, NJ: Lawrence Erlbaum Associates, 1982), 401–18; Rob Withagen et al., "Affordances Can Invite Behavior: Reconsidering the Relationship between Affordances and Agency," *New Ideas in Psychology* 30 (2012): 250–58.

[51] Because they are properties of the physical objects themselves, affordances are, according to Gibson, not a matter of perception. Indeed, Gibson argues, "[t]he observer may or may not perceive or attend to the affordance, according to his needs, but the affordance, being invariant, is always there to be perceived. An affordance is not bestowed upon an object by a need of an observer and his act of perceiving it" (139). We may therefore (mistakenly) perceive a glass door to afford us the ability to pass through it; this does not mean that it will provide that affordance. In cases like this, as Gibson notes, "mistaken perceptions led to inappropriate actions" (142). Yet the affordances of the environment remain unchanged, according to Gibson's theory. Later work on affordances, however, as I discuss below, takes a more expansive view of the relationship between perception, the environment, and affordances. See Gibson, *The Ecological Approach to Visual Perception*.

doorways, and walls, and the choice of what material to construct them from, is therefore an exercise of power—it is a way to get someone to do something they would not otherwise do. And, again, this is true of digital environments as well. Facebook users cannot see the audience of their posts, for example, because the company's developers have decided not to provide users that affordance.[52]

And this exercise of power can be a very effective one. As Don Norman argues in *The Design of Everyday Things*, a foundational design studies text and a cornerstone of contemporary Human-Computer Interaction design practices, "[w]ith the proper use of physical constraints . . . desired actions can be made obvious, usually by being especially salient."[53] By selecting the "right" configuration of characteristics in the built environment, in other words, designers can encourage users to engage in "desired" behaviors. By erecting walls or other barriers, for example, designers, architects, and builders can direct inhabitants to walk certain paths and not others; by limiting the number and types of user engagement options, software designers can likewise encourage users to share certain kinds of content over others.[54]

We can see such design strategies at work in grocery stores, which are built to encourage shoppers to buy more products.[55] Similar tactics are at work in "defensive architecture" practices, which are intended to reduce "loitering" in public spaces,[56] as well as in casinos, which are designed to keep gamblers inside to spend (and lose) more money.[57] In digital environments, design choices like the use of "dark patterns"—such as the choice to display an opt-in option more prominently than the opt-out alternative—follow the same strategy.[58] In all of these examples, whether physical or digital, the built environment is deliberately

[52] We know this is a design choice, and not a technological impossibility, for two reasons. First, there was, at one point in time, a glitch in Facebook that temporarily showed users who viewed their post. Second, Facebook sells this information to advertisers. See, for example, Nick Statt, "Facebook Bug Accidentally Shows You How Popular Your Posts Are," *The Verge*, October 15, 2015.

[53] Don Norman, *The Design of Everyday Things*. Rev. and expanded ed. (New York: Basic Books, 2013), 125.

[54] Amy Chozick, "This Is the Guy Who's Taking Away the Likes," *New York Times*, January 17, 2020.

[55] Rebecca Rupp, "Surviving the Sneaky Psychology of Supermarkets," *National Geographic*, June 14, 2015; Adam P. Vrechopoulos et al., "Virtual Store Layout: An Experimental Comparison in the Context of Grocery Retail," *Journal of Retailing* 80, no. 1 (2004): 13–22.

[56] Oscar Newman, *Defensible Space: People and Design in the Violent City* (New York: Macmillan, 1972).

[57] David Kranes, "Play Grounds," *Journal of Gambling Studies* 11, no. 1 (1995): 91–102; Bill Friedman, *Designing Casinos to Dominate the Competition* (Reno, NV: Institute for the Study of Gambling and Commercial Gaming, University of Nevada, 2000).

[58] Sidney Fussell, "The Endless, Invisible Persuasion Tactics of the Internet," *The Atlantic*, August 2, 2019; Harry Brignull, "Dark Patterns: Inside the Interfaces Designed to Trick You," *The Verge*, August 29, 2013.

designed in ways that, as Norman puts it, provide strong clues as to the type of "desired" user behavior. These deliberate design choices, then, ensure that "people readily determine the proper course of action, even in a novel situation."[59] As a result of specific design choices made by deliberate actors, in other words, these examples show how the built environment often gets us to do things—like spend money and opt-in to spam—that we would not otherwise do.[60]

Of course, the affordances of the built environment, both physical and digital, are always mediated by less tangible institutions, like laws and norms, that we overlay on them. A door marked "Do Not Enter, Alarm Will Sound" *seems* to us more of a blockade than does an unmarked door; a roadway that is marked "One Way" seems to us to have more limited use than a similarly sized street without such a sign. In these examples, we can see how the addition of signage can change our *perception* of a space's affordances, based on the laws and norms of our wider communities. Affordances, then, are not fixed; nor are they determined solely by design. Instead, as I will show throughout this book, we should understand affordances as the product of the interaction between community norms, individual perceptions, and the physical design of a space.[61]

But while it is clearly related, the power of the built environment is distinct from the ways in which these other institutions, like laws or social norms, shape our behavior by suggesting appropriate actions in given circumstances: we *shouldn't* roll through stop signs, because it is against the law. But, of course, we *can* (and often do). The physical characteristics of a stop sign, as opposed to, say, a brick wall, afford us that possibility. But we literally cannot do things—like look outside from a room with no windows, make a phone call with Microsoft Word, or "Dislike" posts on Facebook—if the built environment does not afford those possibilities. And because the encouragements and constraints of the built environment do not require other actors, like police, to enforce them, they often work on us silently and invisibly, even subconsciously. This passivity and subtlety with which the built environment manifests power means it is both very easy and very dangerous to ignore. But the fact of its near-invisible power also reinforces the importance of centering the built environment in any project of democratizing digital technologies.

[59] Norman, *The Design of Everyday Things*, 125.

[60] Importantly, as Sasha Costanza-Chock notes, Norman's discussion of design principles (as with many other canonical texts) tends to ignore "questions of how race, class, gender, disability, and other aspects of the matrix of domination shape and constrain access to affordances" (37). See Sasha Costanza-Chock, *Design Justice: Community-Led Practices to Build the Worlds We Need* (Cambridge, MA: MIT Press, 2020).

[61] For more on the sociological relationships between affordances, perceptions, and users, see Ian Hutchby, "Technologies, Texts, and Affordances," *Sociology* 35, no. 2 (2001): 441–56.

REDESIGNING SPACES TO REDESIGN BEHAVIOR

In order to better understand the power of the built environment—and how it might be deliberately wielded to shape user behaviors in desirous ways, consider the example of a subway car. These spaces are designed to elicit certain responses in riders: brightly lit, with relatively uncomfortable seats, the subway car is designed for efficiency over comfort. Though some do include the affordance, the interior of a subway car is not usually designed to *invite* riders to make themselves comfortable and stay for extended periods of time. Indeed, in some cases, designers remove this affordance altogether, as with cars that split seats so that riders cannot lay down (see Figure 1.1).

Moreover, in comparing different subway car layouts, we can see how seemingly small design choices can have outsized effects on user behavior. The position of a subway car's doors, for example, shapes how riders use that space. When designers position doors symmetrically, riders will often crowd around the doors, leaving much of the car unused. When designers choose to position the doors asymmetrically, however, use of the space is more evenly distributed; passengers can enter and exit the car more efficiently (see Figure 1.2).[62] In these cases, the affordances of both layouts are the same—riders in both environments are afforded the opportunity to use the whole space of the car to sit, stand, and ride. But by changing the location of the doors, designers can reshape riders' *perceptions* of that space, which influences how and whether riders take advantage of this affordance. By moving the position of the subway car doors, in other words, designers can use the power of the built environment to shape rider behavior, getting riders to do something they would not otherwise do.

Of course, the built environment is not the only influence on people's behavior. Scholars have long noted the role of, for example, social norms in regulating human activity; these, too, are evident in the subway.[63] Though subway cars afford talking, as well as sitting in multiple locations, there is often a norm of silence among early-morning commuters, as well as social norms about who gives up seats, when, and to whom.[64] There are also more problematic social norms, such as "manspreading" (when men take up more space than women when seated) and other norms of harassment and dominance, often aimed at

[62] Aaron Berkovich et al., "Observed Customer Seating and Standing Behavior and Seat Preferences Onboard Subway Cars in New York City," *Transportation Research Record: Journal of the Transportation Research Board* 4, no. 2353 (2013): 33–46.

[63] Erving Goffman, *Relations in Public: Microstudies of the Public Order* (New York: Basic Books, 1971); David Patrick Connor and Richard Tewksbury, "Social Control on Public Buses," *Journal of Theoretical and Philosophical Criminology* 4, no. 1 (2012): 1–13.

[64] For an example of a particularly prominent norm for behavior on public transit, one needs only to quickly peruse the debate over proper behavior in "quiet cars" on trains. See Leigh Gallagher, "The Cult of the Amtrak Quiet Car," *Fortune*, September 17, 2014.

Figure 1.1 Washington, DC Metro (top), with split seats, compared to the New York City Subway (bottom) with seats that afford laying down. Top photograph: "Metro 70000-Series railcar debut" by Ben Schumin, available at https://flic.kr/p/iZnpfk and licensed under CC BY-SA 2.0. Bottom photograph: "NYC subway" by frankieleon, available at https://flic.kr/p/qwE93z and licensed under CC BY 2.0.

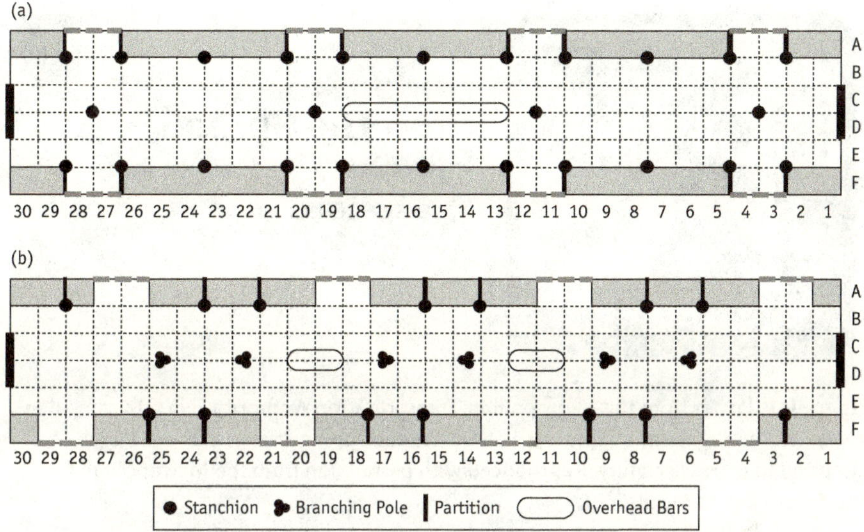

Figure 1.2 Hypothetical subway car layouts: (a) with symmetrical doors, which is more likely to cause crowding around the door areas, and (b) with asymmetrical doors, which shifts riders' perceptions to more effectively uses the space, though the seating capacity and standing room remains the same. Reproduced with permission from Aaron Berkovich, Alex Lu, Brian Levine, and Alla V. Reddy, "Observed Customer Seating and Standing Behavior and Seat Preferences on Board Subway Cars in New York City," *Transportation Research Record: Journal of the Transportation Research Board* no. 2353 (2013): 33–46.

women and members of marginalized groups.[65] In these examples, rider behavior is not shaped by the affordances of the built environment alone; rather, here we see social norms informing behavior in physical spaces as well.

Recognizing that gendered norms like manspreading and harassment are unwelcome—even dangerous—transit authorities have worked to reshape these behaviors. Often, these efforts start with attempts to change the norms themselves. This kind of approach was at work in the New York City Metropolitan Transportation Authority's awareness campaign to prevent "manspreading," which used signs aimed at men to nudge: "Dude . . . Stop the Spread, Please. It's a space issue" (see Figure 1.3).[66] Similarly, we can see this kind of rule-based approach to reshaping rider behavior in restrictions like the Tokyo Metro's "women-only" subway cars intended to prevent groping by restricting men from entering the space of the car in the first place (see Figure 1.4).[67] In both of these

[65] Emma G. Fitzsimmons, "A Scourge Is Spreading. M.T.A.'s Cure? Dude, Close Your Legs," *New York Times*, December 20, 2014.

[66] Fitzsimmons, "A Scourge Is Spreading."

[67] Colin Joyce, "Persistent Gropers Force Japan to Introduce Women-Only Carriages," *The Telegraph*, May 15, 2005.

Dude...
Stop The Spread,
Please

It's a space issue.

Figure 1.3 Poster from the Metropolitan Transportation Authority (NYC)'s campaign to prevent "manspreading," displayed on busses and subway cars as part of a larger campaign to increase civility. Reproduced with permission from the Metropolitan Transportation Authority.

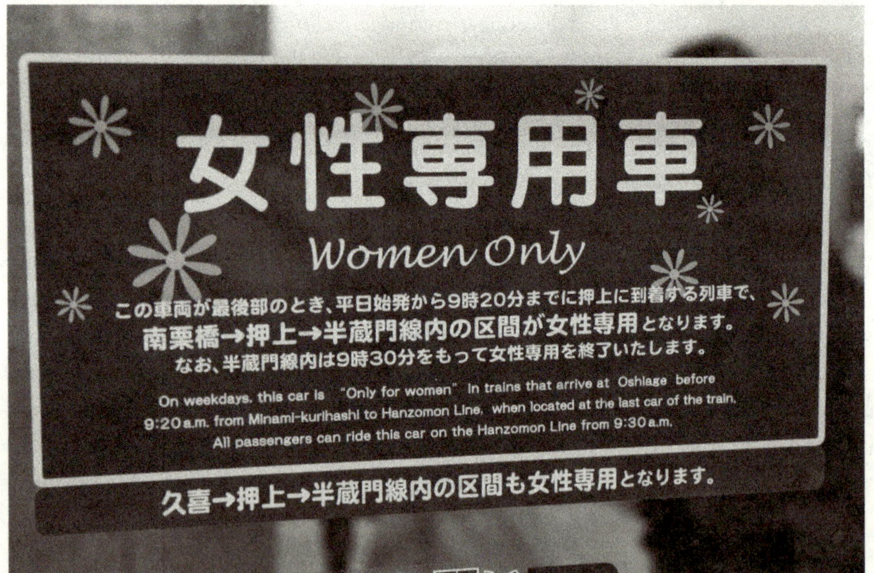

Figure 1.4 Sign from Tokyo Metro, announcing "Women Only" train car. Photograph by Maksym Kozlenko, available at https://commons.wikimedia.org/w/index.php?curid=38771624%20 and licensed under CC BY-SA 4.0.

examples, the affordances of the built environment remained unchanged; the physical space of the subway cars still afforded the opportunity to manspread and grope women. Instead, the transit authorities in both cases focused their efforts to end these unwanted behaviors by targeting the social norms or formal regulations regarding the appropriate behavior in that space.

Figure 1.5 Men reacting to the "penis seat" on Mexico City's Sistema de Transporte Colectivo (STC)-Metro. Sign above the seat reads "For Men Only." Screencapture from "Mexico subway penis seat" by Euronews, available at https://www.youtube.com/watch?v=9wtIaC8FpY4.

As I argue in this book, however, these are not the only available approaches to changing citizens' behavior. Instead, we can also think about how changing the *physical design* of the subway car might achieve the same goals. This environment-oriented strategy was used by Mexico City's Sistema de Transporte Colectivo, when it introduced the "penis seat"—a subway seat shaped like a man's lap, with male genitalia prominent (see Figure 1.5). The logic of the "penis seat" was simple: anyone who sat on (or looked at) the seat would feel—literally—the experience of male sexual harassment. Rather than remind men directly of bad behaviors, like manspreading, or ban men from the spaces of the subway car to prevent groping, the "penis seat" took a spatial approach and redesigned the subway's physical environment to afford men the same discomfort women were regularly made to feel in that space.[68]

As was the case with the "penis seat," redesigning spaces is not a guaranteed solution to changing people's behavior. But neither are traditional approaches that focus only on the laws (like women-only carriages) or the norms (as with manspreading ads) that regulate our collective lives. Rather than advocating for a focus on the built environment *instead of* the formal and informal institutions, like laws and norms, that tend to dominate our discussions of digital technologies, then, it is my argument in this book that any project of democratizing digital

[68] Sopan Deb and Marina Franco, "'Penis Seat' Causes Double Takes on Mexico City Subway," *New York Times*, March 31, 2017.

technologies must consider the built environment *in addition to* these more recognizable manifestations of power. To be sure, our democratic practices are mediated through institutions like norms and laws. But, as we can see from these examples, our practices are also profoundly shaped by the environments we inhabit, the affordances they provide, and our perceptions of those affordances. Yet the question of whether the built environment affords democratic practices—and how to design it to support such ends—has, to date, largely gone unanswered.

Digital Environments and Democratic Affordances

Because it is used to get us to do things we would not otherwise do, the built environment can be an effective, though often invisible, manifestation of power. And this is as true of digital environments as it is of physical ones. "[O]nline platforms," as Zeynep Tufekci notes, "have architectures just as our cities, roads, and buildings do, and those architectures affect how we navigate them."[69] Just as with the physical environments of the subway car, casino, or grocery store, the design of digital platforms like Facebook, Twitter, and Reddit places hard constraints on user behavior. And, as again is the case with the physical built environment, the affordances of digital technologies are also the result of deliberate design choices on the part of software developers. By placing intentionally designed constraints on our behaviors in digital spaces, software architecture functions in much the same way as the walls and sidewalks of the physical built environment: software design is a manifestation of power. It is used to get us to do things we otherwise would not do.

Scholars interested in digital technologies have attended to the design of the digital built environment, the resulting affordances, and their effects on "user behavior" for quite some time. Early studies of digital politics, for example, explored how the internet might help build (democratic) communities in new virtual spaces like Usenet and WELL, as well as its effect on improving offline political participation through "civic networks" in cities like Minneapolis and Santa Monica.[70] Many of these thinkers, in fact, analogized these new digital

[69] Zeynep Tufekci, *Twitter and Tear Gas: The Power and Fragility of Networked Protest* (New Haven: Yale University Press, 2017), 10.

[70] Andrew Chadwick, *Internet Politics: States, Citizens, and New Communication Technologies* (New York: Oxford University Press, 2006); Lincoln Dahlberg, "Extending the Public Sphere through Cyberspace: The Case of Minnesota E-Democracy," *First Monday* 5, no. 3 (2001); William H. Dutton and K. Guthrie, "An Ecology of Games: The Political Construction of Santa Monica's Public Electronic Network," *Informatisation and the Public Sector* 1 (1991): 279–301; Michael Hauben and Ronda Hauben, *Netizens: On the History and Impact of Usenet and the Internet* (New York: Wiley, 1997); William J. Mitchell, *City of Bits: Space, Place, and the Infobahn* (Cambridge, MA: MIT Press, 1995); Damian Tambini, "New Media and Democracy," *New Media and Society* 1, no. 3 (1999): 305–29.

spaces to those of the physical environment, highlighting the internet's potential as an "online third place"[71] that might help "rebuild the aspects of community that were lost when the malt shop became a mall."[72]

In more detailed studies of specific digital communities, scholars tease out the dynamics of these new "third spaces," showing how the affordances of, for example, social media help to build social capital between users as well as how they introduce new dynamics, like context collapse, into networked publics.[73] As Lawrence Lessig famously argued, "code is law."[74] What he meant is that because it affords and invites certain actions and constrains or forecloses others, software's underlying code regulates behavior in the same way as does law—it is used to get us to do things we would not otherwise do. By drawing on the language of affordances, in other words, scholars of digital technologies provide us with nuanced accounts of the power of software design over user behavior.[75]

And yet, for those invested in the work of democratic politics, merely acknowledging this power is insufficient. Indeed, insofar as we hope to build a

[71] Scott Wright, "From 'Third Place' to 'Third Space': Everyday Political Talk in Non-Political Online Spaces," *Javnost—The Public* 19, no. 3 (2012): 5–20.

[72] Howard Rheingold, *The Virtual Community: Homesteading on the Electronic Frontier* (Cambridge, MA: MIT Press, 2000), 56.

[73] Michael Buozis, "Doxing or Deliberative Democracy?: Evidence and Digital Affordances in the Serial Subreddit," *Convergence: The International Journal of Research into New Media Technologies* 25, no. 3 (2019): 357–73; Daniel Halpern and Jennifer Gibbs, "Social Media as Catalyst for Online Deliberation?: Exploring the Affordances of Facebook and YouTube for Political Expression," *Computers in Human Behavior* 29, no. 3 (2013): 1159–68; Christina Shane-Simpson et al., "Why Do College Students Prefer Facebook, Twitter, or Instagram?: Site Affordances, Tensions between Privacy and Self-Expression, and Implications for Social Capital," *Computers in Human Behavior* 86 (2018): 276–89; Taina Bucher and Anne Helmond, "The Affordances of Social Media Platforms," in *The Sage Handbook of Social Media*, ed. Jean Burgess, Thomas Poell, and Alice Marwick (London: Sage Publications, 2018), 233–53; Barry Wellman et al., "The Social Affordances of the Internet for Networked Individualism," *Journal of Computer-Mediated Communication* 8, no. 3 (2003); danah boyd, "Social Network Sites as Networked Publics: Affordances, Dynamics, and Implications," in *Networked Self: Identity, Community, and Culture on Social Network Sites*, ed. Zizi Papacharissi (New York: Routledge, 2010), 39–58; Nicole B. Ellison and Jessica Vitak, "Social Network Site Affordances and Their Relationship to Social Capital Processes," in *The Handbook of the Psychology of Communication Technology*, ed. S. Shyam Sundar (West Sussex, UK: Wiley Blackwell, 2015), 203–27; Tarleton Gillespie, "The Relevance of Algorithms," in *Media Technologies: Essays on Communication, Materiality, and Society*, ed. Tarleton Gillespie, Pablo J. Boczkowski, and Kirsten A. Foot (Cambridge, MA: MIT Press, 2014), 167–94.

[74] Lawrence Lessig, *Code Version 2.0* (New York: Basic Books, 2006). For a contradictory perspective, see James Grimmelmann, "Regulation by Software," *Yale Law Journal* 114 (2005): 1719–58.

[75] For a more nuanced and detailed critical discussion of affordance theory—including its application in technological analysis, see Jenny L. Davis, *How Artifacts Afford: The Power and Politics of Everyday Things* (Cambridge, MA: MIT Press, 2020).

participatory democratic society in which all citizens are able to meaningfully engage in collective decision-making in all areas of their lives, we must ensure that citizens move in spaces that afford them the opportunities to do so. And, as should by now be clear, part of this work involves building environments—both physical and digital—that provide citizens with the specific affordances required for democratic politics. But precisely what *are* these "democratic affordances"?[76]

Democracy, recall, is the collective management of common affairs. It involves both cooperation and disagreement as we work together to care for the things we share with others, collectively managing the consequences of our individual and collective actions. Democracy, in other words, consists not (only) in institutions of formal representation or electoral systems—though these are, of course, important. Instead, democracy is best understood as a *way of life*—a set of practices, attitudes, and relationships that we (should) carry into all the spheres of activity that we share with others. A commitment to democracy, moreover, includes a commitment to *democratization*—to ensuring that all citizens are able to fully participate in the processes of making the decisions that shape their lives and communities.

Starting from this participatory understanding of democracy, as the activity of collective problem-solving, we can identify three conditions necessary for democracy to work. In order to solve problems collectively, for example, we must form communities. These communities, moreover, must sustain themselves over time and must work to improve their decisions and decision-making processes to meet the ever-changing needs of their members. And because democracy is, I argue, best understood as a method or mode of living, each of these conditions is grounded in a corresponding practice or activity in which citizens must participate. These three democratic practices, then—recognition, attachment, and experimentalism—are the affordances that a built environment must provide in order to be a "democratic space."

[76] The concept of "digital democratic affordances" was first introduced by Lincoln Dahlberg (2011) as a way to categorize the relationships between certain digital technologies (like email and listservs) and forms of democratic participation they enable (like deliberation). While Dahlberg and, later, Deseriis (2020) are primarily focused on democratic participation in formal institutions, here I expand the concept of "democratic affordances" to more broadly identify those qualities of the built environment—physical or digital—required to form, sustain, and improve communities, whether online or offline. See Lincoln Dahlberg, "Re-Constructing Digital Democracy: An Outline of Four 'Positions,'" *New Media and Society* 13, no. 6 (2011): 855–72; Marco Deseriis, "Rethinking the Digital Democratic Affordance and Its Impact on Political Representation: Toward a New Framework," *New Media and Society* 23, no. 8 (2021): 2452–2473.

FORMING COMMUNITIES THROUGH MUTUAL RECOGNITION

As the collective management of common affairs, democratic politics is the work of identifying, discussing, and coordinating action to care for the things we share with others. This is, fundamentally, a cooperative activity; it is something we do with other people. And as a collective endeavor, democratic politics is grounded in certain interpersonal relations. More specifically, as many political theorists have noted, citizens must identify their connections to the common endeavor, as well as the other people they share it with, in order to make democratic politics possible.[77]

Forming these interpersonal ties is a feat of *recognition*. In order to identify common aims, citizens must acknowledge that their actions have consequences that extend beyond their own sphere of influence to shape the lives of others. And in order to work collectively with others, citizens must recognize their fellow citizens as co-contributors to the work of managing these common objects and their effects. In order to engage in the work of collective decision-making, in other words, citizens must recognize, first, what they share with others—their common interests. And, second, they must recognize who they share these interests with. Absent this twofold practice of recognition, democratic communities may still exist, but will be "latent." Though citizens will always share interests, in other words, absent the recognition of those interests, and the peers they share those interests with, communities will fail to coalesce.[78] And without clearly defined and acknowledged communities, citizens will be unable to engage in the collective work of identifying and caring for their common affairs—the work of democratic politics.

SUSTAINING COMMUNITIES THROUGH ATTACHMENT

In addition to presuming the existence of communities, democratic politics also assumes their sustainability. The collective management of common affairs is, after all, a forward-looking activity. Collective problem-solving is not just about addressing contemporary challenges; it also involves protecting, maintaining, and providing for the future of the community as well.[79] And this presumes not just that citizens recognize *that* they share things with others, but also that they will feel a sustained commitment to their community and a corresponding

[77] Elinor Ostrom, *Governing the Commons: The Evolution of Institutions for Collective Action* (Cambridge, UK: Cambridge University Press, 1990); Allen, *Talking to Strangers*; Honig, *Public Things*.

[78] Dewey, *The Public and Its Problems*.

[79] Arendt, *The Human Condition*.

investment in the work of maintaining it. Democratic politics requires, in other words, that citizens "stick around"—that their commitment to the work of democracy is not just motivated by immediate short-term benefits but responds to a deeper sense of interdependence and a corresponding obligation to one's fellow citizens and the communities they share.

In order to facilitate this sustainability, democratic politics requires that citizens form *attachments* to their communities and fellow citizens. An affective attachment to one's community, and the peers who comprise it, works to generate civic "buy-in"; it draws citizens out of their myopic private interests and reminds them of their obligations to share in the work of managing common affairs—not only for their own short-term gains, but also for the sake of the community itself. Moreover, cultivating citizens' attachments to their fellow citizens can help to deepen the interpersonal ties that initially form a community; attachment thus helps to strengthen the bonds between citizens, ensuring that the often-frustrating work of democratic politics continues smoothly. Without this twofold attachment—to one's community and one's fellow citizens—citizens are more likely to retreat into their private lives and withdraw from the public work of democratic politics entirely. While communities may still form, in other words, without cultivating citizens' attachments it is unlikely that these communities will see the levels of participation required to sustain themselves over time.

IMPROVING COMMUNITIES THROUGH EXPERIMENTAL HABITS

Of course, not all long-standing communities that act collectively are properly democratic. Indeed, many groups who work together quite well do so at the expense of perceived outsiders. But recall that participatory democracy requires that all citizens participate equally in making the decisions that shape their lives. This is an inclusive ideal; it demands that we constantly ensure that all those subject to decisions are involved in the processes of making them. But this participatory ideal also assumes that such decisions will be made with an eye toward *improving* the community for all those within it; it assumes, in other words, that decisions and decision-making processes will be *self-correcting*—that they become more inclusive and accurate over time. And, if certain options are not open for consideration—if we never hear from new voices and are unable to test our ideas against potentially viable alternatives—then we cannot be sure our chosen path is the right one. Only under conditions in which individuals can interact with multiple, sometimes conflicting, groups and ideas can we be sure that the results of democratic decision-making are the best representation of *all* citizens' diverse, and diversifying, interests.

And this commitment to progress, or self-improvement, is again grounded in a specific civic practice. In order to improve their decisions and decision-making processes—to ensure that collective decisions are inclusive and self-correcting—citizens must regularly check to make sure that both the processes and outcomes of collective problem-solving reflect their members' interests. This habit of *experimentalism* involves a willingness to test, revise, and alter one's decisions and decision-making processes in order to improve their outcomes. Democratic citizens must therefore have a sense of intellectual humility—a willingness to admit when they are wrong—as well as the curiosity and resourcefulness to imagine new possibilities and make changes, when necessary, to their chosen course of action. Absent this experimentalism, it is unlikely that communities will meet the democratic ideal of improvement; instead, they are liable to become static and stagnant, able to engage in collective action, perhaps, but unwilling to pursue the ideal of inclusive and progressive participation that marks participatory democratic politics.

Constructing Democratic Spaces

As the collective management of common affairs, democratic politics requires three conditions: communities must form, must sustain themselves over time, and must work to improve their decisions and decision-making processes to meet the needs of all members. And because democracy involves participation by the citizens themselves, this means democratic citizens must continually work to (1) form communities by *recognizing* what they share and who they share it with; (2) develop *attachments* to those communities to help sustain them over time; and (3) practice *experimental habits* to improve them. To the extent that we are thwarted in one or more of these practices of recognition, attachment, and experimentalism, we should not expect to see robust democratic communities at work. Each of these is, in other words, necessary but insufficient for the work of democratic politics.

These "democratic affordances," of recognition, attachment, and experimentalism, thus serve as the criteria that designers—and users!—should be attentive to when building and inhabiting the spaces of the built environment, both physical and digital.[80] Over the next four chapters, I provide a more sustained

[80] In articulating a set of principles to inform the design of more productive, inclusive, and democratic spaces, I join similar efforts by groups like Civic Signals and the Design Justice Network. Though our specific prescriptions differ, this book shares their commitment to inclusive and participatory design processes and outcomes. See Civic Signals, "Building Better Digital Public Spaces," New_Public, n.d., https://newpublic.org/signals.; "About Us," Design Justice Network, n.d., https://designjustice.org/about-us.

discussion of precisely how we might construct digital environments that afford these democratic practices. Ultimately, I argue, for environments to support democratic politics, they must balance three characteristics: *boundaries*, which afford recognition; *durability*, which affords attachments; and *flexibility*, which affords experimentalism. Taking up each of these characteristics in its own chapter, I first explain how that particular physical characteristic affords or facilitates the corresponding democratic practice. I then pair these theoretical arguments with more contemporary examples of digital spaces—using the examples of Facebook, Twitter, and Reddit—to show how these characteristics of democratic space are (re)negotiated in digital environments.

Boundaries, for example, facilitate recognition; they help communities to form. In chapter 2, I show how boundaries help citizens to identify their common interests and interlocutors; they therefore help to cultivate the interpersonal ties of what Aristotle calls "political friendship" that ground democratic communities. The chapter then turns to the example of Facebook to explain how boundaries can operate in digital environments. I show how design choices made by Facebook—notably, the dissolution of the boundaries imposed by its initial requirement that users register with an .edu email address (thereby limiting membership to students) and the more recent turn to reimpose boundaries with Facebook Groups—have clear consequences for the likelihood that Facebook users can develop political friendships with one another, thereby forming communities on the platform.

Yet even spaces that have clear boundaries may not ultimately lead to the kind of sustainable communities necessary for democratic politics. Democratic spaces must also exhibit the characteristic of durability. In chapter 3, I draw on Alexis de Tocqueville's writing on democracy and individualism to explain how durable spaces can help cultivate the attachments that bind citizens to a community and its members and thus work to sustain that community over time. Turning again to the digital environment, I show how the use of hashtags on Twitter adds boundaries to the platform but that these boundaries lack the durability required for sustainable democratic communities. The result, I argue, is that Twitter facilitates the easy formation of communities on its platform but is ultimately unable to sustain those communities for long periods of time.

But boundaries and durability alone are insufficient for a democratic space. Indeed, just as boundaries can help form communities, and durable spaces sustain them, these physical characteristics can also create exclusive communities that can be violent, offensive, and aggressive toward perceived outsiders. This is why *democratic* spaces must also be flexible. In chapter 4, I show how flexible spaces—those characterized by variety and malleability—facilitate the development of what John Dewey calls the "experimental habit of mind." Returning once more to the digital environment, I show the effects of flexible spaces—or the lack thereof—for two distinct communities on Reddit: r/the_donald (a community of President Trump's supporters) and r/TwoXChromosomes (a community oriented around "women's issues"). I argue that in removing variety from their environment, r/the_donald turned itself into a static and stagnant space that ultimately warped its members habits and attitudes; likewise, while the addition of r/TwoXChromosomes to the list of Reddit defaults led to a more open and diverse community, its overreliance on moderators nevertheless reduces the space's malleability. I conclude this chapter by suggesting how the spaces of Reddit could be redesigned to be more flexible, further facilitating the democratic practice of experimentalism.

After outlining the three characteristics of democratic environments, I turn to address one of the most common challenges to building digital democratic spaces—the question of private ownership and control. Often, scholars argue that it is a combination of (proprietary) corporate ownership, opaque decision-making, and suspect profit motive that leads companies to design and deploy algorithmic environments that prioritize engagement metrics above more "democratic" values. Yet, in chapter 5 I show that these concerns over ownership and control are framed too narrowly; they privilege the characteristic of flexibility at the expense of boundaries and durability. Returning to the examples of Facebook and Twitter, I discuss how these platforms are often critiqued for their opaque sorting algorithms and users' corresponding lack of control over what content they see. As a result, high-profile tools for "fixing" these problems—tools like Gobo—work to increase the flexibility of these platforms by adding variety and making them more malleable. Yet these solutions, while effective, are nevertheless insufficient for building democratic communities. And that is because, while Facebook and Twitter's algorithms could certainly be more flexible, the more pressing concern in both cases is the platforms' lack of clear and durable boundaries. Ultimately, I argue that while questions of ownership and control are important, we must place these questions alongside concerns about the *communal* effects of algorithmic design if we are to build environments supportive of democratic politics.

Finally, in the concluding chapter, I turn attention back to wider questions of democracy, taking up some of the challenges associated with the project of democratization I propose throughout the book. Many are, for example, quite skeptical of the underlying assumption that the "cure" for democracy's problems is *more* democracy. Instead, they argue that there are good reasons to think that building spaces to facilitate greater participation will simply exacerbate the anti-democratic activity we too often see from digital communities that already exist. This lack of faith in citizens leads many to entrust the work of building to experts. And this authoritarian logic, evident in both architecture and technology, is seemingly at odds with the participatory project that I outline in this book.

And yet, as John Dewey reminds us, the solution of "more democracy" does not imply "introducing more machinery of the same kind as that which already exists"; rather, it "indicate[s] the need of returning to the idea itself . . . and of employing our sense of its meaning to criticize and remake its political manifestations."[81] In that spirit, to "remake" democracy in a world dominated by digital technologies, I conclude the book by reaffirming a democratic faith in citizens' capacities, as well as suggesting strategies through which we might begin the work of rebuilding digital spaces democratically.

Of course, this is not a task that should be left solely as the purview of professional political theorists, scholars of media and politics, or software designers. As will be clear throughout this book, I remain committed to the idea that it is the work of *citizens* to engage in this kind of reflective self-examination about our contemporary circumstances and how we might address them collectively. From one citizen to another, then, this book is my best argument for the approach we should take—together—to meet the challenges, and fulfill the promises, that digital technologies present us with. What this book does is provide us with a shared vocabulary with which to begin identifying, explaining, and critically evaluating the ways that the design of the built environment—whether physical or digital—structures our behavior and thus facilitates (or undermines) democratic practices. What we do with this argument is up to us all.

[81] Dewey, *The Public and Its Problems*, 144.

2

Good Fences Make Good Neighbors

Facebook, Boundaries, and Forming Communities

In the wake of the 2016 US presidential election, during which Facebook's political influence became a topic of widespread concern, CEO Mark Zuckerberg took to the site to announce that Facebook was changing its mission. "For the past 10 years," wrote Zuckerberg, "our mission has been to make the world more open and connected."[1] But as of June 2017, he continued, the company was shifting goals, "expanding" its focus to "give people the power to build community and bring the world closer together." In effect, Zuckerberg's announcement laid out a new "product roadmap focused on building 'Meaningful Communities'"[2]—a roadmap that would, over the ensuing months, lead the company to make changes to Facebook with the goal of helping "one billion people join meaningful communities" and, in so doing, "strengthen our social fabric."[3]

These changes included a number of new features such as adjustments to Facebook's News Feed and new tools to help users exercise control over who and what they see—and who can see them—on the platform.[4] The goal of these interventions, the Facebook team argued, was to increase opportunities for users to "interact one-on-one with others in their network" in order to build the kind of "meaningful communities" that Zuckerberg invoked.[5] And Facebook's emphasis on "one-on-one" interactions as the basis for rich community life continues today as Zuckerberg has more recently articulated a "privacy-focused vision for social networking," positioning Facebook as a site for "private interactions" and

[1] Mark Zuckerberg, "Bringing the World Closer Together," *Facebook*, June 22, 2017, https://www.facebook.com/zuck/posts/10154944663901634.

[2] Zuckerberg, "Bringing the World Closer Together."

[3] Zuckerberg, "Bringing the World Closer Together."

[4] David Ginsberg and Moira Burke, "Is Spending Time on Social Media Bad for Us?," *Facebook Newsroom*, December 2017.

[5] Ginsberg and Burke, "Is Spending Time on Social Media Bad for Us?"

Designing for Democracy. Jennifer Forestal, Oxford University Press. © Oxford University Press 2022.
DOI: 10.1093/oso/9780197568750.003.0002

modeling the platform after a "more intimate space like a living room" that cultivates a "sense of privacy and intimacy."[6]

Facebook's new features may be effective at generating higher rates of user engagement; they may also work to counteract criticisms that the platform increases feelings of loneliness in its users.[7] But the company's underlying emphasis on one-on-one interactions, and the private spaces that host them, misunderstands the kind of interpersonal ties that ground the meaningful *communities* that Zuckerberg ostensibly wants to support—the kinds of communities that are required for democratic politics. Rather than insisting, as Facebook does, on individual user control and prioritizing the dyadic Friendship ties that have traditionally formed the basis of Facebook's social graph, a more effective approach to "building community" with Facebook and other digital platforms is to focus on creating the conditions under which users can form the one-to-*many* ties that are the foundation of community life.

Cultivating these one-to-many ties is crucial for the success of democratic politics. As the collective management of common affairs, democracy is a *cooperative* activity. It requires communities to form before they can begin the collective activity of managing their shared interests. To do so, however, citizens must be "activated";[8] they must be made to acknowledge themselves as members of a community with other people and to cultivate the habits, attitudes, and relationships necessary to care for it alongside others. This activation is the basis of what Aristotle calls *political friendship*. And political friendship, as we will see, is the foundation for "building community."

Political friendships are characterized (as all friendships are) by a set of practices through which we learn, as Danielle S. Allen puts it, "when and where to moderate our interests for our own sake" through "practices to equalize benefits

[6] Mark Zuckerberg, "A Privacy-Focused Vision for Social Networking," *Facebook*, March 6, 2019, https://www.facebook.com/notes/mark-zuckerberg/a-privacy-focused-vision-for-social-networking/10156700570096634/.

[7] Jean M. Twenge et al., "Increases in Depressive Symptoms, Suicide-Related Outcomes, and Suicide Rates among U.S. Adolescents after 2010 and Links to Increased New Media Screen Time," *Clinical Psychological Science* 6, no. 1 (2018): 3–17; Philippe Verduyn et al., "Passive Facebook Usage Undermines Affective Well-Being: Experimental and Longitudinal Evidence," *Journal of Experimental Psychology* 144, no. 2 (2015): 480–88; Holly B. Shakya and Nicholas A. Christakis, "Association of Facebook Use with Compromised Well-Being: A Longitudinal Study," *American Journal of Epidemiology* 185, no. 3 (2017): 203–11; Hayeon Song et al., "Does Facebook Make You Lonely?: A Meta Analysis," *Computers in Human Behavior* 36 (2014): 446–52; Stephen Marche, "Is Facebook Making Us Lonely?," *Atlantic Magazine*, May 2012.

[8] Robert J. Sampson, "Neighborhood and Community: Collective Efficacy and Community Safety," *New Economy* 11 (2004): 106–13.

and burdens and power sharing."[9] Unlike in one-to-one friendships, however, where friends distribute these benefits and burdens equally between the two friends personally involved, the specifically *political* friendship Aristotle highlights involves one's willingness to engage in such practices with the many (strangers) who constitute members of one's political community. Political friendship, then, while it shares the same basic practices as more personal forms of friendship, is a one-to-*many* relationship; it involves both the *recognition* that we share interests with the others in our community as well as the *shared activity* of managing those interests with those strangers. Political friendship thus serves as the foundation for democratic communities—it helps these communities form so they can begin the collective work of managing their common concerns.

In what follows, I outline the role of shared interests and interlocutors—and the recognition thereof—in facilitating the formation of democratic communities through ties of "political friendship." And while formal and informal institutions like laws and social norms can and do help facilitate this recognition, I focus my attention in this chapter on the role of the built environment. In particular, drawing from the work of Aristotle, I argue for the importance of clearly identifiable *boundaries* in cultivating citizens' recognition of what they share and with whom they share it. Boundaries—by which I mean clear demarcations that signal to someone that they are entering a particular (and enclosed) space—help to facilitate the activity that generates and sustains the one-to-many ties of political friendship.

By highlighting what they hold in common with one another, physical boundaries like those of a courtyard or city call attention to the shared interests of the citizens within that space. They also help generate feelings of reciprocity and goodwill among those citizens. Boundaries thus play a psychological role in reorienting us away from our individual self-interest and directing our attention—and action—toward our community's shared objects; they afford the recognition that political friendship requires. As a result, they are a constituent element of democratic spaces; they help democratic communities to form.

Recognizing the value of boundaries, architects and urban planners have moved to (re)insert boundaries in and around communal spaces. And there is some evidence this strategy is successful; the addition of elements like fences, front porches, and streets—all of which add boundaries and definition to previously open and undefined spaces—has been correlated with an increased sense of community within a neighborhood.[10] By contrast, in unbounded, and thus

[9] Danielle S. Allen, *Talking to Strangers: Anxieties of Citizenship since Brown v. Board of Education* (Chicago: University of Chicago Press, 2004), 126, 130.

[10] Stephanie E. Bothwell, Raymond Gindroz, and Robert E. Lang, "Restoring Community through Traditional Neighborhood Design: A Case Study of Diggs Town Public Housing," *Housing Policy Debate* 9, no. 1 (1998): 89–114.

ill-defined, spaces, citizens have a harder time recognizing the things they share in common and the people they share them with; in these spaces we are more likely to feel, and act, isolated and alone.

The chapter's argument proceeds as follows: in the next section, I outline the role of *boundaries* in constituting a democratic community. Drawing on Aristotle's concept of "political friendship," I argue that it is the presence of clear and visible boundaries that helps citizens identify their common interests and interlocutors—the things they share and the people they share them with. In clearly bounded spaces, citizens are more likely to form and act upon the one-to-many ties of political friendship based on the recognition of their shared lives.

With this function of boundaries in mind, I then return to the example of Facebook. After first tracing the evolution and effects of Facebook's shifting boundaries, I then show how recent changes to the platform—namely, the reinvigoration of Facebook Groups—function like the fences and front porches of the physical environment; they reimpose boundaries on a platform that was, for most of its existence, defined by its radical openness. Turning Facebook from a collection of individuals to a network of smaller groups, I argue, we would expect these changes to help strengthen communities on the platform, setting the stage for more robust democratic political action by users.

Boundaries, Friendship, and Democratic Politics

Digital technologies, as conventional wisdom has it, are tearing at our social fabric. Though they afford quick and easy access to friends, family, acquaintances, and strangers, the argument goes, social media platforms like Facebook are substituting meaningful intimate relationships with superficial ties.[11] In this, social media are simply the latest in a long line of technologies thought to be undermining or destroying "meaningful communities" by turning us away from traditional civil associations and trivializing public discourse.[12] And while scholars disagree

[11] Sherry Turkle, *Alone Together: Why We Expect More from Technology and Less from Each Other* (New York: Basic Books, 2011); Melissa G. Hunt et al., "No More FOMO: Limiting Social Media Decreases Loneliness and Depression," *Journal of Social and Clinical Psychology* 37, no. 10 (2018): 751–68; Eric J. Vanman, Rosemary Baker, and Stephanie J. Tobin, "The Burden of Online Friends: The Effects of Giving Up Facebook on Stress and Well-Being," *Journal of Social Psychology* 158, no. 4 (2018): 496–508.

[12] Robert D. Putnam, *Bowling Alone: The Collapse and Revival of American Community* (New York: Simon & Schuster, 2000); Neil Postman, *Amusing Ourselves to Death: Public Discourse in the Age of Show Business* (New York: Penguin Books, 1985).

over the severity of the problem—pointing out, for example, the mediating effects of age and activity[13]—this research has led companies like Facebook to change the structure of their platforms to counteract these trends by "rolling out new tools to make it easier for you to build communities."[14]

When diagnosing and proposing solutions to the collective dangers of digital technologies, scholars and practitioners alike tend to use the language of declining social capital.[15] Based in the work of Mark Granovetter and Robert Putnam (among others),[16] this emphasis on social capital has led to debates over the strength of the ties formed using digital technologies (strong versus weak), the people involved in these digital relationships (bonding versus bridging), and the various "uses and gratifications" of specific platforms.[17] These are all important interventions, to be sure. However, at their foundation, all these discussions of social capital understand it to be an *individualized* resource; it refers, as Robert Putnam argues, "to connections among *individuals*—social networks and the norms of reciprocity and trustworthiness that arise from them."[18] The communal

[13] Caroline Bell et al., "Examining Social Media Use among Older Adults," in *Proceedings of the 24th ACM Conference on Hypertext and Social Media* (Paris: ACM, 2013), 158–63; Eric Klinenberg, "Facebook Isn't Making Us Lonely," *Slate*, April 19, 2012.

[14] Zuckerberg, "Bringing the World Closer Together."

[15] Keith Hampton and Barry Wellman, "Neighboring in Netville: How the Internet Supports Community and Social Capital in a Wired Suburb," *City and Community* 2, no. 4 (2003): 277–311; Marko M. Skoric, Deborah Ying, and Ying Ng, "Bowling Online, Not Alone: Online Social Capital and Political Participation in Singapore," *Journal of Computer-Mediated Communication* 14, no. 2 (2009): 414–33; Raquel Recuero, Adriana Amaral, and Camila Monteiro, "Fandoms, Trending Topics and Social Capital in Twitter," *AoIR Selected Papers of Internet Research* 13 (2012): 1–14, https://spir.aoir.org/index.php/spir/article/view/7; Moira Burke, Robert Kraut, and Cameron Marlow, "Social Capital on Facebook: Differentiating Uses and Users," in *Proceedings of the SIGCHI Conference on Human Factors in Computing Systems* (Vancouver, BC, 2011), 571–80.

[16] Mark Granovetter, "The Strength of Weak Ties," *American Journal of Sociology* 78, no. 6 (1973): 1360–80; Robert D. Putnam, "Bowling Alone: America's Declining Social Capital," *Journal of Democracy* 6, no. 1 (1995): 65–78; James Farr, "Social Capital: A Conceptual History," *Political Theory* 32, no. 1 (February 1, 2004): 6–33.

[17] Joe Phua, Seunga Venus Jin, and Jihoon (Jay) Jay, "Uses and Gratifications of Social Networking Sites for Bridging and Bonding Social Capital: A Comparison of Facebook, Twitter, Instagram, and Snapchat," *Computers in Human Behavior* 72 (2017): 115–22; Nicole B. Ellison, Charles Steinfield, and Cliff Lampe, "Connection Strategies: Social Capital Implications of Facebook-Enabled Communication Practices," *New Media and Society* 13, no. 6 (2010): 873–92; Jessica Vitak, Nicole B. Ellison, and Charles Steinfield, "The Ties That Bond: Re-Examining the Relationship between Facebook Use and Bonding Social Capital," in *Proceedings of the 44th Hawaii International Conference on System Sciences* (Piscataway, NJ: IEEE, 2011), 1530–1605.

[18] Putnam, *Bowling Alone*, 19. Emphasis mine.

dimension of social capital is, by contrast, relegated to those "'externalities' that affect the wider community."[19]

The concept of social capital is, in other words, focused on the resources individuals draw from their social networks. But social networks are, as Nancy K. Baym argues, fundamentally different from *communities*. "Social networks," she notes, "are egocentric and . . . no two SNS [social networking site] users will have access to the same set of people or messages, giving them each an experience of the site that is individualized yet overlapping with others."[20] In communities, by contrast, members have a "sense of shared space, rituals of shared practices, and exchange of social support," as well as a shared identity as members of that community.[21] The interpersonal ties that ground communities, in other words, are not the same as the individually connected one-to-one ties of a social network—the ties captured by the concept of social capital. Instead, communities are marked by one-to-*many* ties based in the collective recognition that members have a shared existence and, as a result, have a shared interest in directing it.

If democracy is, as I have been arguing, a way of life through which we collectively manage common affairs, then these one-to-many ties that ground communities are an integral component of this work. "Building meaningful communities" suited to the work of democratic politics, then, is not only a matter of strengthening the individualized, one-to-one relationships of social capital that comprise one's personal network; rather, democratic citizens must develop certain habits of shared agency oriented toward the many other strangers in their community. Rather than treat them as "externalities," in other words, the collective consequences of one's activity must be *central* to citizens' relationships. But this requires citizens' mutual recognition that a shared interest or endeavor exists in the first place.

Facilitating this recognition is no easy feat. Indeed, many of the long-standing problems of political science—like the provision of public goods and the "free-rider" problem[22]—are problems of collective action; they occur as the direct result of citizens' inability or unwillingness to acknowledge a shared interest or common advantage. Instead, these collective action problems speak to how easily citizens act with "rivalrous self-interest," ignoring the collective consequences of their individual actions.[23] They are therefore best understood as problems of

[19] Putnam, *Bowling Alone*, 20.

[20] Nancy K. Baym, *Personal Connections in the Digital Age*, 2nd ed. (Cambridge, UK: Polity Press, 2016), 101.

[21] Baym, *Personal Connections in the Digital Age*, 96.

[22] Mancur Olson Jr., *The Logic of Collective Action: Public Goods and the Theory of Groups* (Cambridge, MA: Harvard University Press, 1971).

[23] Allen, *Talking to Strangers*.

recognition; the breakdown of collective action occurs in these cases because citizens fail to recognize their one-to-many relationship to a larger community and its members.

In order to form the communities required to act collectively, then, simply building social capital between individuals is insufficient. Instead, democratic politics requires that citizens reconceptualize their relationship to others and the interests they share—that they form self-conscious communities. And in order to form these communities, citizens must agree upon the goods, goals, and resources they share with others, as well as acknowledge those with whom they share them. They must recognize one another—and act—not with social capital, but as political friends.

In this section, I turn to Aristotle—one of the first democratic thinkers—to clarify the nature and requirements of this "political friendship," emphasizing, in particular, the environmental requirements needed to achieve it. Living and writing in the fourth century BCE, Aristotle spent considerable time thinking about the interpersonal ties that ground democratic politics. And while much of the secondary scholarship in this area has focused on exploring the intricacies of Aristotelian friendship[24] and teasing out its role in his political theory,[25] Aristotle also recognized that the built environment can have an effect on how we relate to one another as friends and citizens.

Though he did not frame his arguments using the language of the built environment, I nevertheless use Aristotle's work to identify two key democratic functions of boundaries. Boundaries, I argue, facilitate political friendship by helping citizens (1) identify their common interests; and (2) recognize, and act with reciprocated goodwill toward, their interlocutors. In so doing, boundaries structure citizens' interpersonal relationships in a way that makes democratic politics possible; boundaries help communities form. Absent clear boundaries, I argue, it becomes much more difficult to form communities because citizens cannot identify what they share and with whom—the foundation of political friendship, in other words, is harder to cultivate.

[24] John M. Cooper, "Aristotle on the Forms of Friendship," *Review of Metaphysics* 30, no. 4 (1977): 619–48; John M. Cooper, "Friendship and the Good in Aristotle," *Philosophical Review* 86, no. 3 (1977): 290–315; Lorraine Smith Pangle, *Aristotle and the Philosophy of Friendship* (Cambridge, UK: Cambridge University Press, 2003).

[25] Allen, *Talking to Strangers*; Bernard Yack, *The Problems of a Political Animal: Community, Justice, and Conflict in Aristotelian Political Thought* (Berkeley: University of California Press, 1993); Susan Bickford, "Beyond Friendship: Aristotle on Conflict, Deliberation, and Attention," *Journal of Politics* 58, no. 2 (1996): 398–421; Jill Frank, *A Democracy of Distinction: Aristotle and the Work of Politics* (Chicago: University of Chicago Press, 2005), chap. 5.

DEMOCRACY AND (POLITICAL) FRIENDSHIP

Democratic politics, as Aristotle describes it, involves collective "deliberation or decision" (P 1275b19) over the things shared by a community.[26] As the collective management of common affairs, in other words, democratic politics is the work of identifying, discussing, and coordinating action to care for the things we share with others. And as a mode of cooperative activity, democratic politics rests on interpersonal relations. More specifically, democracy works best when citizens are bound by ties of reciprocity, trust, and accommodation[27]—ties of what Aristotle calls "political friendship." To properly call themselves (political) friends, Aristotle tells us, citizens must identify and work together toward a common advantage and, in so doing, both recognize and act with reciprocated goodwill toward their peers.

It may seem strange to characterize the interpersonal ties between citizens as "friendship." But the Ancient Greek concept of friendship, as many have noted, is more capacious than our modern understanding; in addition to "friends" as we commonly think of them, the Greek term also encompasses relationships between family members, business associates, and citizens.[28] At the foundation of all these relationships, however—the thing that marks them all as types of friendship—are feelings of mutual goodwill, mutually recognized; friendship, in other words, is "reciprocated goodwill" (NE 1155b33–1156a6).

A friend, then, is someone we wish the best for—though the reason for this goodwill may differ in different relationships. While in "complete friendship," says Aristotle, friends hold feelings of goodwill because of their virtuous characters, in "pleasure" or "utility" friendships, friends wish well for one another "because he is pleasant to them" or "insofar as they gain some good for themselves from him" (NE 1156a10–15).[29] In all cases, though, while the object of friendship may differ, the underlying feeling of goodwill remains; friends, for whatever the reason, want what is best for their friends.

Goodwill is an important feature of friendship—but it is not the entirety of it. Goodwill, Aristotle reminds us, "arises even toward people we do not know, and without their noting it" (NE 1166b30). For a relationship to be a meaningful

[26] Throughout this chapter, I use the abbreviation P to refer to Aristotle's *Politics*, NE to refer to the *Nichomachean Ethics*, and EE to refer to the *Eudemian Ethics*. See Aristotle, *Aristotle's Politics*, trans. Carnes Lord, 2nd ed. (Chicago: University of Chicago Press, 2013); Aristotle, *The Eudemian Ethics*, trans. Anthony Kenny (Oxford: Oxford University Press, 2011); Aristotle, *Nichomachean Ethics*, trans. Terence Irwin, 2nd ed. (Indianapolis: Hackett Publishing Company, 1999).

[27] Amy Gutmann and Dennis Thompson, *Democracy and Disagreement* (Cambridge, MA: Harvard University Press, 1996).

[28] Cooper, "Aristotle on the Forms of Friendship."

[29] See also Cooper, "Aristotle on the Forms of Friendship," esp. 633–34.

friendship, however, it requires a kind of mutuality—friends must not just "have goodwill to each other," they must also "be aware of it" (NE 1156a3). Friendship, in other words, rests on a mutual *recognition*—more than generalized feelings of goodwill, the basis of friendship is goodwill grounded in a mutually recognized shared interest (whether pleasure, utility, or virtue). Absent that recognition, and the familiarity it generates, we might say that people have goodwill toward one another, but we cannot properly call them friends.

Yet even this mutually recognized, reciprocated goodwill is insufficient for Aristotelian friendship. Friendship, Aristotle notes repeatedly, is an *activity*.[30] This is why, Aristotle tells us in the *Nichomachean Ethics*, "concord also appears to be a feature of friendship" (NE 1167a23). More than "sharing a belief, since this may happen among people who do not know each other" (NE 1167a23), concord "concerns questions for action, and, more exactly, large questions where both or all can get what they want" (NE 1167a30). To be in concord—to be a friend—means not just goodwill and the recognition thereof; it also means that friends "agree on what is advantageous, make the same decision, and act on their common resolution" (NE 1167a29). Concord, in other words, is cooperative activity oriented toward a common advantage—whether pleasurable activities or useful exchanges. Friendship, then, consists of two components: mutually recognized goodwill and collective action around a shared interest. Absent one or more of these characteristics—mutually recognized goodwill and cooperative activity—we may still have virtue or decency, but we do not have friendship.

And though today we tend to think of friendship as a "private" or apolitical human relationship, the concept has a central place in Aristotle's political theory. Friendship not only involves association, Aristotle tells us (NE 1159b25–35), but it is the very foundation of a democratic community; it is the glue that "would seem to hold cities together" (NE 1155a23). As a specific form of utility friendship, moreover, political friendships are based on mutual advantage—citizens, as political friends, recognize that they can gain something from one another.

In the context of political friendship, the common advantage and concord that ground ties between citizens concern questions of justice—questions

[30] See Cooper, "Friendship and the Good in Aristotle"; Pangle, *Aristotle and the Philosophy of Friendship*. "Shared activities are especially valuable for any human being since they, more than purely private activities, enable one to be continuously and happily engaged in things. This is so, in sum, for three reasons: (1) they provide one with an immediate and continuing sense that what one finds interesting and worthwhile is really so, since the experience of others is seen to agree with one's own in this respect; (2) they enhance one's attachment to and interest in one's own personal, direct activities by putting them within the context of a broader group activity which is itself a source of pleasure and interest; and (3) they expand the scope of one's activity by enabling one to participate, through membership in a group of jointly active persons, in the actions of others" (Cooper, "Friendship and the Good in Aristotle," 308).

regarding "the advantageous and the harmful, and hence also the just and the unjust" (P 1253a15).[31] Political friendships, then, are organized around the mutual desire to create the conditions under which we successfully "live together with strangers."[32] In order for political friendships—and thus democratic communities—to form, citizens must both recognize this shared interest in living well together and act cooperatively to secure it.

Both formal and informal institutions, like laws and social norms, can help facilitate this twofold behavior of recognition and cooperative action. But so, too, can the built environment.[33] Friendship, Aristotle tells us, "is the intentional choice of living together" (P 1280b35–40). And while it is the activity of friendship—the sharing of conversation and thought—that matters most to Aristotle, this nevertheless has a spatial dimension. Distance, Aristotle reminds us, has a detrimental effect on friendship: while it "does not dissolve the friendship unconditionally," it does eliminate "its activity" (NE 1157b10–14). But friendship, as we have seen, *requires* activity; it demands that citizens continually engage one another with mutual goodwill and actively pursue a shared effort toward a common goal. And it is easier to engage in the coordinated activity of concord when friends share space. This is because we must recognize our (potential) collaborators and identify a common pursuit before we can act together as political friends. A shared environment can help us do both.

It is *boundaries*, in particular, that help cultivate these ties of political friendship. Clearly bounded spaces—spaces that are clearly demarcated—are environments that help to direct generalized feelings of goodwill into the focused and reciprocated goodwill of friends. In so doing, bounded spaces also set the stage for the activity of concord—the collective action of democratic politics. Clearly identified boundaries thus have a twofold effect: they help us recognize what we share (the mutual advantage and object of democratic politics) as well as with whom we share it (our fellow citizens; those for whom we feel reciprocated goodwill). Absent this recognition, there is no guarantee that we will form

[31] This is why, Aristotle notes, lawmakers should be more concerned with facilitating friendship than justice, because "friendship and justice would seem to be about the same things and to be found in the same people" (NE 1159b27). That shared object between justice and friendship is the reciprocated goodwill that "converts rivalrous into equitable self-interest" (Allen, *Talking to Strangers*, 137). Just as justice demands equitable treatment, so too do the practices of friendship. As political friends, we recognize and act with one another as equal co-contributors in a shared endeavor.

[32] Allen, *Talking to Strangers*, 135.

[33] Aristotle was clearly attentive to the power of the built environment. In Book II of the *Politics*, in the context of his comparative evaluation of good governments, Aristotle introduces Hippodamus of Miletus as the man who "invented the art of planning cities" and who was "the first person not a statesman who made inquiries about the best form of government."

the political friendships that ground democratic communities; these communities will simply fail to coalesce.

IDENTIFYING COMMON INTERESTS

Friends are, as we have seen, brought together by a common good or advantage; it is this common object that clarifies their relationships with one another (NE 1159b25–30; NE 1160a30). For utility or pleasure friendships, this common advantage is the usefulness or pleasure the friends receive from one another's company; as a particular form of utility friendship, then, the political friendship of citizens "seems both to have been originally formed and to endure for advantage" (NE 1160a12–14)—specifically, for the sake of the good life (P 1253a1–5; NE 1160a20–25). Political friendships, in other words, rest on citizens' recognition that they share an interest in justice, in living well together with the others in their community.

Laws and other formal institutions can help citizens recognize this shared interest; the US Constitution, for example, identifies certain ideals—such as "domestic tranquility," "common defense," and "general welfare"—that are ostensibly the shared interests of the citizens who make up "the people." The Constitution, like the contracts that Aristotle says mark utility friendships (EE 1242b35–1243a10), thus helps outline for citizens what they share; it directs their attention to a common advantage around which they can begin arguing, deliberating, and acting collectively. But the built environment, too, can help facilitate this recognition.

Boundaries, in particular, help citizens identify their shared interests by shaping individuals' perceptions of the world in which they live. Clear boundaries highlight the collective experiences of a given shared space. By distinguishing one space from others, boundaries help clarify the common advantage of the community housed in that space.[34] Using the metaphor of travel, Bernard Yack explains this dynamic in more detail:

> We are usually far more inclined to put ourselves out to help someone with whom we are sharing a plane or bus ride than we are willing to do after we have reached our destination. When we share a journey, the sense of being "all in the same boat"—the sense that we are all unavoidably stuck, whatever our differences, with the difficulties and

[34] Sheila R. Foster, "Collective Action and the Urban Commons," *Notre Dame Law Review* 87 (2011): 57–134; Russell Weaver, "A Cross-Level Exploratory Analysis of 'Neighborhood Effects' on Urban Behavior: An Evolutionary Perspective," *Social Sciences* 4 (2015): 1046–66; George Galster, "On the Nature of Neighborhood," *Urban Studies* 38, no. 12 (2001): 2111–24.

> inconveniences created by our shared means of transport—disposes us to make much more of an effort than we ordinarily make to help strangers.[35]

The fellow travelers in this example are like political friends: in recognizing their shared condition, they also recognize a common advantage; safe passage, in this case, can only be achieved with collective efforts. But while Yack, like many scholars of Aristotelian friendship, emphasizes the shared *experience* of traveling—the "difficulties and inconveniences created by our shared means of transport"—he nevertheless fails to explore how it is the *physical space* of the plane or bus that brings this shared experience into relief. That shared "sense of being 'all in the same boat' " is generated through the physical design of the boat itself; we recognize those fellow travelers *as* fellow travelers only because the walls and seats of the boat have the psychological effect of helping us to conceptualize their relationships to us.

Consider airplane passengers before and after travel versus during the flight itself. The same people might be sitting nearby in the airport prior to take-off. They might stand next to one another waiting for their bags to be unloaded after arrival. In either case, the same kind of recognition of, and coordination around, a shared interest that Yack describes is not present. Indeed, the less-defined area of the airport gate or baggage claim makes it more difficult to identify not only those around us who share our experiences, but even what those experiences might be. We cannot easily tell, for example, who is on *our* flight and who is not, because the lack of clear boundaries fails to signal to us this shared endeavor. If political friendship rests on the "sense of being 'all in the same boat,' " in other words, then the construction and visibility of the boat has an enormous impact on whether travelers will recognize that sense of being or not—as well as how they will act once they do.

The same dynamic is at work in a courtyard clearly "bounded by the dwellings it serves"[36] (see Figure 2.1). The courtyard is clearly demarcated by its boundaries; residents' houses visibly form its limits. As a result of these clear boundaries, it becomes easier for residents to acknowledge that they share the space with others (their neighbors) and thus have a shared (collective) interest in, and responsibility for, participating in its upkeep and maintenance.[37] Within a space defined by clear boundaries, in other words, residents are more likely to

[35] Yack, *The Problems of a Political Animal*, 37.

[36] Clare Cooper Marcus, "Shared Outdoor Space and Community Life," *Places* 15, no. 2 (2003): 32–41.

[37] Marcus, "Shared Outdoor Space and Community Life."

Figure 2.1 Example of shared courtyard. The courtyard is clearly bounded by the houses around it, making it easier for residents to recognize their shared interest in its maintenance. Photograph: "Autumn Courtyard" by Jocelyn Erskine-Kellie, available at https://flic.kr/p/2auj5Up and licensed under CC BY-SA 2.0.

enter into concord—to understand both the magnitude of the shared object as well as their role in cooperatively managing it.[38]

Despite the increasing prevalence of digital technologies that facilitate frequent, low-cost communication between individuals, moreover, there is evidence that boundaries still play an important psychological role in facilitating this recognition of shared interests and the cooperative activity it generates—even among strangers in digital environments. Testing the effectiveness of computer-mediated collaborative tools like video conferencing and instant messaging applications, for example, researchers found significant differences between respondents who believed they were communicating with a partner located in a distant locale versus those who believed they were communicating with a partner located in their own city. Subjects were more immediately willing to cooperate with someone located in their own

[38] Elinor Ostrom, *Governing the Commons: The Evolution of Institutions for Collective Action* (Cambridge, UK: Cambridge University Press, 1990); Sara Singleton and Michael Taylor, "Common Property, Collective Action and Community," *Journal of Theoretical Politics* 4, no. 3 (1992): 309–15.

city and considered their interactions to be much closer in distance than they were.[39]

What this study shows is the psychological impact of clearly bounded, shared space on subjects' perceptions. Despite their never having met their digital interlocutor, and despite the rather large geographical area of a city, the fact that the shared object (the city) was clearly defined meant that subjects could conceptualize what they shared with their partner—and it had noticeable effects on their behavior, leading to more cooperation.[40] As with the examples of the boat and the courtyard, the clear boundaries of the city helped participants conceptualize what they had in common with the strangers they encountered.

By connecting what would otherwise be disparate elements of a given environment, boundaries help us to clearly identify the things we share with others. And this identification is the first crucial step in acting cooperatively to care for them. In helping us to identify a common advantage, boundaries set the foundation for political friendships—and thus for democratic politics.

RECOGNIZING MUTUAL GOODWILL

A democratic community, as we have seen, arises out of mutual advantage: recognizing their shared goals and the mutual benefits of collaboration, citizens turn their efforts to securing those collective goals and activities by working together. Recognizing a common interest is thus a necessary component in developing political friendship. But just having a shared space is not enough. A common space and collective goods must, Aristotle tells us, "necessarily be present if there is to be a city, but not even when all of them are present is it yet a city" (P 1280b30–35). Recall that friendship also requires mutual recognition—friends must not just have shared interests, they must also be "aware of the reciprocated goodwill" (NE 1155b35) they have toward one another as co-contributors to maintaining that shared interest. What Aristotle is highlighting, here, is the importance of what he elsewhere calls the "work of affection" (P 1280b35–40). By this, he means that citizens, as political friends, do not just have a generalized sense of goodwill toward others, but actively recognize their shared life and act collectively, and with goodwill, with those with whom they share their lives.

[39] Erin Bradner and Gloria Mark, "Why Distance Matters: Effects on Cooperation, Persuasion and Deception," in *Proceedings of the 2002 ACM Conference on Computer Supported Cooperative Work* (New Orleans, LA, 2002), 226–35.

[40] When asked to explain why they were willing to cooperate, for instance, subjects expressed an expectation of eventually meeting partners from their own city. Because they conceived of themselves as sharing the space of the city with their interlocutor, in other words, subjects thought it was much more likely that they would meet their partner in person. The importance of repeated interactions in durable spaces (like that of a city) is explored in more detail in chapter 3.

In discussing how to form these affectionate interpersonal ties, Aristotle notes the importance of "marriage connections . . . clans, festivals, and the pastimes of living together" (P 1280b35–36); through these kinds of institutionalize practices, citizens repeatedly come to recognize and embody the "intentional choice of living together" (P 1280b35–40) that Aristotle terms "affection." Through these institutional practices, in other words, citizens not only come to see one another as co-contributors to the common good; they also develop the recognition of mutual goodwill and habits of reciprocity that, ultimately, leads them to act collectively and equitably as citizens and (political) friends.

Institutions like marriage and other formal celebrations can be important tools for cultivating this goodwill. But just as the built environment can shape our perceptions of a shared object, so too can it play a role in generating goodwill among those who share it. Consider again Yack's metaphor of travel. It is travelers' recognition of their common advantage that also "disposes [them] to make much more of an effort than [they] ordinarily make to help strangers."[41] In recognizing their common advantage, in other words, the travelers (or citizens) are more likely to develop feelings of goodwill and reciprocity toward those they share the journey with. The two elements of political friendship—reciprocated goodwill and coordinated action around common interests—are therefore mutually reinforcing. The result is a trip that runs much more smoothly. And, again, it is the clearly bounded space of the boat that helps generate these feelings of mutuality and accommodation for those with whom we share a space.

We can see this at work in other clearly bounded spaces as well. In an office kitchen, for example, workers can easily identify those who share a stake in the cleanliness of the microwave; those who work in the office have the same claim to that common space. If the kitchen were unbounded, however, and use of that resource were not clearly limited to those who share in the office space, it would be much more difficult for the workers to conceptualize the "kitchen community" and develop feelings of mutual goodwill with the other members of it.

This psychological effect of boundaries in helping citizens cultivate the mutually recognized goodwill required to form communities is at the core of the New Urbanism movement. An influential approach to urban planning, New Urbanism gained prominence throughout the 1980s and 1990s with its commitment to "reestablishing the relationship between the art of building and the making of community."[42] Emphasizing compact, walkable towns, New Urbanism's guiding principles include a recognition of the role of well-defined spaces in facilitating residents' sense of community: "metropolitan regions," proclaims the first principle of New

[41] Yack, *The Problems of a Political Animal*, 37.

[42] The Congress for the New Urbanism, "The Charter of the New Urbanism," accessed October 31, 2016, https://www.cnu.org/who-we-are/charter-new-urbanism.

Urbanism, "are finite places with geographic boundaries."[43] Thus, "a primary task of all urban architecture and landscape design is the physical definition of streets and public spaces as places of shared use.... Properly configured, they encourage walking and enable neighbors to know each other and protect their communities."[44] The "proper" configuration, moreover, is one of clear boundaries; boundaries, reinforced during the urban planning process, create "a better way of defining what a neighborhood is, which contributes to establishing its identity and meaning."[45] By clearly inscribing the boundaries of a given locale, in other words, the principles of New Urbanism seek to facilitate residents' feelings of mutual goodwill toward their fellow citizens—and there is some evidence that they succeed.[46]

Take, for example, the Five Oaks neighborhood in Dayton, Ohio. Originally a thoroughfare between the city's downtown and its outlying suburbs, the Five Oaks neighborhood aimed to build community among its residents by following the principles of Oscar Newman's (in)famous "Defensible Space" approach to urban design.[47] Like the New Urbanists, Newman advocated for the creation of clearly defined spaces as a way to facilitate feelings of goodwill and collective action among neighbors. When spaces are clearly defined, argued Newman—bounded in a way that makes it easy for residents to identify what is shared and with whom—residents can "control the public spaces better" because they can "more readily recognize residents from strangers and feel they have a say in determining accepted behavior."[48] The strategic use of boundaries, in other words, can help citizens reorient their perceptions of one another, helping to identify citizens (and political friends) from outsiders and to direct their attention to issues of common concern, facilitating concord.

In order to impose boundaries in Five Oaks, Dayton placed gates on certain streets—pedestrians and cyclists could move freely through the space, but cars were permitted only one entrance (see Figure 2.2). The goal of this change was to add definition to a previously ill-defined space, creating "mini-neighborhoods" that would "make it easier [for residents] to recognize neighbors—and strangers."[49] By imposing boundaries on a formerly too-permeable space, in other words, Newman and the Dayton city planners hoped that residents would "come

[43] The Congress for the New Urbanism, "The Charter of the New Urbanism."

[44] The Congress for the New Urbanism, "The Charter of the New Urbanism."

[45] Emily Talen, "The Social Goals of New Urbanism," *Housing Policy Debate* 13, no. 1 (2002): 182.

[46] Bothwell, Gindroz, and Lang, "Restoring Community through Traditional Neighborhood Design."

[47] Oscar Newman, *Creating Defensible Space* (Washington, DC: US Department of Housing and Urban Development, 1996). See also Oscar Newman, *Defensible Space: People and Design in the Violent City* (New York: Macmillan, 1972).

[48] Newman, *Creating Defensible Space*, 22–23.

[49] Newman, *Creating Defensible Space*, 41.

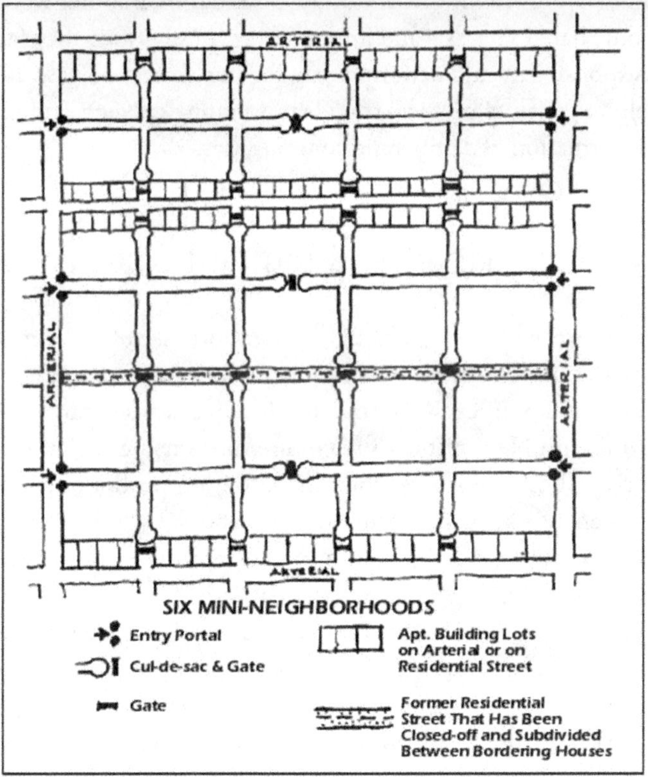

Figure 2.2 Photo (top) and sketch (bottom) of the Five Oaks mini-neighborhood plan, designed by Oscar Newman and featuring gated streets to create clearer boundaries. From Oscar Newman, *Creating Defensible Space* (Washington, DC: US Department of Housing and Urban Development Office of Policy Development and Research, 1996).

to know each other through greater association" and "develop standards of mutually acceptable behavior together."[50] And there is some evidence that these changes to the built environment fostered precisely the kind of mutual goodwill and concord that Aristotle argues is the foundation for political friendship.[51]

Boundaries, as we have seen, help citizens come to recognize what they share with others. Within clearly demarcated spaces—within the boundaries of a neighborhood, for example, or a boat, courtyard, or city—it is much easier for citizens to identify what they share with others; they are thus more likely to adjust their behavior and act collectively in order to maintain the common interest or advantage. But boundaries also facilitate citizens' recognition of the other community members with whom they share the space; they help cultivate feelings of mutual goodwill, mutually recognized that make the collective activity of democratic politics run more smoothly. Boundaries, in other words, help us to identify our shared interests and interlocutors. In so doing, they facilitate the collective responsibility and action to care for our shared objects. Boundaries, in short, help to generate political friendships among citizens, and in so doing, facilitate the formation of democratic communities.

Facebook, Boundaries, and Digital Democracies

Boundaries, as we have seen, can play an important role in generating the one-to-many ties of political friendship that help form communities and thus ground democratic politics. With this in mind, we can see how conventional responses to the problem of building communities using digital technologies overlook a crucial dimension. By focusing attention on the one-to-one interactions between users on platforms like Facebook, scholars and practitioners largely misunderstand the nature of the interpersonal ties that ground communities, as well as the practices that sustain those ties. As we consider how best to cultivate democratic communities in digital environments, then, we must expand our approach to focus more specifically on the relations of *political friends*—ties that rest on coordinated action and mutual goodwill in one-to-many relationships—and work to secure the environmental conditions required to cultivate those ties.

To that end, in this section I use the analysis of boundaries outlined earlier—their role in helping us to (1) identify common interests and (2) recognize

[50] Newman, *Creating Defensible Space*, 41.

[51] Patrick G. Donnelly and Charles E. Kimble, "An Evaluation of the Effects of Neighborhood Mobilization on Community Problems," *Journal of Prevention and Intervention in the Community* 32, no. 1–2 (2006): 61–80.

and act with reciprocity toward our interlocutors—and return to the example of Facebook to show how the presence or absence of boundaries might facilitate or thwart the formation of political friendships in digital environments. Though Facebook began as a Harvard-exclusive social networking site, it soon after expanded its membership requirement to include anyone with a valid email address. The Facebook story up until 2015, then, was one of disappearing boundaries; this can help explain why we saw a gradual loosening of communal ties on the platform during that time. More recently, with the company's "expanded" mission, the platform has reimposed boundaries by emphasizing Groups—a move that we would expect to strengthen political friendships, and thus help communities form on the platform. Facebook's evolution throughout the years thus serves to elucidate how boundaries can function, perhaps unexpectedly, in digital environments—as well as the effects that boundary changes impart on the democratic potential of these spaces.

GEOGRAPHIC BOUNDARIES: EARLY FACEBOOK

Facebook debuted in 2004 as a site available only to Harvard-affiliated users; access to the platform required a harvard.edu email address. Though the site quickly expanded to include other colleges and universities, this requirement remained in place: joining the site—which, at the time, consisted of a series of connected networks, each dedicated to a particular college or university—required an official .edu email address. And upon joining the site, Facebook users could view the profiles of anyone they knew directly (and who acknowledged that relationship by accepting a "Friend" request) as well as anyone in their institutional network, Friend or not. The earliest iteration of Facebook thus operated as an interconnected web of smaller college- and university-based communities; users knew that those they encountered on the platform were verified members of the same institutional communities to which they also belonged. And this structural design cultivated the kind of communal feelings we would expect: at the time, users perceived Facebook to be "an intimate, private community"[52]—one in which it was easy for users to identify what they shared with others they encountered in that space (see Figure 2.3).

Though the Facebook population was relatively small at the time—particularly when compared to the two-billion-plus-user behemoth it is today—I argue that it was not primarily the platform's size that contributed to users' feeling of belonging. Instead, the .edu requirement functioned as a kind of boundary that

[52] danah m. boyd and Nicole B. Ellison, "Social Network Sites: Definition, History, and Scholarship," *Journal of Computer-Mediated Communication* 13 (2007): 210–30.

Figure 2.3 Mark Zuckerberg's Facebook profile circa 2006. Notice the clearly marked "Harvard" network membership in the upper right corner, as well as the list of networks in the lower left (by this time, Facebook networks had expanded to include both geographic networks, like "San Francisco, CA" as well as employment-based networks like "Facebook").

clearly delimited spaces on the platform and helped users to easily conceptualize what they held in common with other users they encountered. Just as physical walls of a classroom or office help inhabitants to identify what they share with one another in those spaces, so too did the .edu requirement facilitate this recognition in Facebook users. Because an institutional email was required for membership, and because the platform allowed users into only those networks they had emails for, Facebook users at the time knew that they shared at least one common interest—their institutional affiliation—with the other users whose profiles they could see and with whom they interacted.

Thus, the .edu requirement functioned as, to return to Yack's travel metaphor, the sides of a boat; Facebook users knew they were "all in the same boat" with those they encountered on the platform because they knew everyone on the site had met the requirements for entry, much as travelers are barred from boarding a boat or plane without a ticket. Imposing the .edu requirement, and prominently separating users into institutional networks, meant that users could more easily recognize what they held in common with others—their shared college or university.

And we can see the effects of these boundaries in users' experiences on the platform. While Facebook was, even from the beginning, a space for existing friends to maintain their relationships, it was also, in this early iteration, an environment in which users could more easily form new interpersonal ties characteristic of political friendship, including mutually recognized goodwill grounded in a common advantage. A 2007 study, for example, found the vast majority of student respondents at Michigan State University (MSU) understood the "primary audience" of their Facebook profile to be "people in my classes" (around 90%), "total strangers at MSU" (around 80%), and "someone I met at a party" (around 80%). In all these cases, Facebook served to reinforce the recognition of users' shared community membership; even the "total strangers" users encountered on the site were acknowledged members of the shared MSU community.

Indeed, students primarily used Facebook at the time to "maintain or intensify relationships characterized by some form of offline connection such as dormitory proximity or a shared class."[53] Facebook, in other words, rendered visible latent ties between members of a shared campus community who may not have otherwise acknowledged one another directly.[54] Though they may not have had strong, personalized one-on-one relationships with most others on the platform, in other words, Facebook users at the time clearly acknowledged that they shared the space of Facebook with acquaintances and strangers that they nevertheless recognized as members of their shared college or university community.

In addition to facilitating the recognition of mutual goodwill among users, however, this .edu-gated Facebook also facilitated the kind of coordinated activity characteristic of political friends. By "making visible one's connections to a wide range of individuals," Facebook helped users "identify those who might be useful in some capacity"[55]—such as finding potential collaborators or classmates. In so doing, the platform facilitated the kind of concord Aristotle

[53] Nicole B. Ellison, Charles Steinfield, and Cliff Lampe, "The Benefits of Facebook 'Friends': Social Capital and College Students' Use of Online Social Network Sites," *Journal of Computer-Mediated Communication* 12 (2007): 1162.

[54] Ellison, Steinfield, and Lampe, "The Benefits of Facebook 'Friends,'" 1162.

[55] Ellison, Steinfield, and Lampe, "The Benefits of Facebook 'Friends,'" 1162.

identifies as the foundation of political friendship—the acting together for a common advantage. In helping users identify shared interests and act collectively to achieve shared goals, Facebook facilitated the formation of the political friendships that ground community life—the basis of democratic politics.[56]

In building a platform with clearly defined boundaries, this early iteration of Facebook effectively provided an additional common space to those already existing on the various campuses it served. In this respect, the early Facebook platform functioned similarly to other "wired neighborhoods" in providing further opportunities for social contact between those who lived in physical proximity and thus already shared geographic space.[57] The result was, as we would expect, that Facebook use in these early years helped users not just to maintain and intensify their relationships with existing offline connections, but also to form new political friendships with other users—members of their community they recognized as "useful in some capacity." By translating the geographic boundaries of a campus into the digital environment of the Facebook platform, the .edu requirement served as a boundary marker that helped Facebook users generate mutually recognized goodwill and engage in the cooperative activity of political friendship to an extent that "ungated" internet use could not provide.

DISSOLVING BOUNDARIES: FACEBOOK GOES PUBLIC

With its .edu entry requirement and institutionally specific networks, the earliest iteration of Facebook was designed as a set of interconnected gated communities. This made it easier for users to identify common interests and interlocutors; acting as an extension of physical campus communities, the platform could successfully set the stage for political friendships in a way that the ungated internet could not. But this structure was not to last.

As early as September 2005, Facebook began slowly expanding its borders to be more inclusive of high school students, corporate professionals, and, finally, anyone with a valid email address.[58] At last, in 2009, the platform did away with these institutional and regional groupings altogether—instead of determining visibility based on one's verified network memberships, each individual Facebook user controlled their own, personalized privacy settings.[59] By default,

[56] Charles Steinfield, Nicole B. Ellison, and Cliff Lampe, "Social Capital, Self-Esteem, and Use of Online Social Network Sites: A Longitudinal Analysis," *Journal of Applied Developmental Psychology* 29, no. 6 (2008): 434–45.

[57] Keith Hampton, "Place-Based and IT Mediated 'Community,'" *Planning Theory and Practice* 3, no. 2 (2002): 228–31; Skoric, Ying, and Ng, "Bowling Online, Not Alone."

[58] boyd and Ellison, "Social Network Sites: Definition, History, and Scholarship."

[59] Kathy H. Chan, "Growing Beyond Regional Networks," *Facebook*, June 9, 2009, https://www.facebook.com/notes/facebook/growing-beyond-regional-networks/91242982130/.

one's information on Facebook was "public," meaning users' profiles, posts, and pictures were available to everyone on the platform, though users also had options of limiting this content to "Friends," "Friends of Friends," or a customized list of one's connections. In making these changes, Facebook in effect tore down its walls and erased the boundaries previously created by the .edu requirement. In the name of radical openness, the platform did away with anything that might be construed as a barrier to entry (see Figure 2.4).

This commitment to openness was reaffirmed when Facebook filed for an initial public offering in 2012. As part of the proceedings, Zuckerberg penned a letter to prospective investors that clearly outlined a commitment to the platform's "social mission—to make the world more open and connected."[60] Throughout the document, Zuckerberg reveals the conception of social relations that grounded Facebook at the time:

> At Facebook, we build tools to help people connect with the people they want and share what they want, and by doing this we are extending people's capacity to build and maintain relationships. People sharing more—even if just with their close friends or families—creates a more open culture and leads to a better understanding of the lives and perspectives of others. We believe that this creates a greater number of stronger relationships between people, and that it helps people get exposed to a greater number of diverse perspectives.[61]

Openness, according to Zuckerberg at the time, was valuable for its own sake. Moreover, it was through openness and connectedness that the platform would help "give everyone a voice and help transform society for the future."[62] Walls and boundaries were antithetical to this project because they act as barriers to building relationships and prevent sharing. As a result, Zuckerberg implied, boundaries lead to social stagnation and even regression. Instead, Zuckerberg and Facebook envisioned a platform that developed "stronger relationships"—meaning individualized one-to-one relationships—through a "more open culture."

Yet boundaries, as we have seen, are critical for facilitating the one-to-many ties of political friendship that help democratic communities to form. Absent boundaries, which give definition and meaning to any given space, inhabitants have a more difficult time recognizing what they share with others and with

[60] WIRED Staff, "Mark Zuckerberg's Letter to Investors: 'The Hacker Way,'" *WIRED*, February 1, 2012.

[61] Zuckerberg, quoted in Wired Staff, "Mark Zuckerberg's Letter to Investors."

[62] Zuckerberg, quoted in Wired Staff, "Mark Zuckerberg's Letter to Investors."

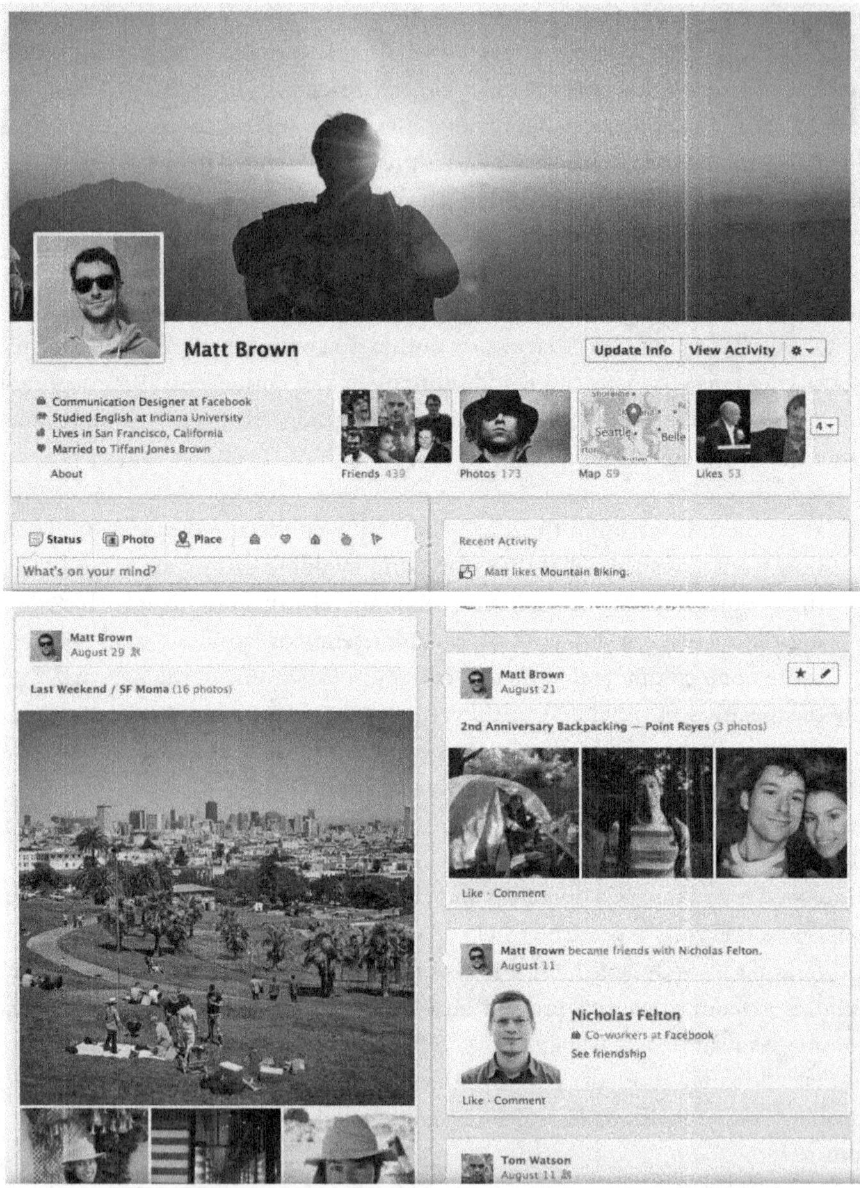

Figure 2.4 Example Facebook profile circa 2011. With the release of "Timeline," Facebook profiles privileged individual actions and networks over the bounded .edu communities. Images from MG Siegler, "Here's What Facebook Timeline Looks Like," *TechCrunch*, September 11, 2011, available at https://techcrunch.com/2011/09/22/facebook-timeline-pictures/.

whom they share it—their communal relationships, as a result, become much more difficult to conceptualize.

And, Zuckerberg's claims notwithstanding, there is evidence that this shift to a more "open and connected" platform failed to live up to even his own expectations. What social connections Facebook did facilitate during this time were weak and individualized.[63] Though individuals were able to connect, one-to-one, with many more users in this unbounded environment, there was little evidence these connections were characterized by the mutually recognized goodwill and cooperative activity that defines political friendships.[64] By removing the site's boundaries, which helped to define users' relationships, Facebook's commitment to openness and connectivity not only made it more difficult for users to recognize their shared interests, but it also failed to provide fertile ground for the cooperative *activity* of friendship.

In removing the .edu requirement—a boundary that helped users conceptualize their communal relationships—Facebook's shift to radical openness and universal connectivity fundamentally reshaped the interpersonal dynamics of the platform. Instead of building environments in which friends were encouraged to act together, the open Facebook instead facilitated "networked individualism" in which "[e]ach person is a switchboard, between ties and networks. People remain connected, but as individuals. Each person operates a separate personal community network, and switches rapidly among multiple subnetworks."[65] Where the early Facebook was organized around common (institutional) ground, forming communities by highlighting for users what they shared with others and with whom they shared it, this new "open and connected" iteration was built around individuals, creating the kind of social networks Baym contrasts with communities. Centering on one's personal preferences, the wide-open Facebook ceded control to *individuals*; the reciprocal behavioral and attitudinal adjustment of political friends, developed through the process of working together, was lost.

The result of Facebook's unbounding its platform, in other words, was the disintegration of the site's communal bonds. Unable to conceptualize their common interests, and released from the ties of mutual goodwill and cooperative

[63] J. Donath and d. boyd, "Public Displays of Connection," *BT Technology Journal* 22, no. 4 (2004): 71–82; Dmitri Williams, "The Impact of Time Online: Social Capital and Cyberbalkanization," *CyberPsychology and Behavior* 8 (2007): 580–84; Pasquale De Meo et al., "On Facebook, Most Ties Are Weak," *Communications of the ACM* 57, no. 11 (2014): 78–84.

[64] Ellison, Steinfield, and Lampe, "Connection Strategies"; Donath and boyd, "Public Displays of Connection."

[65] Barry Wellman et al., "The Social Affordances of the Internet for Networked Individualism," *Journal of Computer-Mediated Communication* 8, no. 3 (2003).

activity that ground political friendships, Facebook users shifted from treating the platform as a shared space to using it as a personal one.[66] Consequently, Facebook users retreated from the public engagements of political friends into their own individually curated and intimate private networks. The platform shifted from a collection of connected communities, in other words, to become a aggregation of individual users, oblivious to what they held in common and unable to act collectively to maintain it.[67]

REINSCRIBING BOUNDARIES: FACEBOOK GROUPS

In February 2017, four months before his debut of the company's new "product roadmap," Zuckerberg made an unexpected announcement. Posting a "manifesto" to the site, Zuckerberg outlined a new direction for Facebook. Entitled "Building Global Community," the 5,700-word essay was a dramatic departure from Zuckerberg's letter to investors from five years earlier. Instead of openness and connectedness, the new vision was of a Facebook that stood for "bringing us closer together and building a global community." Drawing heavily on the language of infrastructure, Facebook's new mission, according to Zuckerberg, would begin "with the millions of smaller communities and intimate social structures we turn to for our personal, emotional, and spiritual needs."[68]

Citing "churches, sports teams, unions or other local groups," Zuckerberg's description of the new social context for Facebook was more complex and multilayered than its previous iterations. Indeed, Zuckerberg suggested that online communities could act as a supplement to existing structures, one that would

[66] Another, related consequence of this shift was that Facebook users began to experience "context collapse"—the flattening of audience and subsequent difficulty in self-presentation. Within clearly bounded spaces, like a school or office or campus social network, individuals can take behavioral cues from the boundary markers and act in a contextually appropriate manner for the intended audience. In the radically open Facebook environment, however, these boundaries had disappeared, combining audiences and collapsing contexts and making this kind of contextualized and communal behavior much more difficult.

[67] An additional effect of this shift can be seen in the number of novel mechanisms that Facebook introduced to reduce trolling and other bad behavior. Strategies like "public displays of connection," a "real name" policy (later phased out), and "report abuse" flags are all intended to reintroduce accountability into the unbounded digital space of the site. See Donath and boyd, "Public Displays of Connection." Though they vary in method and effectiveness, all these tactics are attempts to recapture the kind of mutuality that Aristotle understands to be generated by the activity of friendship—habits and attitudes that are more likely to develop, as I have argued, in bounded spaces. See Jennifer Forestal, "The Architecture of Political Spaces: Trolls, Digital Media, and Deweyan Democracy," *American Political Science Review* 111, no. 1 (2017): 149–61.

[68] Mark Zuckerberg, "Building Global Community," *Facebook*, February 16, 2017, https://www.facebook.com/notes/mark-zuckerberg/building-global-community/10154544292806634/.

"strengthen existing physical communities by helping people come together online as well as offline." Through Facebook, he continued, "this infrastructure will strengthen these communities, as well as enable completely new ones to form."[69] Positioning Facebook as "infrastructure" that would work in tandem with more traditional physical communities, this shift was in many ways a return to form. It was an attempt to rein in the limitless expanse that Facebook had become and once again tie Facebook to distinct communities of interest. And, like the site's original .edu-only iteration, many—though not all—of these communities had offline equivalents.

Abandoning the language of connection and openness, the platform's goal was now to "[g]ive people the power to build community and bring the world closer together." Yet this adjustment in Facebook's mission was not simply a reversion to the clear boundaries from the early days of the platform's .edu requirement. Facebook, as is clear from the 2017 "product roadmap" and its subsequent changes, is still largely working within a frame of one-to-one interactions, giving users more individual control over—and thus de-emphasizing the communal aspects of—their News Feeds. Yet in the midst of these changes, the platform nevertheless also began slowly reintroducing boundaries to users' experiences by heavily promoting a previously underutilized feature of the platform: Groups (see Figure 2.5).

Facebook introduced Groups in 2010, as a way to make it "easy for you to build a space for important groups of people in your life."[70] Groups are user-created spaces with which to "communicate about shared interests with certain people";[71] members can either search and find Groups to join themselves, or else can be invited by existing members (see Figure 2.6).[72] Whatever their substantive focus, the existence of Facebook Groups works to reintroduce boundaries and definition into users' otherwise undefined News Feeds. With clear names and descriptions, Groups clearly highlight members' shared interests; they, in effect, build walls around certain segments of the general Facebook population (see Figure 2.7). In so doing, they clarify relationships that would otherwise be

[69] Zuckerberg, "Building Global Community."

[70] Matt Hicks, "New Groups: Stay Closer to Groups of People in Your Life," *Facebook*, October 6, 2010, https://www.facebook.com/notes/facebook/new-groups-stay-closer-to-groups-of-people-in-your-life/434700832130/.

[71] Facebook, "Groups," *Facebook Help Center*, n.d., https://www.facebook.com/help/1629740080681586.

[72] More recently, Facebook has begun to more rigorously moderate—and ban—some Groups for violating the platform's policies on hate speech and harassment. See Kim Lyons, "Facebook Bans One of the Largest QAnon Groups for Violating Harassment, Hate Speech Policies," *The Verge*, August 2020. For more on anti-democratic digital communities, see chapter 4.

Figure 2.5 Examples of advertisements for Facebook Groups, as part of Facebook's #MoreTogether campaign. Groups exist for any number of interests, including (as pictured clockwise from top left), basset hounds ("Nothing Better than a Basset"), big trees ("Big Tree Seekers"), fat cats ("This Cat Is Chonky"), and older women who love horses ("Aging Horsewomen Intl.™"). Photographs by author.

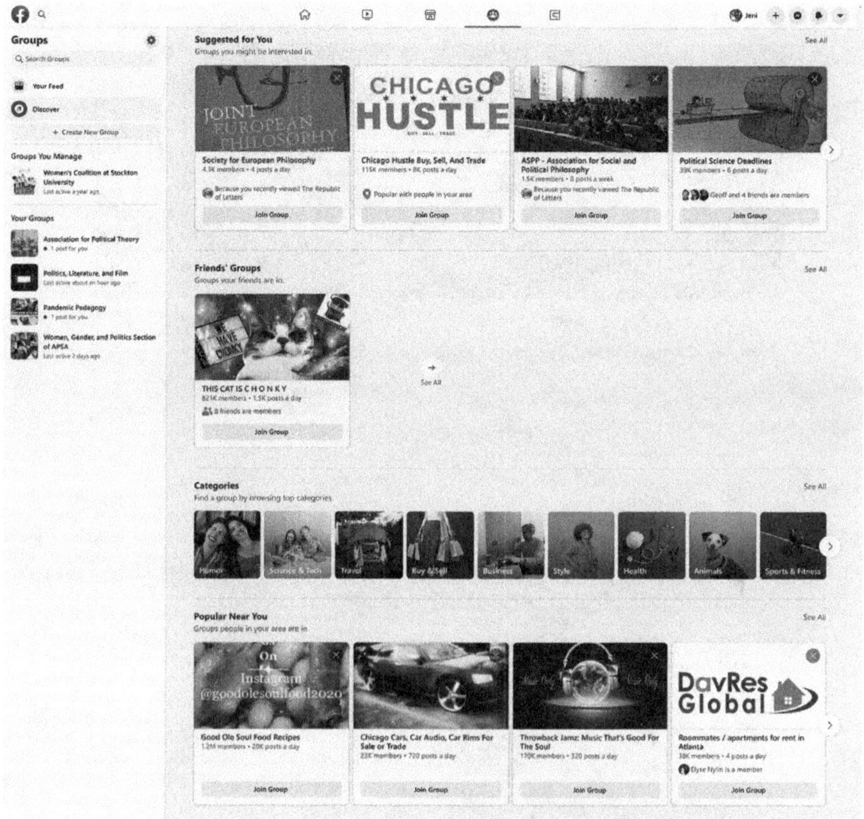

Figure 2.6 Screenshot of the Facebook Groups "Discover" page, where users can find Groups they want to join. Notice how Groups are suggested to users based on, for example, their own interests and the interests (and Group memberships) of their Friends, as well as the Group memberships of other users in the same geographic areas. Photograph by author.

hard to identify, just as do rooms in an office building. As a result, they help otherwise latent communities form on the platform.

And, as with bounded physical spaces, like an office or university campus or the early .edu-bounded version of Facebook, Facebook Groups can both support existing relationships as well as introduce new ones. Imagine, for example, a block party taking place on a neighborhood street. Blocks are spaces with well-defined boundaries; residents can clearly identify who lives on their block and who does not. Invitations for a block party would therefore presumably include all residents of the block. The party, in this case, is a designated—and clearly bounded—space for neighbors to gather, talk, and share in each other's lives. Yet the space need not be exclusive to residents: we can easily imagine a scenario

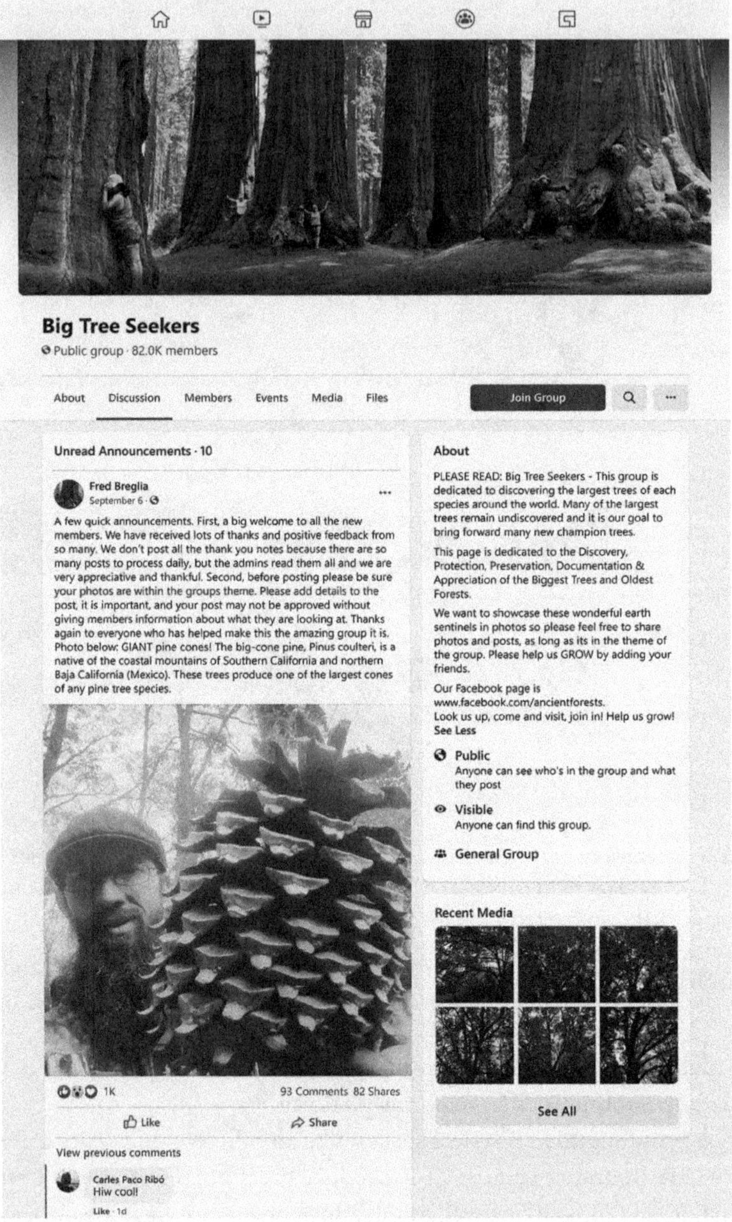

Figure 2.7 Screenshot of the main page of the "Big Tree Seekers" Group, which is "dedicated to discovering the largest trees of each species around the world." Each Facebook Group has a main page, which serves as a clearly bounded space within which users can easily identify shared interests and engage with other Group members. Photograph by author.

in which neighbors invite their own personal (non-neighbor) friends to join the event.

At this point, the street on which the block party is taking place is not only a space for neighbors to deepen their existing communal ties, but it also provides opportunities for them to meet new people and make new friends—all the while recognizing that their very presence at the party signals that all attendees have something in common: they are connected in some way to the block itself and the residents who live on it. Likewise with Facebook Groups; Groups may consist of members with whom one is already familiar, but Groups can also include Facebook users with whom one has never previously interacted. In both cases, the Group structure introduces boundaries that help users to more easily identify what they hold in common (the Group's focus) and with whom (the other members); in so doing, Groups help to create the environmental conditions in which users can also begin to generate mutual goodwill by recognizing one another as peers and political friends.

Facebook Groups help users to recognize their fellow citizens and act with mutual goodwill toward them. But they also help users engage in the cooperative activity of political friendship. Posting to your own Facebook Feed—the default mode of communication on Facebook—does not guarantee a known audience. Because the algorithm that organizes information on one's News Feed is opaque to the public, users can never be sure who among their Friends can see any given post; this opacity prioritizes individual self-interest and eschews the reciprocity and collective activity of political friendship. Groups, by contrast, because they are clearly delimited, give users a clearer idea of who will see their content—and, as a result, who might censure them for bad behavior. Users posting content to a *Group's* Feed, in other words, are more directly incentivized to craft their post in a way that further advances the Group's shared interest.[73] Groups thus build reciprocity and cooperative activity back into Facebook's user interactions because Group posts are oriented toward the Group's common advantage in a way individual posts are not.

Moreover, there is evidence that Facebook is tweaking its algorithms to privilege Group posts—meaning that users are more likely to repeatedly encounter other Group members and content. By emphasizing Group interactions in this way, Facebook is further facilitating the reciprocated goodwill and cooperative action between users that is necessary for the collective action of democratic politics.[74]

[73] Much of the content regulation in Facebook Groups is carried out by Group Admins and Moderators, roles in which Facebook users take on additional responsibilities to manage the Group, including approving and removing posts, removing or blocking users, and maintaining the Group's settings. For more on the role of moderators in online communities, see chapter 4.

[74] Kevin Roose, "Behind the Velvet Ropes of Facebook's Private Groups," *New York Times*, July 16, 2017. The importance of repeated encounters, as well as the role of the built environment in sustaining them, is discussed at greater length in chapter 3.

Circumscribing users, Groups make it more likely that users will see and be seen by other members; as a result, Groups make it likely that members will hold one another accountable for their actions (at least by the standards of their shared Group). In bolstering Groups by prioritizing their content in users' News Feeds, Facebook is reintroducing boundaries without the explicit geographical connection of the .edu requirement. In so doing, Facebook is also modeling a strategy for building boundaries into digital spaces, thus providing environments within which democratic communities might more easily form.

Contesting Boundaries?

In throwing its support behind Groups, Facebook appears to be transforming the platform from a single, massive, ill-defined social *network* to an environment more similar to a collection of clearly-defined micro-*communities* along the lines of Reddit or 4chan.[75] As we have seen, this reintroduction of boundaries, which adds structure and definition to Facebook's mass of over two billion users, is a much-needed first step toward the goal of building digital democratic communities.

Boundaries, whether physical or digital, can help citizens come to understand what they hold in common with their peers. And boundaries, by delimiting a certain area, help inhabitants recognize those with whom they share these common experiences, which facilitates the mutual goodwill and cooperative activity characteristic of political friends. Boundaries, in other words, have a psychological effect on those within them, reshaping their habits and attitudes in ways that provide the foundation for the ties of political friendship that—as the basis for community life—are necessary for the work of democratic politics.

Facebook, as we have seen, has, at least partially (and perhaps accidentally) arrived at a similar conclusion. From its early start as a collection of clearly bounded, geographically based communities limited by the requirement of an institutional .edu email address, to its later expansion into an unbounded and undefined two-billion-member global behemoth, Facebook's evolution is a story of shifting boundaries. More recently, the platform has once again changed course, reintroducing structure and definition by emphasizing closeness and community over openness and connectivity. Recognizing, as one *New York Times* writer put it, that "the marketplace of ideas could be improved with a few

[75] For a sustained discussion of Reddit as a democratic space, see chapter 4; for a discussion of Reddit's algorithmic front page, see chapter 5.

more walls,"[76] Facebook has turned to Groups as one solution to the "networked individualism" characterizing the platform for most of its existence. Rather than treat the platform as a single, limitless space, it seems Zuckerberg's current vision for Facebook is as a massive convention center—a space with rooms for every community of interest, but one that also encourages plenty of mingling in the hallways.

Yet the reintroduction of boundaries into Facebook also introduces new problems for those invested in designing digital technologies to support democratic politics. Just as boundaries can bring together those who live inside of them, they can also homogenize these communities and exclude non-members. Often, the existence of a wall—an object which clearly marks borders and boundaries—signals distrust, rigidity, and exclusion. From the "peace lines" in Northern Ireland to the DMZ demarcating North and South Korea, walls are used to separate communities and divide nations; they are, moreover, often used as symbols of exclusionary public policy. Indeed, political and social theorists have explored the effect of this exclusion on the possibilities for democratic politics. As Susan Bickford observes, these kinds of boundaries "function not just to keep some people out, but to keep people on each side separate from one another—or, to put it paradoxically, to actively construct relations of separation."[77] There is a long history of drawing boundaries, in other words—from redlines to highways—with the intention to exclude, remove, separate, and segregate.[78]

But in addition to these problems of (self-)segregation and exclusion, which I take up at length in chapter 4, digital spaces like Facebook paradoxically pose even more difficulties for *maintaining* boundaries around the spaces of digital democratic life. Drawing boundaries can be a difficult, and highly contestable, task. But boundaries are, as we have seen, also an important element of democratic space; they signal to us that we share things with others, facilitating the formation of the communities required for democratic political action. And they serve this purpose, crucially, through their *visibility*—it is because we can clearly identify boundaries that they have the psychological effects that they do. It is this tangibility, moreover, that ensures the boundaries themselves can be shared objects at the center of democratic contestation, deliberation, and action.

[76] Roose, "Behind the Velvet Ropes of Facebook's Private Groups."

[77] Susan Bickford, "Constructing Inequality: City Spaces and the Architecture of Citizenship," *Political Theory* 28, no. 3 (2000): 361.

[78] See Douglas S. Massey and Nancy A. Denton, *American Apartheid: Segregation and the Making of the Underclass* (Cambridge, MA: Harvard University Press, 1993); Edward J. Blakely and Mary Gail Snyder, "Divided We Fall: Gated and Walled Communities in the United States," in *Architecture of Fear*, ed. Nan Ellin (Princeton, NJ: Princeton University Press, 1997), 85–99.

The tangibility of (physical) boundaries does not necessarily translate, however, to the constantly shifting and easily alterable digital environment. Unlike the walls and fences that often mark boundaries in physical spaces, digital platforms like Facebook can be frequently—and invisibly—redesigned and removed with little notice or fanfare from the perspective of users. Other digital boundaries fail to outlast the activity within them; they disappear as soon as users stop using them. In other words, what looks one minute like a well-designed, democratic digital space might, overnight, simply disappear or radically transform; indeed, this is precisely what happened with Facebook's shift away from the .edu email requirement. This impermanence of digital boundaries thus undermines their role in supporting democratic communities.

This is because democratic communities, as we know, must not only form; they must also persist. Democratic politics is, after all, a sustained practice. It is clear, then, that boundaries alone are insufficient for building democratic spaces. The boundaries that define democratic environments—whether physical or digital—must also be characterized by *durability* if they are to support the kind of sustainable communities and practices necessary for democratic action. We often take for granted the durability of physical boundaries and the spaces they create. As new digital environments highlight, however, we can no longer afford to leave this assumption uninterrogated. To that end, in the next chapter, I take up this question of durability by turning to the work of Alexis de Tocqueville and the example of Twitter.

3

Sustaining Democracy

Durability, Attachment, and Twitter

On January 28, 2017, in response to Executive Order 13769, commonly referred to as the "travel ban" or "Muslim ban," thousands of people gathered at airports across the United States to protest the designation of certain predominantly Muslim countries as "unsafe." Starting with thirty or so people at JFK's Terminal 4 around 11 A.M., the crowds steadily grew as activists and advocacy groups took to social media—and Twitter in particular—to spread the word that protests were forming. Using hashtags like #NoBanNoWall to help identify their shared interests and coordinate with other interested parties, these protests spread across the United States, appearing in airports from Los Angeles to Washington, DC, including large cities like Chicago as well as smaller locales like Portland and Indianapolis.

As instances of coordinated activity, organized quickly and effectively using social media, the 2017 airport protests showcase the power of digital technologies to spur collective action by facilitating citizens' recognition of issues of common concern. Within the digital spaces created by hashtags, group chats, and listservs, citizens were quickly able to identify and act as communities of interest, coordinating protest activity against the Trump administration's Executive Order. #NoBanNoWall and similar hashtags, on this reading, mobilized citizens precisely because they functioned like the clear boundaries of a city or campus. Followers of these hashtags could quickly identify what they shared, and with whom; the hashtag made it easier for citizens to identify their peers and to organize gatherings at airports across the country. Yet the airport protests were also striking for another reason: their relatively short duration. While some protests continued for multiple days, the vast majority dissipated after a few hours; though the

Designing for Democracy. Jennifer Forestal, Oxford University Press. © Oxford University Press 2022.
DOI: 10.1093/oso/9780197568750.003.0003

"travel ban" remained in place for years, moreover, the collective protest response waned.[1]

With their high visibility yet relatively short life cycle, the airport protests call attention to the ways that digital technologies intersect with another long-standing challenge for democratic politics: not that of forming communities of interest, but of *sustaining* communities once they are formed. As the collective management of common affairs, democratic politics involves more than discrete instances of collective action, like protests. Instead, democracy is best understood as a set of *repeated* practices—as a way of life. Recall, for example, that Aristotle's political friendship is a habit; it involves the *ongoing* activity of sharing, speaking, arguing, negotiating, and compromising in the work of managing our common objects and interests. Because we will always have things in common, and because we will always disagree about what they are and how to care for them, the work of democratic politics is never finished. More than just mobilizing citizens by recognizing communities of interest, then—the dimension of democratic politics readily evident in the 2017 airport protests—democracy also requires that citizens sustain their public engagement and work to maintain these communities over time.

Just as digital technologies are, as we saw in chapter 2, shifting the ways we recognize our shared interests and interlocutors, so too are these new technologies reshaping the patterns of activity that occur *after* this initial moment of recognition. By providing "shortcuts" so that citizens can easily communicate without prior relationships, and incentivizing more personalized modes of participation, digital technologies can make it easier to mobilize citizens. Yet these same affordances, as scholars like Zeynep Tufekci have argued, can also undermine the attachments that sustain political communities—and collective action—over time.[2] As we consider how best to construct digital environments that support democratic politics, then, we must determine not only how to facilitate the recognition of shared interests and interlocutors through which communities are formed, but also how to cultivate the practices that sustain these communities even after their initial "founding" moments.

In this chapter, I do just that. Turning to the work of Alexis de Tocqueville, I show how the built environment can play an important role in generating

[1] On February 3, 2017—a few days after the protests—a US District Court in Seattle issued a restraining order that blocked key elements of the original executive order; a month later, in March, President Trump announced a new, "watered down version" of the ban, which subsequently received another restraining order, this time from a US District Court in Hawaii. The Trump administration appealed these rulings up to the Supreme Court, while also, in September 2017, issuing a third version of the ban, this time with an indefinite end date. In June 2018, in a 5–4 vote, the Supreme Court upheld this ban. See Nausheen Husain, "Timeline: Legal Fight over Trump's 'Muslim Ban' and the Supreme Court Ruling," *Chicago Tribune*, June 26, 2018.

[2] Zeynep Tufekci, *Twitter and Tear Gas: The Power and Fragility of Networked Protest* (New Haven, CT: Yale University Press, 2017).

citizens' attachments to their communities and their fellow citizens—how well-designed spaces can help cultivate affective ties that increase the likelihood that citizens will continue to engage in the often-difficult work of collectively managing common affairs.

Writing in the nineteenth century, watching the "approaching and irresistible and universal spread of democracy throughout the world,"[3] Tocqueville was preoccupied with precisely this question of how to sustain citizens' participation in public affairs in the face of a new democratic threat: individualism, or the withdrawal of citizens from public life. And this retreat—when citizens think of themselves in isolation and prioritize their own individual interests—remains a source of anxiety today as digital technologies make it easier to mobilize citizens by appealing to their self-interest, but often fail to sustain citizens' political engagement once the initial moment of mobilization has passed.

This problem is not one of recognition. Insofar as digital technologies make it easier to show citizens how a given issue affects their self-interest, we should not be surprised to see them mobilize in response. But sustained participation in democratic life requires more than these episodic bursts of personalized engagement; it demands thicker commitments to one's community and those within it. Only when citizens properly feel the communal attachments of political friendship—and recognize the obligations they share to maintain them—will they be primed for the sacrifices democratic politics asks of us all. The "personalization of politics" we often see associated with digital technologies, then, is not a new problem. Rather, it exemplifies one of the dangers inherent in democracy itself: citizens forming and acting as communities only as long as their participation advances a narrowly conceived idea of individual self-interest. This is better than nothing, of course, but—as Tocqueville warns—it is ultimately unsustainable.

Tocqueville's suggestions for combating individualism are famously, like Aristotle's political friendship, practice-based. Throughout *Democracy in America* (hereafter, DA), he identifies certain social institutions, like law, religion, newspapers, and "associations," as critical for developing citizens' attachments to their communities. What all of these institutions do, according to Tocqueville, is to draw citizens out of their personal circles of family and friends and reconnect them with their fellow citizens. In so doing, Tocqueville argues, these institutions, first, remind citizens of their social obligations and, second, provide the repeated encounters that sustain habits of concord and goodwill—of Aristotelian political friendship—among citizens. Following Tocqueville,

[3] Alexis de Tocqueville, *Democracy in America*, ed. J. P. Mayer, trans. George Lawrence (New York: HarperPerennial Modern Classics, 1969).

scholars have noted the success of formal education, as well as informal participation in civil society organizations, in cultivating these feelings of attachment and obligation, as well as sustaining the habits of political friendship, that make democratic politics possible.[4]

This work is no doubt important—certainly these various social institutions play an important role in sustaining democratic engagement among citizens. Yet, as I argue throughout this book, approaches that prioritize social institutions are not exhaustive. Indeed, throughout Tocqueville's work we can see an attentiveness not only to the role of social institutions, but also to the ways the built environment can have similar effects on developing citizens' attachments to their community and their peers. In his discussions of aristocratic family estates, as well as his praise of the New England township, for example, Tocqueville suggests ways the built environment—and, in particular, the *durability* of its spaces—affords opportunities for citizens to engage in the kinds of practices that develop attachments and thus sustain democratic participation.

Durable spaces are those—like a township or family estate—which retain a sense of continuity. They are spaces that people can return to time and again with some familiarity. And while durability does not preclude change, durable spaces remain recognizable over time. While the specific configuration of stores, and even buildings, may change between visits to Chicago, for example, it is unlikely the streets themselves would shift or disappear so as to render the city utterly alien to residents and repeat visitors. These streets, then, are durable spaces. And it is by virtue of this durability that citizens are ultimately able to form affective attachments to their communities and fellow citizens. These attachments, in turn, make it more likely that citizens will be willing to enact their obligations and maintain their engagement with the community. The attachments cultivated by the durable spaces of the built environment, in short, help to sustain democratic communities over time.

But durability can be difficult to come by in digital environments. The difference in building materials—computer code instead of concrete—can make it easier for software developers and the companies they work for to alter or destroy digital spaces relative to physical ones; such changes are, moreover, often immediate and invisible to users—an experience that is almost inconceivable in physical environments. And digital platforms are, in addition, often designed to prioritize novelty. While things can certainly linger on the internet, in other

[4] John Dewey, "Democracy and Education," in *John Dewey: The Middle Works, Vol. 9, 1899–1924*, ed. Jo Ann Boydston (Carbondale: Southern Illinois University Press, 1916); Robert D. Putnam, *Bowling Alone: The Collapse and Revival of American Community* (New York: Simon & Schuster, 2000); Danielle S. Allen, *Talking to Strangers: Anxieties of Citizenship since Brown v. Board of Education* (Chicago: University of Chicago Press, 2004).

words, many digital platforms are not designed to facilitate repeated interactions with familiar content and users. Rather than generating attachments through continuity and repetition, many digital platforms are instead built to incentivize "fresh" experiences. This results in platforms that are well equipped to catalyze initial moments of acting but are perhaps less suited for supporting the sustained work of democratic politics.

But this need not be the case. In what follows, I draw from Tocqueville's work to suggest ways that the *durability* of the built environment can support sustainable democratic communities, even in digital environments. In the next section, I return to Tocqueville's writing on democracy to elaborate the threat of individualism and the role of durable spaces in countering its effects and sustaining democratic communities. The built environment, I argue, can be a powerful resource for generating the attachments that sustain democratic politics by (1) continually reminding citizens of their social obligations and (2) facilitating repeated interactions between citizens. I then turn to the example of Twitter—and, in particular, the mechanism of hashtags—to explore these dynamics in a digital environment. Hashtags, I argue, provide temporary boundaries that are useful for mobilizing—but not sustaining—communities of interest; the result is that Twitter can often help users identify what they share and with whom, but it is not a platform well suited for cultivating the attachments required for longer-term cooperative activity. Finally, I conclude with suggestions as to how we might design more durable spaces—and sustainable communities—in digital environments.

Tocqueville, Political Habits, and the Built Environment

Digital technologies, as is now well established, are reshaping political engagement. Even as platforms like Twitter lower the costs of communication and make it easier to mobilize large numbers of people quickly, these same platforms often provide "shortcuts" that ultimately result in a "lack of organizational depth and experience, of tools or culture for collective decision-making and strategic, long-term action."[5] Instead, these technologies have facilitated the rise of new forms of political membership and civic action, characterized by what David Karpf calls "passive democratic feedback," where citizens' input is collected through mechanisms like A/B testing and personalized calls to action rather than active

[5] Tufekci, *Twitter and Tear Gas*, xxvii.

processes of collective decision-making.[6] The result is, as Tufekci argues, a de-emphasis on the development of "resilience and collective decision-making and acting capacity that emerge from the long-term work of negotiation and interaction."[7] By making it easier to mobilize around common interests, it seems, digital technologies are undermining those practices which ensure the resulting communities will be sustainable.

Scholars interested in digital technology and democracy tend to frame this problem in terms of the changing social context. The digital age, they argue, is marked by a rise in the "personalization of politics" in which citizens seek "more flexible association with causes, ideas, and political organizations"[8] and "[m]atters previously thought to require debate and struggle are now addressed as personal issues or technical concerns."[9] As a result, scholars invested in using digital technologies to support democratic politics have called for organizations to adapt to this new context and work to develop methods of engagement that are better suited for the new, personalized logic of "connective action."[10] Or else they have argued that activists should turn away from an overreliance on digital technologies and instead reinvest in the organizational capacities of groups, invoking more traditional social movement organizations or political parties as examples of the kind of infrastructure required for the sustained collective decision-making and action that characterizes democratic politics.[11]

While both of these approaches may lead to increased participation, however, neither challenges the underlying assumption that it is digital technologies that are to blame for the "personalization of politics"; the choices, it seems, are to fully embrace this new logic of connective action, or else limit the role of digital technologies in democratic life. In framing the problem as one of technological affordances and their effects, however, these scholars misidentify the root of the problem; as a result, they are unable to identify strategies for harnessing the power of digital technologies to host sustained democratic activity.

Democracy, as I have been arguing, is best understood as a set of practices; it is a way of life in which we collectively identify and care for those interests

[6] David Karpf, *The MoveOn Effect: The Unexpected Transformation of American Political Advocacy* (New York: Oxford University Press, 2012).

[7] Tufekci, *Twitter and Tear Gas*, 269–70.

[8] W. Lance Bennett and Alexandra Segerberg, *The Logic of Connective Action: Digital Media and the Personalization of Contentious Politics* (Cambridge, UK: Cambridge University Press, 2013), 5.

[9] Jodi Dean, "Communicative Capitalism: Circulation and the Foreclosure of Politics," *Cultural Politics* 1, no. 1 (2005): 56.

[10] David Karpf, *Analytic Activism: Digital Listening and the New Political Strategy* (New York: Oxford University Press, 2016); Bennett and Segerberg, *The Logic of Connective Action*.

[11] Tufekci, *Twitter and Tear Gas*; Jodi Dean, "Communicative Capitalism and Revolutionary Form," *Millennium: Journal of International Studies* 47, no. 3 (2019): 326–40.

we share with others. This requires not just a recognition *that* we share things in common, but also a sustained commitment to stick around and participate in the often-difficult cooperative work of caring for them—not because we see the immediate short-term benefit, but because we recognize that we have an obligation to our fellow citizens to do so. In order to sustain democratic communities in an era of "personalized politics," then, we must find a way not just to mobilize citizens by engaging them on their own terms, but also to generate the requisite attachments that will compel those same citizens to stay engaged for the sake of the community's. Traditional social movement organizations can do this, of course. But if we are to use digital technologies to this end, we must find ways to cultivate these attachments in digital environments as well. And by (re)designing the digital built environment, I argue, we can begin to do precisely that.

In this section, I turn to the work of French thinker Alexis de Tocqueville to outline both the forms of attachment that sustain democratic politics as well as the role of the built environment in cultivating them. Writing in the nineteenth century, Tocqueville identifies the problem of "individualism," citizens' gradual withdrawal from public life. Like more recent scholars writing on the "personalization of politics," Tocqueville noticed that democratic citizens were increasingly motivated to engage in political activity on their own terms, to advance their self-interest, narrowly conceived. Unlike modern scholars, however, Tocqueville did not see this as a problem of technology. Individualism, he argued, is a problem of *democracy*; it is a consequence of democratic equality. While much of the secondary literature on Tocqueville's writing, like subsequent work on digital technologies, has focused on the role of associations as an antidote to individualism, however, Tocqueville was also attentive to the role of the built environment in structuring citizens' habits, attitudes, and relationships. Certain spaces of the built environment, he recognized, could cultivate those practices which sustain political engagement and thus combat individualism's pernicious effects.

In particular, I argue here that it is the *durability* of the built environment that helps counteract individualism and thus sustain democratic communities. Durable spaces—spaces that have a sense of continuity and to which citizens can therefore return with some familiarity—help to sustain democratic practices in two ways. First, by cultivating attachments to one's community, durable spaces generate the "buy-in" that draws citizens out of their private spheres and reminds them of their obligations to share in the work of caring for their common interests. And, second, by facilitating repeated interactions between citizens, durable spaces help to strengthen the ties of reciprocity and goodwill—ties of political friendship—that ensure citizens will continue to work together smoothly. By developing a more accurate understanding of how the built environment influences these dynamics, we can better determine how to build digital spaces that are helpful not just for political mobilization, but also for sustaining the resulting communities over time.

THE PROBLEM OF INDIVIDUALISM

More than occasional interest or activity, democracy is sustained participation in the work of cooperation and compromise as we negotiate the best decisions for our communities and stick around to see them through. Democracy thus requires not just the recognition that we share things in common; it also rests on a sustained commitment to working with others in caring for those interests, both now and in the future. And this necessitates an acknowledgment of one's entanglements with their community: "[E]ach man being equally weak" in a democracy, says Tocqueville, ideally "would feel a like need for the help of his companions, and knowing that he would not get their support without supplying his, he would easily appreciate that for him private interest was mixed up with public interest" (DA 15). The sustained engagement with public affairs required for democratic politics, in other words, requires that we properly conceptualize our relationship to the community and to our fellow citizens—that we understand our interdependence and, importantly, feel the weight of the obligations that fall out of that fact.

However, in democratic societies, as Tocqueville famously argues, it is immensely difficult for citizens to feel these obligations. The social structure of democracy is such that democratic citizens are encouraged to see things only from the limited perspective of our individual interests and to eschew the collective dimensions—and corresponding obligations—of our shared existence. And part of the reason for this, Tocqueville argues, is the disappearance of those "permanent associations" of family and class that formed the basis of aristocratic societies.

These permanent associations, while fundamentally inegalitarian, nevertheless had "the effect of linking each man closely with several of his fellows" (DA 507). As a result of their rigidly defined social positions, in other words, citizens in an aristocratic society "are almost always closely involved with something outside themselves, and they are often inclined to forget about themselves" (DA 507). Aristocratic institutions constantly remind citizens of their connections to others; individuals are made not only to recognize what interests they share, but also to feel the common advantages—and corresponding obligations—that fall out of those shared interests. The result, says Tocqueville, is that in an aristocratic society, citizens are unequal in status but "men do often make sacrifices for the sake of certain other men" (DA 507). They are better prepared to sacrifice their narrow self-interest in the name of specific social obligations.

In democracies, by contrast, the leveling effect of equality has largely destroyed these permanent associations. Rather than linking citizens together through interlocking relationships of family and class, Tocqueville tells us, "[d]emocracy breaks the chain and frees each link" (DA 508). Instead, with the democratic promise of class mobility and the corresponding loss of importance of family name and rank, "nobody's position is quite stable" (DA 507). And without these permanent associations of family and class, which remind citizens of their connections to others, past, present, and future, "[t]he woof of time is ever being broken and the track of past generations lost. Those who have gone before are easily forgotten, and no one gives a thought to those who will follow. *All a man's interests are limited to those near himself*" (DA 507; emphasis mine). It is easy, in other words, for democratic citizens to think themselves independent; in leveling our relationships, the democratic social structure has also obscured the ties that bind citizens together. Though we *are* still interconnected—we still share interests and thus have obligations to share in the work of managing them—democratic equality cultivates a sense of independence that encourages citizens to turn away from these attachments and obligations.

The result is what Tocqueville calls the problem of "individualism": when a citizen is disposed to "isolate himself from the mass of his fellows and withdraw into the circle of family and friends . . . [and] gladly leaves the greater society to look after itself" (DA 506). Individualism is the general detachment from public affairs that accompanies the loss of those permanent associations that tie citizens together and involve them in the affairs of wider society. Instead, individualism encourages democratic citizens to retreat from the complexities of public work and eschew our collective obligations—to leave them for others to care about.

Importantly, individualism does not preclude political action; rather, individualism *transforms* citizens' orientations toward public work. The result, Tocqueville argues in language that presages more recent work on the "personalization of politics," is that "private interest will more than ever become the chief if not the only driving force behind all behavior" (DA 527). Even under conditions of individualism, citizens may still become involved in democratic politics. But they are motivated to do so because of narrow personal concerns—and their interest, and participation, lasts only so long as they directly benefit. Rather than an effect of new digital technologies and the contemporary social context, then, Tocqueville's work shows us that individualism, and the corresponding "personalization of politics," is a consequence of the "equality of conditions" that necessarily accompanies democracy; individualism is a problem with democracy itself.

Happily, there are steps we can take to combat individualism's potentially devastating effects. Individualism, Tocqueville reminds us, is at its core a problem of (self-)perception. It "is based on misguided judgment" and "inadequate understanding" (DA 506) on the part of democratic citizens. Though they are, in reality, as interdependent as citizens in aristocracies, democratic citizens *misunderstand* their relationship with their communities and their fellow citizens. Rather than remaining "closely involved with something outside themselves," democratic citizens' warped perceptions of their social ties mean they instead "form the habit of thinking of themselves in isolation and imagine that their whole destiny is in their own hands" (DA 508). This, however, is a *mistaken* notion; combating individualism thus means correcting this misperception.

Ensuring that citizens sustain their democratic participation, then, requires more than citizens' recognition of their shared interests. It also necessitates that they adjust their (mis)understanding of their relationships to others, and form attachments to the community as a whole as well as to the other citizens within it. This reeducation of democratic citizens can be, as Tocqueville well recognized, quite difficult. The inegalitarian institutions of class and family—the permanent associations that linked citizens in aristocratic societies—are no longer appropriate for a democratic society premised on equality. Instead, Tocqueville proposes a number of new "artificial" institutions, suitable for democracy, which would nevertheless "provide a thousand continual reminders to every citizen that he lives in society" (DA 512). These new institutions have the effect of re-linking democratic citizens, correcting their misguided notions of independence, and reconnecting them to society by cultivating the requisite attachments.

Tocqueville, as well as those writing in the almost two centuries since *Democracy in America* was published, largely focused on the role of social institutions—like associations, newspapers, and organized religion—to provide citizens with these "thousand continual reminders." But the built environment can also, as we have seen, help citizens cultivate the habits, attitudes, and relationships that democracy requires. The built environment, recall, can provide cues that help citizens recognize their shared interests and interlocutors. In the same way, the built environment can also help remind citizens of their interdependence, and can thus help generate feelings of attachment and obligation to the community and maintain ties of political friendship between citizens. The built environment, in other words, can help citizens form the attachments that ultimately combat individualism and sustain democratic communities. But to do so, the spaces of the built environment must be durable.

CONTINUITY, ATTACHMENT, AND OBLIGATION

Democratic politics, as the continued work of managing our common affairs, requires a sustained commitment to take part in this work. This involves recognition that we share interests, of course, as "[c]itizens who are bound to take part in public affairs must turn from the private interests and occasionally take a look at something other than themselves" (DA 510). But it also relies on a deeper sense of attachment and obligation—citizens must not only recognize *that* they share interests, but must also "appreciate that in order to enjoy the benefits of society one must shoulder its obligations" (DA 14). Democracy, in other words, requires that citizens both recognize their shared interests and interlocutors—their connections to others—and also feel the corresponding responsibility to care for them. Though formed through an initial moment of recognition, democratic communities are *sustained* through these thicker affective attachments between citizens and the communities to which they belong.

Facilitating this attachment, and developing "firm and lasting ties" (DA 517) between citizens, is one reason Tocqueville praises the Americans' use of associations—what we might now call interest groups, clubs, or civil society organizations. Associations bring citizens into close contact with one another and highlight their common causes; in so doing, an association "draws a lot of people at the same time out of their own circle" (DA 521). As artificial institutions, democratic associations perform the role that the "permanent associations" of family and class played in aristocratic societies; they re-link citizens, reminding them of their obligations and providing continued opportunities for members to act collectively. Associations can, in other words, serve as powerful reminders that we live with others, share interests, and therefore have obligations to care for them collectively.

But the built environment also serves this function of drawing us out of our individual perspectives and reconnecting us with our fellow citizens. Indeed, Tocqueville acknowledges this effect of the built environment in his discussion of landed family estates. In aristocracies, he argues, "families maintain the same station for centuries *and often live in the same place*" (DA 507, emphasis mine). The result of this extended habitation in the same physical location is that "family feeling finds a sort of physical expression in the land. The family represents the land, and the land the family, perpetuating its name, origin, glory, power, and virtue. It is an *imperishable witness* to the past and a precious earnest of the future" (DA 52, emphasis mine). In aristocratic societies, in other words, the physical spaces of family estates stand as inescapable, "imperishable," reminders of citizens' obligations and attachments to a common (family) interest outside their narrow (individual) perspectives.

This connection between aristocratic families and their landed estates is an example of what psychologists and human geographers call "place attachment," the "dynamic but enduring positive bonds between people and prized socio-physical settings, such as homes."[12] Attachments to place "promote and provide

[12] Barbara Brown, Douglas D. Perkins, and Graham Brown, "Place Attachment in a Revitalizing Neighborhood: Individual and Block Levels of Analysis," *Journal of Environmental Psychology* 23 (2003): 259. See also Irwin Altman and Setha M. Low, eds., *Place Attachment* (New York: Plenum Press, 1992).

stability, familiarity, and security"[13] and lead to greater quality of life.[14] And, just as Tocqueville argued that an aristocratic attachment to family land would help cultivate citizens who are inclined to fulfill their communal obligations, so too does more recent research show that when residents form attachments to certain spaces, they are more likely to engage in civic action to preserve and maintain them.[15] When we develop this sense of place attachment, in other words, we are drawn out of our individual interests and reminded of our communal concerns and our shared obligations to manage them.

Crucially, however, not all spaces can foster the kind of place attachment necessary for sustained collective action; the *kinds* of spaces matter for generating these attachments. It is the continuity and accompanying familiarity of the aristocratic family estate—as an "imperishable witness"—that make it likely to foster these attachments.[16] And this is because the formation of place attachments requires *durable* spaces; we must have interacted with a space enough times to form a "sense of place"—to know what to expect and want to preserve it—before our place attachment is strong enough to draw us into public life.[17] It is precisely because the family estate endures throughout multiple generations, in other words, that each member of the family can more easily imagine their connections and obligations to past and future generations who might inhabit that space; it is due to the estate's durability that "there is a sense," as Tocqueville says, "in which all the generations are contemporaneous" (DA 507). And it is

[13] Brown, Perkins, and Brown, "Place Attachment in a Revitalizing Neighborhood," 259.

[14] Paul B. Harris et al., "Relocation and Privacy Regulation: A Cross-Cultural Analysis," *Journal of Environmental Psychology* 15 (1995): 311–20.

[15] Jacqueline Leavitt and Susan Saegert, "The Community-Household: Responding to Housing Abandonment in New York City," *Journal of the American Planning Association* 54, no. 4 (1988): 489–500; Clare L. Twigger-Ross and David L. Uzzell, "Place and Identity Processes," *Journal of Environmental Psychology* 16 (1996): 205–20; Marco Lalli, "Urban-Related Identity: Theory, Measurement, and Empirical Findings," *Journal of Environmental Psychology* 12 (1992): 285–303; Michelle A. Payton, David C. Fulton, and Dorothy H. Anderson, "Influence of Place Attachment and Trust on Civic Action: A Study at Sherburne National Wildlife Refuge," *Society and Natural Resources* 18, no. 6 (2005): 511–28.

[16] Maria Lewicka, "Place Attachment: How Far Have We Come in the Last 40 Years?," *Journal of Environmental Psychology* 31, no. 3 (2011): 207–30; Leila Scannell and Robert Gifford, "The Relations between Natural and Civic Place Attachment and Pro-Environmental Behavior," *Journal of Environmental Psychology* 30, no. 3 (2010): 289–97; Lalli, "Urban-Related Identity"; Kalevi M. Korpela et al., "Stability of Self-Reported Favourite Places and Place Attachment over a 10-Month Period," *Journal of Environmental Psychology* 29, no. 1 (2009): 95–100; Marino Bonaiuto et al., "Multidimensional Perception of Residential Environment," *Journal of Environmental Psychology* 19 (1999): 331–52.

[17] Melinda J. Milligan, "Interactional Past and Potential: The Social Construction of Place Attachment," *Symbolic Interaction* 21, no. 1 (1998): 1–33.

this connection, not just to what we hold in common at any given moment, but also to the imagined community of the past and future, that facilitates *sustained* democratic engagement to care for these shared interests.

We can see, moreover, the importance of durable spaces for sustaining democratic politics by exploring the consequences of their absence. In democracies, Tocqueville argues, "landowners are deprived of their strong sentimental attachment to the land, based on memories and pride" (DA 53) due in large part to laws of equal inheritance. Because democratic laws mandate "the equal sharing of a father's property among his children" (DA 52), family land is continually divided with each generation. As a result, these laws, in the name of equality, break "that intimate connection between family feeling and preservation of the land" such that "the land no longer represents the family" (DA 53). Because it exchanges hands more often, the land is more easily altered beyond recognition. The family land, in other words, becomes less durable; it therefore cannot serve the same role as a physical reminder of one's familial obligations. And without the "*spatial continuity* of experience"[18] provided by a durable space, which helps to connect one's experiences to those of the past and future, "the [democratic] family is felt to be a vague, indeterminate, uncertain conception" (DA 53)—it fails to cultivate the same communal attachments as the aristocratic families (and their estates) once did.

And, again, more recent research bears out these claims. In more mobile societies, individuals form place attachments differently—or not at all.[19] Rather than attaching to concrete locations, for example, highly mobile individuals tend to cultivate general "settlement identities," identifying as, for example, "city people" rather than residents of a particular city like Philadelphia.[20] And without a "rooted sense of place"[21] and the place attachment it generates, these citizens are more likely to turn their attention inward, to focus on their own individual interests instead of recognizing their entanglements with, and obligations toward, the *specific* communities of which they are members. It is the durability of the built environment that helps to generate the "strong sentimental attachment" to one's

[18] Milligan, "Interactional Past and Potential," 9.

[19] Harold M. Proshansky, Abbe K. Fabian, and Robert Kaminoff, "Place-Identity: Physical World Socialization of the Self," *Journal of Environmental Psychology* 3 (1983): 57–83; Marc Fried, "Grieving for a Lost Home: Psychological Costs of Relocation," in *Urban Renewal: The Record and the Controversy*, ed. James Q. Wilson (Cambridge, MA: MIT Press, 1966), 359–60.

[20] Roberta M. Feldman, "Settlement-Identity: Psychological Bonds with Home Places in a Mobile Society," *Environment and Behavior* 22, no. 2 (1990): 183–229.

[21] Robert Bruce Hay, "Sense of Place in Developmental Context," *Journal of Environmental Psychology* 18, no. 1 (1998): 5–29.

community that keeps one invested in it. And in facilitating these communal attachments, it is the durability of the built environment that reminds us of our obligations to care for them.

REPEATED INTERACTIONS AND GOODWILL

Durable spaces, as we have seen, play an important role in facilitating attachment to one's community; they remind citizens of their obligations to care for the things they share with others and, in so doing, help to sustain the communities that form around them. But while attachment to one's community is necessary, democratic politics is not reducible to this feeling. And "attachment," while important in drawing citizens out of their personal lives, is not synonymous with the work of democracy itself. As the collective management of common affairs, democratic politics requires not just recognizing that we share things in common and enacting our obligations to care for them; it also, as we saw in the previous chapter, involves certain interpersonal relations—like political friendship—that help to ensure that cooperative democratic engagements are productive and sustainable. And, again, the durability of the built environment can help to maintain and deepen these interpersonal ties.

The mutual goodwill that marks political friendships is not, Tocqueville reminds us, the result of a single "brilliant achievement" (DA 511); rather, it takes time to cultivate this kind of relationship—"a long succession of little services rendered and of obscure good deeds, a constant habit of kindness and an established reputation for disinterestedness are required" (DA 511). Indeed, when people "only occasionally . . . come together in the same places," Tocqueville notes, "they often lose sight of one another" and thus "no lasting bonds form between them" (DA 511).

The mechanism Tocqueville identifies here for sustaining ties of cooperation and affection—for sustaining political friendships—is one of repeated interactions.[22] If we know we are likely to meet someone again, that fact shapes how we treat them; we are likely to be on our best behavior because we want to ensure that future encounters will go smoothly. Knowing we will

[22] See also Amy Gutmann and Dennis Thompson, *The Spirit of Compromise: Why Governing Demands It and Campaigning Undermines It* (Princeton, NJ: Princeton University Press, 2012); Elinor Ostrom and T. K. Ahn, eds., *Foundations of Social Capital, Foundations of Social Capital* (Northampton, MA: Edward Elgar, 2003); Robert D. Putnam, *Making Democracy Work: Civic Traditions in Modern Italy* (Princeton, NJ: Princeton University Press, 1993); Mark E. Warren and Jane Mansbridge, "Deliberative Negotiation," in *Negotiating Agreement in Politics*, ed. Jane Mansbridge and Cathie Jo Martin (Washington, DC: American Political Science Association, 2013), 86–120.

likely meet again, we are more inclined to cooperate with our fellow citizens, to act as a "good neighbor"—or as a (political) friend.

Key here is that repeated interactions take *time*; repetition requires a certain continuity of experience. And as a permanent association, the township—like the aristocratic family estate—provides that continuity.[23] This is due, in part, to the durability of its physical spaces; the township, Tocqueville tells us, "has a more pronounced physiognomy than is found elsewhere" and is "shaped to form the nucleus of strong attachments" (DA 69).[24] In the township, citizens are repeatedly brought together to "look after the particular affairs of [their] district," such that "the same people are always meeting and they are forced, in a manner to know and adapt themselves to one another" (DA 511). The result, says Tocqueville, is the generation of new habits: "what had been calculation becomes instinct" (DA 512). And it is this *habit* of goodwill and cooperation—of political friendship—that ultimately sustains a community.

Though these civic ties may begin from the recognition of mutual advantage, in other words, citizens soon come to deepen these interpersonal attachments and feelings of goodwill toward their neighbors; over time, the practices of cooperation and compromise become second nature.[25] And this, again, is in part a function of the built environment. While the township's boundaries help to clarify for citizens what the "public interest" is, it is the *durability* of those boundaries that help citizens form these "strong attachments"—not only to the community, but also to their fellow citizens—and develop the habits to sustain them.

Moreover, the effects of repeated interactions are, like the effects of place attachments, not limited to the township. Historically, scholars have noted the role of durable spaces in sustaining the democratic participation of workers in

[23] For more on Tocqueville's distinctions between different "forms" of association, including the relationship between the "permanent association" of the township and voluntary associations, which are "episodic" and "shifting in membership," see Dana Villa, *Public Freedom* (Princeton, NJ: Princeton University Press, 2008).

[24] Importantly, the value of the township does not seem to be reducible to size alone in this account. Tocqueville spends little time on the question of size and instead presents his findings—that an American township "generally has from two to three thousand inhabitants" (DA 63)—as descriptive rather than normative. Size only matters, for Tocqueville, insofar as the township is "not too large for all inhabitants to have roughly the same interests, but is big enough to be sure of finding the elements of a good administration within itself" (DA 63). The political value of townships is not, therefore, the specific number of citizens who live in it. It is, rather, the greater likelihood of shared interests held by a township's residents that is the source of their value. And, as we know from chapter 2, it is the township's boundaries that help citizens recognize these interests.

[25] Robert Kraut, Carmen Egido, and Jolene Galegher, "Patterns of Contact and Communication in Scientific Research Collaboration," in *Proceedings of the 1988 ACM Conference on Computer-Supported Cooperative Work* (Portland, OR: ACM, 1988), 1–12.

nineteenth-century Paris[26] as well as students during the 1989 Beijing protests.[27] In both cases, durable spaces (of neighborhoods and university campuses) strengthened collective identities and incentivized citizens to sustain their participation by reminding them of their communal obligations. And, as decades of work in geography, sociology, and social and environmental psychology has continued to show in the spaces of neighborhoods,[28] offices,[29] and college dorms and classrooms,[30] people who live and work within bounded and durable spaces are more likely to associate and collaborate, and form and sustain friendships. In all these examples, boundaries are not the only feature that matters. There is an element of durability at work in these environments as well. Citizens in these spaces can be reasonably sure that, for example, their neighborhoods, classrooms, dorms, cities, or office buildings will not disappear from one moment to the next; this continuity, and the repeated encounters it invites, is what helps citizens more easily feel the weight of their obligations to one another and work cooperatively to manage them.

Alongside social institutions, like newspapers and associations, then, the durability of the built environment can play an important role in counteracting the impulse toward individualism and the corresponding "personalization of politics" by keeping us engaged in our communities. By facilitating place attachment, durable spaces reconnect us to things outside the limited sphere of our own personal interests; they serve as "continual reminders" of our dependence on others, past, present, and future, and thus remind us of our obligations to care for the interests we share. Moreover, durable spaces provide opportunities for the repeated encounters through which we deepen our habits of reciprocated goodwill and concord—of political friendship—that underlie sustainable

[26] Roger V. Gould, *Insurgent Identities: Class, Community, and Protest in Paris from 1848 to the Commune* (Chicago: University of Chicago Press, 1995).

[27] Dingxin Zhao, "Ecologies of Social Movements: Student Mobilization during the 1989 Prodemocracy Movement in Beijing," *American Journal of Sociology* 103, no. 6 (1998): 1493–529.

[28] David L. DuBois and Barton J. Hirsch, "School and Neighborhood Friendship Patterns of Blacks and Whites in Early Adolescence," *Child Development* 61, no. 2 (1990): 524–36; R. Robert Huckfeldt, "Social Contexts, Social Networks, and Urban Neighborhoods: Environmental Constraints on Friendship Choice," *American Journal of Sociology* 89, no. 3 (1983): 651–69; Ted Mouw and Barbara Entwisle, "Residential Segregation and Interracial Friendship in Schools," *American Journal of Sociology* 112, no. 2 (2006): 394–441; Lucille Nahemow and M. Powell Lawton, "Similarity and Propinquity in Friendship Formation," *Journal of Personality and Social Psychology* 32, no. 2 (1975): 205–13.

[29] Kraut, Egido, and Galegher, "Patterns of Contact and Communication in Scientific Research Collaboration."

[30] Theodore M. Newcomb, *The Acquaintance Process* (New York: Holt, Rinehart and Winston, 1961); Leon Festinger, Stanley Schachter, and Kurt Back, *Social Pressures in Informal Groups: A Study of Human Factors in Housing* (Stanford, CA: Stanford University Press, 1950).

democratic communities. While boundaries may help us recognize *that* we share things in common with others, then, it is the durability of these boundaries that helps us to *sustain* the collective activity of managing them. Yet it is precisely this element of durability that can be difficult to capture in digital environments.

Problems with Digital Durability: The Case of Twitter

Digital platforms like Twitter are often recognized for their role in mobilizing citizens to engage in public action. While scholars disagree over precisely how much influence to attribute to these technologies, there is nevertheless a strong consensus that their affordances of quick, easy, and efficient communication have helped citizens quickly raise the visibility of particular issues of concern and form communities around these issues. But in addition to accelerating these instances of mobilization, scholars argue, digital technologies are also changing the very ways that citizens act together. Reflecting and exacerbating the modern "logic of connective action"—with its emphasis on the personalization of politics and the use of digital tools to enable it—digital technologies, it seems, have accompanied a new era of political action.

Scholars studying the political uses of digital technologies have largely tended to embrace the new possibilities of connective action, convincingly demonstrating the ways that technological affordances introduce more flexible and effective forms of political mobilization. Certainly, there are reasons to celebrate the creative potential of this new networked civic action. And yet we should also be wary of what is lost when we engage in political activity primarily on our own terms. As Tufekci argues, these patterns of digital engagement—while efficient—can lead to lost capacities; more specifically, as Tocqueville reminds us, when we lose sight of our interdependence, we more easily fall victim to the misguided judgment of individualism. We wrongly think that we are independent and isolated and thus fail to sufficiently feel the weight of our obligations toward others. The result is a slow withdrawal from public life and the corresponding collapse of democratic communities—a context ripe for despotism.

As we consider how to harness the power of digital technologies to sustain democratic communities, then, we must consider how to ensure that citizens form the necessary attachments to both their communities and the other members of them. In this section, I turn to the example of Twitter not only to show how the lack of durability of certain digital environments can contribute to this loss of sustained political engagement, but also to suggest strategies for improving the durability of digital spaces. Over the course of the last decade, scholars have examined Twitter's effects on political engagement,[31] particularly its role in campaigns of awareness-raising and mobilization as part of social movements.[32] This work tends to focus on how citizens use Twitter to communicate, reflecting the same emphasis on the *activity* of politics that motivates our traditional focus on associations as engines of civic engagement.

Yet, as I have been arguing, Tocqueville's remarks on the "permanent associations" of the aristocratic family estate and the New England township—and especially the role of the built environment in supporting their permanence—invite us to also examine the durability of Twitter as a discrete space in the digital built environment. Here, then, I analyze the mechanism of hashtags, which have become synonymous with the platform, as a factor influencing the sustainability of the communities it hosts. Ultimately, I argue that Twitter's reliance on the hashtag as a device for forming communities on the site is largely successful because hashtags impose clear boundaries. Yet hashtags also ultimately lack the durability required to sustain these communities over time. The result is that Twitter can be very effective at mobilizing citizens, but that it is also rather ill-suited to host sustained democratic communities. I then conclude with some suggestions for making the spaces of Twitter more durable and thus rendering the platform more hospitable for democratic politics.

TWITTER: UNBOUNDED SPACE

Founded in March 2006, Twitter has variously been characterized as a microblogging site, news service, and social networking site.[33] Despite this diverse

[31] Chang Sup Park, "Does Twitter Motivate Involvement in Politics? Tweeting, Opinion Leadership, and Political Engagement," *Computers in Human Behavior* 29, no. 4 (2013): 1641–48; Anders Olof Larsson and Hallvard Moe, "Studying Political Microblogging: Twitter Users in the 2010 Swedish Election Campaign," *New Media and Society* 14, no. 5 (2011): 729–47; Leticia Bode and Kajsa E. Dalrymple, "Politics in 140 Characters or Less: Campaign Communication, Network Interaction, and Political Participation on Twitter," *Journal of Political Marketing* 15, no. 4 (2016): 311–32.

[32] Rebecca Kay LeFebvre and Crystal Armstrong, "Grievance-Based Social Movement Mobilization in the #Ferguson Twitter Storm," *New Media and Society* 20, no. 1 (2018): 8–28; Yannis Theocharis et al., "Using Twitter to Mobilize Protest Action: Online Mobilization Patterns and Action Repertoires in the Occupy Wall Street, Indignados, and Aganaktismenoi Movements," *Information, Communication and Society* 18, no. 2 (2014): 202–20; Simon Lindgren and Randy Lundström, "Pirate Culture and Hacktivist Mobilization: The Cultural and Social Protocols of #WikiLeaks on Twitter," *New Media and Society* 13, no. 6 (2011): 999–1018.

[33] Akshay Java et al., "Why We Twitter: Understanding Microblogging Usage and Communities," in *Proceedings of the 9th WebKDD and 1st SNA-KDD 2007 Workshop on Web Mining and Social Network Analysis* (San Jose, CA, 2007), 56–65; Barry Ritholtz, "How Twitter Is Becoming Your First Source of Investment News," *ABC News*, April 20, 2013; Haewoon Kwak et al., "What Is Twitter, a Social Network or a News Media?," in *International World Wide Web Conference Committee* (Raleigh, NC, 2010), 591–600.

categorization, the basic function of the platform is simple. Upon logging in to Twitter, users are prompted to "tweet" short messages of no more than 280 characters in response to the question "What's happening?"[34] Tweets then appear on the timelines of one's followers, in a more-or-less reverse chronological order, with newer tweets appearing near the top of one's feed.[35] Users can opt to "follow" those users whose tweets they wish to see regularly; there is no obligation, however, that anyone will "follow back." Unlike Facebook, then, on which "Friendships" must be reciprocated, Twitter's user relationships are often asymmetrical, with less than half of users' followings reciprocated, on average.[36] As a result, Twitter encourages "a one-to-many form of social interaction, and thereby may facilitate the formation and maintenance of looser, distal ties, or a mix of close and loose ties wherein reciprocity is more arbitrary."[37] Unlike the closer-knit relationships that characterized Facebook in its bounded phases, in other words, Twitter is "like a giant hangout—an open and rich chat room that's happening in public."[38]

This looser network structure is due, in part, to Twitter's design: the platform is a relatively unbounded space. Though individual Twitter users can be connected to one another, there are no clear markers that signal users' collectively shared interests. As a result, unlike the communal ties of political friendship generated by Facebook in its .edu incarnation, Twitter is characterized by

[34] For most of its existence, tweets were limited to 140 characters. In November 2017, however, the site expanded this limit to 280 characters. See Sarah Perez, "Twitter Officially Expands Its Character Count to 280 Starting Today," *TechCrunch*, November 7, 2017; Aliza Rosen and Ikuhiro Ihara, "Giving You More Characters to Express Yourself," *Twitter Blog*, September 26, 2017.

[35] In 2016, Twitter introduced algorithmic sorting of tweets in users' timeline, meaning they were presented in terms of "best fit" rather than strict reverse chronology. In late 2018, Twitter introduced a feature that allowed users to quickly switch between "top" tweets (as determined by the algorithm) and "latest" tweets (that would display tweets in strict reverse-chronology). The implications of the sorting algorithm will be discussed in more detail in chapter 5. See Jon Porter, "Twitter Is Making It Easier to Toggle between Latest and Top Tweets," *The Verge*, November 1, 2018.

[36] Seth A. Myers et al., "Information Network or Social Network? The Structure of the Twitter Follow Graph," in *WWW'14 Companion: Proceedings of the 23rd International Conference on World Wide Web* (23rd International Conference on World Wide Web, Seoul: ACM, 2014), 493–98.

[37] Christina Shane-Simpson et al., "Why Do College Students Prefer Facebook, Twitter, or Instagram? Site Affordances, Tensions between Privacy and Self-Expression, and Implications for Social Capital," *Computers in Human Behavior* 86 (2018): 285.

[38] April Glaser, "How to Use Twitter: Critical Tips for New Users," *WIRED*, May 6, 2016.

"diverse, loosely-linked connections."[39] Because it lacks the kind of clear, durable boundaries that we know help to develop and sustain ties of political friendship, in other words, Twitter is built as a space for those who "want to try new things, and come into contact with new people."[40] It is an environment designed to encourage heterogeneity, novelty, and unreciprocated interactions rather than a space that will facilitate recognition of shared interests, generate attachment to a given community of interest, and incentivize the repeated interactions necessary to sustain ties of political friendship among members.[41] Instead of reminding users of their connections to others, Twitter facilitates the individualism that concerned Tocqueville—users' experiences are largely guided by their own personal interests and perspectives.

And we can see the effects of Twitter's lack of durable boundaries in how users interact with one another on the platform. Unlike Facebook, which hosts users who are "more motivated to maintain social contact through reciprocal communication," Twitter emphasizes "self-disclosure in one-sided status updates."[42] In 2010, for instance, over three-quarters of Twitter users had only unidirectional connections, while over two-thirds of users were not followed by any of the people they followed, meaning they had *no* reciprocal relationships on the site.[43] As a result of this asymmetry, Twitter "provides fewer obvious opportunities to speak than Facebook."[44] "Conversations" on Twitter are often not conversations at all—they are one-way transmissions, individual monologues rather than dialogues between mutually recognized members of a shared community. Indeed, the most common type of tweet on the platform is the "singleton"—meaning a tweet that had no reply or retweet. "Mentions," by contrast, where a user addresses another specific user in their tweet, are the least common

[39] Joe Phua, Seunga Venus Jin, and Jihoon (Jay) Jay, "Uses and Gratifications of Social Networking Sites for Bridging and Bonding Social Capital: A Comparison of Facebook, Twitter, Instagram, and Snapchat," *Computers in Human Behavior* 72 (2017): 119. These loose ties "allow for diffusion of new information, as seen on users' Twitter feeds, which includes tweets from others they follow, as well as retweets and other re-broadcast posts."

[40] Phua, Jin, and Jay, "Uses and Gratifications of Social Networking Sites," 119.

[41] In November 2020, Twitter introduced a new feature—"Fleets," which (like Instagram "Stories") disappear within 24 hours of posting—that introduced even more impermanence into its spaces. Joshua Harris and Sam Haveson, "Fleets: A New Way to Join the Conversation," *Twitter Blog*, November 17, 2020.

[42] Shane-Simpson et al., "Why Do College Students Prefer Facebook, Twitter, or Instagram?," 285. See also David John Hughes et al., "A Tale of Two Sites: Twitter vs. Facebook and the Personality Predictors of Social Media Usage," *Computers in Human Behavior* 28, no. 2 (2012): 561–69.

[43] Kwak et al., "What Is Twitter, a Social Network or a News Media?."

[44] Amy Binns, "Twitter City and Facebook Village: Teenage Girls' Personas and Experiences Influenced by Choice Architecture in Social Networking Sites," *Journal of Media Practice* 15, no. 2 (2014): 85.

type of tweet.[45] Rather than serve as a space where users can easily recognize themselves as members of a community, form attachments, and engage in the repeated interactions required to sustain them, Twitter is designed as a space with "flexible opportunities to connect with loose ties."[46]

Of course, there is more to Twitter than the relationships between individual users. One of the most prominent features of the platform is the hashtag—a mechanism through which users can identify issues of concern that are, in theory, shared with others on the site. Hashtags, as we will see, work to impose boundaries on Twitter. Yet while they can be, as a result, quite effective at helping users form communities, hashtags as they are currently deployed ultimately lack the durability necessary to ensure those communities can maintain themselves over time. As a result, hashtag-housed communities on Twitter can easily—and often—form, but they are much more difficult to sustain.

HASHTAGS: TEMPORARY COMMUNITIES

When Twitter was first created, there were no mechanisms through which users could sort and aggregate tweets—a tweet would simply appear in one's timeline as a wholly isolated post, disconnected from any context except its author. About a year after the platform was launched, however, and with little aid from the company itself, Twitter users began using hashtags to organize information on the site.[47] In August 2007, Twitter user Chris Messina used #barcamp to help participants of BarCamp, an ad-hoc, participatory workshop/conference event, organize group activities online. Drawing on a history of Internet Relay Chat (IRC) chatroom titles, Messina set off the tag "barcamp" with a # sign in the hopes that it would be easier for event participants to identify one another's tweets. The hashtag concept did not fully catch on, however, until October of that year, when Twitter user Nate Ridder (and, subsequently, others) used the hashtag #SanDiegoFire to compile and disseminate information about wildfires raging in the area. Following the popularity of these user-created interventions, Twitter later officially adopted the hashtag feature by linking it to the platform's "search" function.[48]

[45] Kwak et al., "What Is Twitter, a Social Network or a News Media?."

[46] Shane-Simpson et al., "Why Do College Students Prefer Facebook, Twitter, or Instagram?," 278.

[47] Jeff Huang, Katherine M. Thornton, and Efthimis N. Efthimiadis, "Conversational Tagging in Twitter," in *Proceedings of the 21st ACM Conference on Hypertext and Hypermedia—HT '10* (Toronto, 2010), 173. For more, see Joe Rosenberg, "Interrobang," 99% Invisible, 2018, https://99percentinvisible.org/episode/interrobang/.

[48] Lexi Pandell, "An Oral History of the #Hashtag," *WIRED*, May 19, 2017.

With Twitter's integration of hashtags into the site's search, the platform effectively added boundaries to users' experiences on the platform. Hashtags are labels—following the format #topic—that users can add to "tag" their tweets as part of a specific conversation happening on Twitter.[49] In so doing, hashtags create particular spaces within which users can clearly identify what they have in common with others who are also using those hashtags.[50] A tweet tagged with #WomenAlsoKnow, for example, is likely to contribute to a larger effort at raising women's visibility in political science scholarship, much like tweets tagged #APSAonFire relate to discussions around the 2014 American Political Science Association (APSA) conference, during which a "series of suspicious fires" broke out in one of the conference hotels.[51]

Though there are a number of popular, recurring hashtags—like #FollowFriday, where users recommend other users to follow, or #AcademicTwitter, which signals a shared interest in academic life—hashtags can be created for whatever users choose; simply placing the # sign immediately before a string of alphanumeric characters will turn those characters into an aggregable hashtag. Hashtags then appear in tweets as hyperlinks, such that clicking on a hashtag in any given tweet will generate a feed of all tweets that include that tag (see Figure 3.1).[52] By adding boundaries to Twitter, hashtags make it easy for Twitter users to identify common interests (those designated by the hashtag), as well as those who share them (the others using that hashtag). It should be unsurprising, then, that Twitter hashtags are often used to help coordinate collective action, share information during crises, and respond in real time to current events.

Because they effectively help users identify shared interests and interlocutors, moreover, the boundaries provided by hashtags are a foundational element of community life on Twitter. "Hashtags," writes André Brock, "enable Twitter to mediate communal identities in near-real time; allowing participants to act individually yet en masse while still being heard."[53] Consider the example of "Black Twitter." Black Twitter, argues Meredith Clark, is a "hashtag public" that is "formed through the uniting of individuals who share some of the interest and characteristics reflective of each participant's physical and virtual identities."[54]

[49] David Laniado and Peter Mika, "Making Sense of Twitter," in *9th International Semantic Web Conference, ISWC 2010*, ed. Peter F. Patel-Schneider et al. (Shanghai, China: Springer, 2010), 470–85.

[50] Laniado and Mika, "Making Sense of Twitter," 471–72.

[51] Daniel W. Drezner, "Who Is Targeting America's Greatest Political Scientists?," *Washington Post*, September 2, 2014.

[52] These searches are presented to uses with a curated list of "top" tweets using that hashtag, though users can also choose to see a list of the "latest" tweets using the hashtag as well.

[53] André Brock, "From the Blackhand Side: Twitter as a Cultural Conversation," *Journal of Broadcasting and Electronic Media* 56, no. 4 (2012): 539.

[54] Meredith Clark, "Black Twitter: Building Connection through Cultural Conversation," in *Hashtag Publics: The Power and Politics of Discursive Networks*, ed. Nathan Rambukkana

Figure 3.1 Sample search results for #AcademicTwitter. Twitter hashtags act as boundaries that gather users and help them to identify what they share with others using the same hashtag. In this case, the hashtag #AcademicTwitter collects tweets from different users who are discussing various aspects of academic life. Photograph by author.

(New York: Peter Lang Publishing, 2015), 207. There is, however, some debate over the value of characterizing "Black Twitter" as a cohesive community, with some arguing that it implies a monolith that is not reflective of its members' diverse interests. See Sarah Florini, "Tweets, Tweeps, and Signifyin': Communication and Cultural Performance on 'Black Twitter,'" *Television and New Media* 15, no. 3 (2014): 233–37.

And it is in the spaces of hashtags that this community gathers together; through the "creative use of Twitter's hashtag function and subsequent domination of Twitter's 'trending topics,' "[55] Black Twitter participants both "invite[] an audience" and "signal that the Twitterer is part of a larger community."[56] The clear boundaries of Twitter's hashtags, in other words, make it easy for users to identify what they share. And, in so doing, they invite a collective response that is integral in forming communities—like Black Twitter—on the platform.

Yet hashtags, while bounded, are not durable. While they can help users identify shared interests and interlocutors, any given hashtag is often short-lived. Hashtags are frequently connected to "micro-memes" that "catch on and then die-out quickly."[57] The spaces created by hashtags, in other words, rarely last beyond the moment in which they are actively used; as a result, they provide little of the continuity that we know is so important for a space to act as an "imperishable witness" that helps us form the communal attachments and experience the repeated encounters required for sustained democratic engagements. Instead, communities formed through the use of hashtags are perhaps best understood as "ad-hoc issue publics"[58]—they effectively engage in collective action for short periods but are often not sustainable over time.

We can see this dynamic at work in prominent "hashtag publics." While communities like Black Twitter and #GirlsLikeUs (a "self-organized community of trans women"[59]) are sometimes described as cohesive—and sustained—"counterpublics,"[60] they often operate more like networks of networks, consisting of overlapping personal networks reinforced and made public with the occasional use of hashtags. Indeed, as Brock argues, Black Twitter is "best understood as a 'public group of specific Twitter users' rather than a 'Black online public.' "[61] As an "active meta-network,"[62] Black Twitter is "grouped into personal communities

[55] Brock, "From the Blackhand Side," 545. "Trending topics" is a list, created by Twitter, of the most-used hashtags at any given moment.

[56] Brock, "From the Blackhand Side," 539.

[57] Huang, Thornton, and Efthimiadis, "Conversational Tagging in Twitter," 5.

[58] Axel Bruns and Jean Burgess, "Twitter Hashtags: From Ad-Hoc to Calculated Publics," in *Hashtag Publics: The Power and Politics of Discursive Networks*, ed. Nathan Rambukkana (New York: Peter Lang Publishing, 2015), 13–28.

[59] Sarah J. Jackson, Moya Bailey, and Brooke Foucault Welles, "#GirlsLikeUs: Trans Advocacy and Community Building Online," *New Media and Society* 20, no. 5 (2018): 1869.

[60] Roderick Graham and Shawn Smith, "The Content of Our #Characters: Black Twitter as Counterpublic," *Sociology of Race and Ethnicity* 2, no. 4 (2016): 433–49; Jackson, Bailey, and Foucault Welles, "#GirlsLikeUs."

[61] Brock, "From the Blackhand Side," 545.

[62] Clark, "Black Twitter," 209.

and interconnected thematic nodes" and periodically reflected in hashtags.[63] Rather than a sustained, clearly bounded community, in other words, Black Twitter has instead been described as a "constantly shifting"[64] network of "interpersonal connections and shared interests" that "has been leveraged to mobilize users around various political and cultural issues."[65]

Likewise, #GirlsLikeUs is better characterized as a "broadcast network . . . in which most people retweet messages authored by a small number of prominent users"; in particular, #GirlsLikeUs is largely centered on two key celebrity figures: Janet Mock and Laverne Cox, who together originated almost one third of the #GirlsLikeUs-tagged tweets.[66] And while the hashtag does provide a space for users to "locate other trans people, find social support, and share the 'microstresses' of trans living,"[67] the resulting conversations are largely focused around personal disclosures, "shaping cultural solidarity and providing important emotional and psychological support."[68] Within the space of the hashtag, in other words, engagement with the #GirlsLikeUs network is still largely driven by users' own personal interests.

This is not to dismiss these networks as passive or unimportant. Nor is it to claim that the periodic mobilizations of these networks are ineffective. Indeed, the "ad-hoc" publics of Twitter hashtags—and particularly those of the counterpublics discussed here—have very successfully organized offline protests, corrected media biases in representation, and critiqued dominant discourses especially around questions of identity.[69] But these are perhaps better understood in terms of the quick mobilization and personalized politics of "connective

[63] Clark, "Black Twitter," 207.

[64] Clark, "Black Twitter," 206.

[65] Sarah Florini, *Beyond Hashtags: Racial Politics and Black Digital Networks* (New York: NYU Press, 2019), 22. Importantly, as Florini's book shows, Black Twitter is situated within a larger assemblage of Black digital networks, where hashtags (like #BLACKandSTEM and #BlackLivesMatter) are often given more durable spaces like blogs and websites. We might expect, then, that those hashtags connected with more durable spaces host more sustained community interactions on Twitter—though the communal attachments are cultivated elsewhere. For more on #BLACKandSTEM, for example, see David Zax, "#BLACKandSTEM: The Hashtag as Community," *Fast Company*, March 4, 2014; DNLee, "You Should Know: Stephani Page and #BLACKandSTEM," *Scientific American*, July 13, 2014.

[66] Sarah J. Jackson, Moya Bailey, and Brooke Foucault Welles, *#HashtagActivism: Networks of Race and Gender Justice* (Cambridge, MA: MIT Press, 2020), 78.

[67] Jackson, Bailey, and Foucault Welles, *#Hashtag Activism*, 90.

[68] Jackson, Bailey, and Foucault Welles, *#Hashtag Activism*, 78.

[69] Jackson, Bailey, and Foucault Welles, *#Hashtag Activism*; Logan Rhoades and Adrian Carrasquillo, "How the Powerful #IfTheyGunnedMeDown Movement Changed the Conversation about Michael Brown's Death," *BuzzFeed News*, August 13, 2014; Mikki Kendall, "#SolidarityIsForWhiteWomen: Women of Color's Issue with Digital Feminism," *The Guardian*, August 14, 2013; Clark, "Black Twitter."

action" rather than the sustained and coordinated activity of self-conscious democratic communities.[70]

And, again, this is largely due to hashtags' lack of durability. Hashtags are only "rarely used to retrieve old tweets"; rather, they are more often "used to funnel related tweets into common streams."[71] While hashtags—as boundaries—might successfully collect individual experiences and mark them as similar, in other words, their lack of durability means they are not able to keep this collection of individuals together as a cohesive, and self-conscious, *community* that sustains itself over time. Instead of serving as an "imperishable witness" to a community outside one's own interests, in other words, hashtags' lack of durability means they are most commonly used to aggregate personalized experiences. Rather than turning our attention to something outside of ourselves and reminding users of their interdependence, as did the aristocratic family estate and the New England township, hashtags keep our perceptions squarely centered on our personal interests—interests that we might happen to share with others. Even with hashtags, then, Twitter largely fails to incentivize the communal attachments and repeated interactions that might turn this aggregation of individuals into more sustained and self-conscious communities.

CREATING DURABLE HASHTAGS

Hashtags provide the boundaries necessary to help Twitter users identify communities of interest and act together for short periods of time and on their own individual terms. But hashtags ultimately lack the durability required to sustain political communities on the platform for significant periods. Instead, the boundaries created by hashtags are temporary and self-selected. While they are extraordinarily effective at aggregating users' experiences and mobilizing around those personalized concerns, they largely fail to facilitate repeated and reciprocal interactions between citizens and remind them of communal obligations.

As they are currently configured, in other words, hashtags largely fail to effectively draw users out of their personal experiences and foster attachments to a wider community and its members. In order to redesign Twitter in a way that would sustain democratic communities, however, the platform might develop hashtags into more "permanent" spaces that both cultivate users' attachments to their communities and facilitate repeated interactions among those users. By bolstering hashtags' durability, Twitter could help users to more easily form

[70] Anke Wonneberger, Iina R. Hellsten, and Sandra H. J. Jacobs, "Hashtag Activism and the Configuration of Counterpublics: Dutch Animal Welfare Debates on Twitter," *Information, Communication and Society* 24, no. 12 (2021): 1694–1711.

[71] Huang, Thornton, and Efthimiadis, "Conversational Tagging in Twitter," 3.

attachments to the various communities of interest on the platform, stabilizing those communities that currently form and disappear.

This is not a new recommendation. For years, there have been calls for Twitter to introduce "Groups"[72] or Rooms"[73] that would serve as these durable spaces (see Figure 3.2). What these recommendations have in common is that they give the "ad-hoc publics" currently facilitated by hashtags a more permanent home. In one formulation, Rex Sorgatz suggests turning hashtags into Groups, such that "[w]hen you tweet from within a Group, your message is placed directly into the context of that Group" and tweets are then "suppressed from the main timeline unless the viewer has also joined that Group."[74] Like Facebook Groups, then, this structural change would work to "direct [users] into distinct venues of conversation and community."[75] Similarly, Daniel Rakhamimov's proposed "Rooms" feature would offer "a gathering place for people with similar interests."[76]

In all their various suggested forms, these durable hashtags would work like the "channels" of Internet Relay Chat (IRC) or Slack (see Figure 3.3)—as dedicated spaces that persist, that users can return to repeatedly to find the same users and interests. By providing more durable spaces, these changes would help to add communal context to users' hashtagged tweets, giving users a sense of continuity. In so doing, these durable spaces would help generate the attachments and facilitate the repeated interactions that help to sustain democratic communities.

Hashtags, in this more durable iteration, would thus serve as an enduring, external reminder of one's communal interests and obligations, in the same way as did the aristocratic family estate and the New England township. Constructing durable hashtags would allow for content on Twitter to be organized—and, importantly, *presented to users*—in a way that reminds users of their embeddedness within a wider community and their interdependence with other users therein. As a result, users would be induced to compose tweets in response to a community—and an ongoing conversation—that preexists and outlasts their individual contribution.

Contrast this with the current practice of composing a tweet in isolation *then* affixing a hashtag to it to ensure it is seen by others "following" that hashtag. While users currently use hashtags to categorize and aggregate tweets

[72] Rex Sorgatz, "Twitter Should Have Groups and Here Is How They Should Work," *Medium*, February 20, 2019.

[73] Daniel Rakhamimov, "The Global Town Square," *Medium*, November 5, 2015.

[74] Sorgatz, "Twitter Should Have Groups and Here Is How They Should Work."

[75] Sorgatz, "Twitter Should Have Groups and Here Is How They Should Work."

[76] Rakhamimov, "The Global Town Square."

Figure 3.2 Example of how "Groups" might work on Twitter. Notice how the content is organized by hashtag—users are channeled into the spaces formed by hashtags and invited to engage with other users around those shared interests. Reproduced with permission from Rex Sorgatz, "Twitter Should Have Groups and Here Is How They Should Work," *Medium*, February 20, 2019, available at https://medium.com/@rexsorgatz/twitter-groups-hashtags-5932bb54e27c.

after the fact, in other words, more durable hashtags—like Rooms, Groups, or channels—might induce users to respond to discussions in their communities they might otherwise ignore; because of their recognized membership in a community, in other words, these users would be more inclined to acknowledge, as Tocqueville put it, that their "private interest was mixed up with public interest" (DA 15). More durable hashtags, like the permanent associations of family and

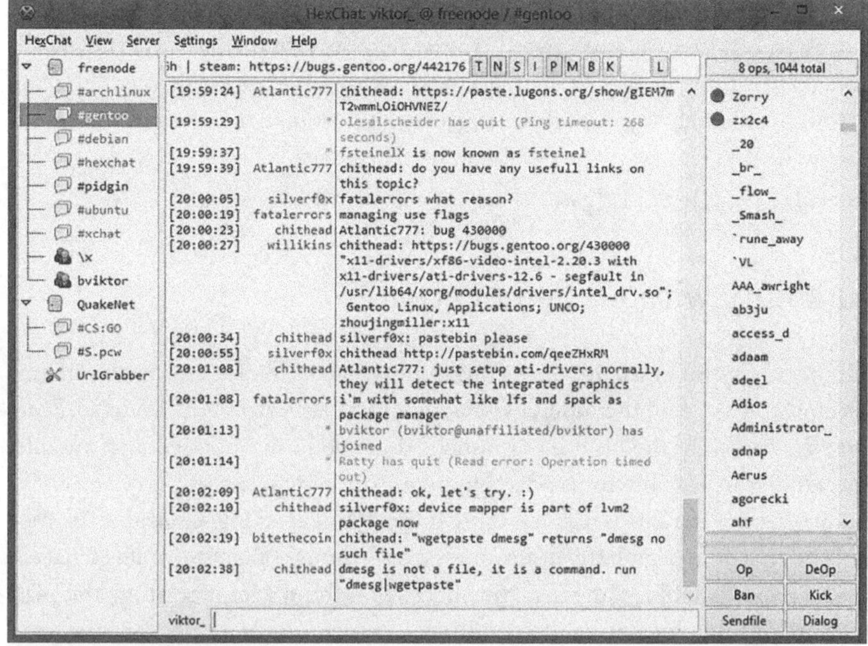

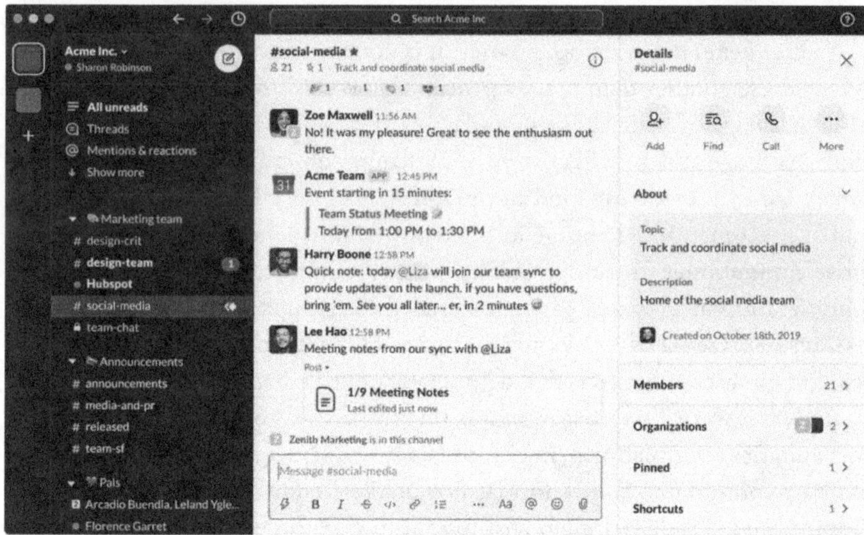

Figure 3.3 Screenshots of Internet Relay Chat (IRC; top) and Slack (bottom) layouts. Both IRC and Slack use "channels," also set off by # symbols, to organize conversations on their platforms (see left menu in both images). But unlike Twitter's hashtags, the channels are durable—they persist without being actively used. Top image by Berke Viktor, available at https://commons.wikimedia.org/wiki/File:Screenshot_of_HexChat_in_Windows_8.png and licensed under GNU General Public License. Bottom image from Tom Warren, "Slack Unveils Its Biggest Redesign Yet," *The Verge*, March 18, 2020, available at https://www.theverge.com/2020/3/18/21184865/slack-redesign-update-sidebar-changes-available-now-download.

township, would thus help turn users' attention away from their own narrowly conceived self-interest and toward "something outside themselves" (DA 507). By making minor changes to the ways that hashtags operate on Twitter, then, the platform could help to support the existence of sustained democratic communities on the site.

Durability without Segregation?

Democracy, as we know, requires communities to both form and sustain themselves over time. And the built environment can help with both. To do so, however, the spaces of the built environment must be both bounded and durable. But while it is possible to impose boundaries in digital spaces, ensuring these boundaries are durable is a much more difficult undertaking. Consider the case of Twitter; while the platform itself persists—though changes to its structure can be unpredictable from users' perspectives—the spaces created by the platform are not durable enough to sustain democratic communities for long periods of time.

Twitter generally lacks boundaries, incentivizing asymmetrical interactions between users rather than the reciprocal relationships of political friends. And while hashtags provide those boundaries, they are often fleeting. As a result, while hashtags can be effective at mobilizing communities of interest, they largely fail to provide the kind of durability necessary for users to form communal attachments and engage in the repeated interactions required to sustain those communities over time. While Twitter, with its hashtags, can help communities form in its spaces, in other words, these groups often exist as loose collections of personal networks and ad-hoc publics rather than the sustained and self-conscious communities that democratic politics demands.

If Twitter were interested in supporting these kinds of sustained democratic communities, the platform might consider rendering the spaces created by hashtags more durable, in a format not unlike Reddit's subreddits, Facebook Groups, or IRC and Slack channels. The addition of these more durable hashtags to the otherwise boundless Twitter environment would work to keep groups of users together, cultivating their attachments to communities of interest, and facilitating the repeated interactions that sustain citizens' participation in democratic political activity. While boundaries help facilitate users' recognition of shared interests—which can help mobilize collective action—it is clear from the case of Twitter that this recognition is not enough. Democratic politics requires *sustained* engagement with communal interests; durable spaces help to sustain this activity.

Yet the introduction of durability into digital spaces like Twitter also raises new concerns. Durable spaces can facilitate communal attachments that are unhealthy; this call to provide communities of interest with durable spaces raises, for example, the specters of "filter bubbles," self-segregation, and "echo chambers" that plague other digital spaces.[77] And by encouraging repeated interactions, durable spaces can direct collective action toward increasingly dangerous and extremist ends—as is evident in the rise of white supremacist groups organizing and radicalizing through apps like Discord.[78] Certain online communities—especially those that operate in clearly bounded and durable digital spaces like 4chan—can be violent, offensive, and aggressive toward perceived outsiders. They are, moreover, consistently (and correctly) criticized for allowing "bad actors" to thrive. These are all credible threats to the functioning of a healthy democracy and should therefore not be readily dismissed.

And yet, digital spaces are quickly becoming entrenched in our public lives. As we cannot simply abandon them, the challenge is thus to redesign them to better support a specifically *democratic* politics—one that is inclusive, expansive, and self-correcting in addition to sustained and communal. Boundaries and durability are certainly integral to this project. Democratic politics does require that we form attachments and recognize our long-standing ties to our communities and those within them; it requires a shared and sustained commitment to common goals. A specifically *democratic* community, however, must also be an inclusive one, a community that continually seeks to grow and improve itself, reflecting the needs of all its members. As we continue to think of how to build democratic spaces (particularly in digital environments), we must therefore balance these competing inclinations of durability and stagnation, political friendship and exclusivity.

To achieve this balance, I turn in the next chapter to explore the importance of *flexibility* as the final essential characteristic of democratic space. Drawing from the work of John Dewey, who emphasized the role of local spaces like the neighborhood and school in developing citizens' democratic habit of experimentalism, I argue that bounded, durable spaces must also be flexible if they are to cultivate a democratic ethos of experimentation and improvement in their inhabitants. Only by exhibiting all three characteristics—boundaries, durability, and flexibility—can the built environment support the work of democratic politics.

[77] Cass R. Sunstein, *#Republic: Divided Democracy in the Age of Social Media* (Princeton, NJ: Princeton University Press, 2017); Eli Pariser, *The Filter Bubble: What the Internet Is Hiding from You* (New York: Penguin Press, 2011).

[78] Kevin Roose, "This Was the Alt-Right's Favorite Chat App. Then Came Charlottesville," *New York Times*, August 15, 2017.

4

r/democracy

Flexible Spaces, Experimental Habits, and the Problem of Self-Segregation

On December 4, 2016, a twenty-eight-year-old man from North Carolina named Edgar M. Welch walked into a Washington, DC, pizza restaurant and fired three shots from an AR-15-style rifle.[1] Though the attack on Comet Ping Pong led to no injuries, and Welch soon surrendered himself into police custody, the incident was nevertheless a striking reminder of the potentially dangerous consequences of our online activities. When asked about his motives for the attack, Welch replied that "he had read online that the Comet [Ping Pong] restaurant was harboring child sex slaves and that he wanted to see for himself if they were there."[2] What Welch had "read online" was a well-traveled conspiracy theory—one that came to be known as "Pizzagate"—that falsely connected Hillary Clinton and other Democratic Party leaders with human trafficking rings that were allegedly run out of a number of DC-area pizza restaurants.

By the time Welch read them, Pizzagate stories had been spreading throughout digital spaces for over a month. In late October, claims that Clinton was involved with a child sex-trafficking ring began to appear on Twitter, conspiracy theory message boards, and fringe news sites, as well as the notorious anonymous message board 4chan. And though the Pizzagate conspiracy flourished on these sites, it was not confined to these spaces; it also circulated to a much wider audience by way of more popular digital media platforms like Facebook and Reddit.[3] Initially the subject of much discussion by members of the

[1] Marc Fisher, John Woodrow Cox, and Peter Hermann, "Pizzagate: From Rumor, to Hashtag, to Gunfire in D.C.," *Washington Post*, December 6, 2016.

[2] Fisher, Cox, and Hermann, "Pizzagate."

[3] Craig Silverman, "How the Bizarre Conspiracy Theory behind 'Pizzagate' Was Spread," *BuzzFeed News*, November 4, 2016.

Designing for Democracy. Jennifer Forestal, Oxford University Press. © Oxford University Press 2022.
DOI: 10.1093/oso/9780197568750.003.0004

r/the_donald subreddit, a community of then-candidate Donald Trump supporters, for example, redditors' interest in the Pizzagate conspiracy ultimately led to the formation of a dedicated subreddit. Created on November 7, slightly under one month before Welch's attack on Comet Ping Pong, r/pizzagate quickly attracted over 20,000 members before it was banned by Reddit site administrators after only a few weeks—though the ban was not successful in preventing Edgar Welch's attack on Comet Ping Pong two weeks later.[4]

Pizzagate is, unfortunately, not unique. Over the past few years, similar instances of (potentially) deadly violence, often informed by extremist conspiracies, have fueled anxieties about the role of "filter bubbles" and "echo chambers" in users' online experiences.[5] It is the growth of digital technologies that afford users an unprecedented ability to self-select into homogenous content and communities, scholars argue, that makes it easier for dangerous movements to thrive. Algorithmically fueled social media feeds can, for example, incentivize users to post certain kinds of (extreme) content,[6] while moderation and feedback mechanisms can enforce social norms that encourage digital communities to close ranks and react with hostility toward perceived outsiders.[7] As a particularly vivid illustration of the threats that the resulting exclusive and extremist communities pose, Pizzagate highlights perhaps *the* major challenge facing democracy in a digital age: how can we cultivate communities that expand opportunities for democratic decision-making while also preventing them from becoming unwelcoming, hostile, or aggressive to new ideas and perceived outsiders?

Democratic politics, as we have seen, requires communities to form and sustain themselves over time. Yet democracy is not reducible to citizens' recognition

[4] Abby Ohlheiser, "Fearing Yet Another Witch Hunt, Reddit Bans 'Pizzagate,'" *Washington Post*, November 24, 2016.

[5] Eli Pariser, *The Filter Bubble: What the Internet Is Hiding from You* (New York: Penguin Press, 2011); Eric Lawrence, John Sides, and Henry Farrell, "Self-Segregation or Deliberation? Blog Readership, Participation, and Polarization in American Politics," *Perspectives on Politics* 8, no. 1 (2010): 141–57; Jack Nicas, "Alex Jones and Infowars Content Is Removed from Apple, Facebook and YouTube," *New York Times*, August 6, 2018; Allie Conti, "Why the Ridiculous 'Paid Protester' Myth Refuses to Die," *Vice*, March 1, 2017; Jane Coaston, "#QAnon, the Scarily Popular pro-Trump Conspiracy Theory, Explained," *Vox*, August 2, 2018.

[6] Amit Chowdhry, "Facebook Confirms Emoji 'Reactions' Affects Your News Feed," *Forbes Magazine*, March 2, 2017; Karissa Bell, "You Might Want to Rethink What You're 'Liking' on Facebook Now," *Mashable*, February 27, 2017; Will Oremus, "Twitter's New Order: Inside the Changes That Could Save Its Business—and Reshape Civil Discourse," *Slate*, March 5, 2017.

[7] Cliff Lampe and Erik Johnston, "Follow the (Slash) Dot: Effects of Feedback on New Members in an Online Community," in *Proceedings of the 2005 International ACM SIGGROUP Conference on Supporting Group Work—GROUP '05* (New York: Association for Computing Machinery, 2005), 11–20; Justin Cheng, Cristian Danescu-Niculescu-Mizil, and Jure Leskovec, "How Community Feedback Shapes User Behavior," in *Proceedings of the Eighth International AAAI Conference on Weblogs and Social Media*, 41–50, (Ann Arbor, MI), 2014.

of their shared interests or their ongoing participation in managing them. Indeed, as we can see clearly in these cases of (digital) extremism, robust and sustainable communities often organize around shared interests that are hostile and unwelcoming to outsiders; they can—and often do—sustain high levels of participation towards those ends. A specifically *democratic* politics, then, requires that citizens' participation take a particular form.

Participatory democracy is a progressive ideal—it envisions communities engaged in self-improvement. Thus, for collective action to properly be called "democratic," it must be premised on continued "readaptation and readjustment"[8] with an eye toward expanding the richness and variety of opportunities available to all (potential) participants. Democratic politics consists in more than simple participation, in other words. It also entails a twofold commitment: to widening the scope of participation to be more inclusive, as well as to continually seeking out new and better solutions to our collective problems. And these are mutually reinforcing goals; we can only reach our best decisions when everyone participates and when that participation involves a diverse array of experiences and information. Absent these conditions, we cannot be sure that our decisions reflect the best possible outcomes for our community.

To properly meet the demands of democratic citizenship, then, it is clear that citizens must do more than simply recognize their shared interests and form attachments to their communities. They must also demonstrate a particular orientation—to decision-making, to their community, and to knowledge itself. In short, democratic citizens must cultivate and act with an "*experimental* habit of mind"[9]—a kind of empowered open-mindedness without which we cannot properly "do" democracy.[10]

While formal institutions, like the school, can and do cultivate this experimental habit, I focus my attention in this chapter on the role of the built environment in facilitating this practice. Drawing from the work of prominent twentieth-century philosopher John Dewey—a public intellectual perhaps most famous for his contributions to the theory and practice of democratic education—I argue that we can only develop the experimental habit in a built environment characterized by *flexibility*, meaning spaces that (1) host a *variety* of perspectives and experiences and (2) are *malleable*, affording citizens control over their environment so they might reshape the space to fit their needs. Absent this flexibility,

[8] John Dewey, "The Bearings of Pragmatism upon Education," in *The Middle Works of John Dewey, Volume 4, 1899–1924: Essays on Pragmatism and Truth, 1907–1909* (Carbondale: Southern Illinois University Press, 2008), 182.

[9] Dewey, "The Bearings of Pragmatism upon Education," 188.

[10] William Hare, "Education for an Unsettled World: Dewey's Conception of Open-Mindedness," *Journal of Thought* 39, no. 3 (2004): 111–27.

the built environment will not afford citizens the ability to practice the requisite democratic experimentalism—even if they possess an open-minded attitude or a willingness to collaborate. Like boundaries and durability, then, flexibility is a necessary, though insufficient, characteristic of democratic spaces.

The chapter's argument proceeds as follows: in the next section, I outline the role of flexible spaces in providing an environment in which citizens can develop the experimental habit required for democratic politics. In flexible spaces—spaces characterized by both variety and malleability—citizens will not only encounter difference but will also be able to use it in the process of democratic decision-making. Only in flexible spaces, in other words, are citizens provided an environment that facilitates the democratic practice of improving their communities.

With this concept of flexibility in mind, I turn to the case of Reddit as an example of a digital democratic space. Comparing two subreddits, r/the_donald and r/TwoXChromosomes, I show how r/the_donald slowly, but intentionally, reaffirmed and reified its boundaries by redesigning the subreddit to exclude new ideas, thereby eschewing variety. But this was not an inevitability. Faced with a similar situation—the influx of new and diverse users—the subreddit r/TwoXChromosomes chose to open its boundaries and welcome these potentially disruptive newcomers. The result was a thriving and relatively diverse space—but one that was still not, I argue, as malleable as we might hope. I therefore conclude with recommendations for improving r/TwoXChromosomes' democratic potential by increasing its malleability, thus creating an environment more suitable to supporting the experimental practices of specifically democratic communities.

Dewey, Democracy, and the Role of Design

Digital technologies, it seems, are destroying democracy. Even as they expand access to information, sites like YouTube and Google filter our searches with algorithms that can reinforce our biases and radicalize our views.[11] Platforms like Facebook and Twitter can amplify messages of hate and anger, making our worst sentiments "go viral" with surprising ease.[12] And through mechanisms

[11] Safiya Umoja Noble, *Algorithms of Oppression: How Search Engines Reinforce Racism* (New York: NYU Press, 2018); Zeynep Tufekci, "YouTube, the Great Radicalizer," *New York Times*, March 10, 2018; Cathy O'Neil, *Weapons of Math Destruction: How Big Data Increases Inequality and Threatens Democracy* (New York: Crown Publishers, 2016).

[12] Siva Vaidhyanathan, *Antisocial Media: How Facebook Disconnects Us and Undermines Democracy* (New York: Oxford University Press, 2018).

of personalization, designed to capture our attention for longer and longer stretches, digital platforms afford us an unprecedented ability to select out of the things and people we do not want to see, and to be inundated with those we do.[13] Digital technologies are thus, as Zeynep Tufekci says of YouTube, enabling our worst habits by feeding us an endless buffet of the information equivalent to a diet of sugar and fat.[14] As a result, they are, as Siva Vaidhyanathan argues about Facebook, "undermining our ability to think collectively"[15] and, in so doing, undermining democracy itself.

Certainly, scholars are right to point out these problems. The rise of extremist "alt-right" groups, for example, point to the dangers posed by the unprecedented ability to self-select using digital technologies. But when diagnosing these dangers, scholars and practitioners alike tend to frame the problem in terms of individual users' bad habits that are amplified by digital technologies. As a result, solutions tend to include some combination of "regulation, self-regulation and education":[16] either teach users how to avoid problematic groups and content, or else redesign and regulate platforms so that those groups and content are not accessible to users in the first place.[17] These solutions may be effective at reducing citizens' exposure to incorrect, extremist, or biased information, as well as forcing them to engage with new or different perspectives. But in imposing external constraints on where, when, and how digital communities interact with users, groups, and information—and thereby removing users' ability to make those judgments for themselves—these approaches fundamentally misunderstand the nature of democratic politics.

Throughout this book, I have argued that democracy is best understood not as a formal mode of government but instead as a set of practices, a method through which we identify and solve problems collectively. The process here is important—as much as, if not more than, the answers we come up with. Democracy is, recall, a process of cooperative decision-making that demands

[13] Pariser, *The Filter Bubble*; Cass R. Sunstein, *#Republic: Divided Democracy in the Age of Social Media* (Princeton, NJ: Princeton University Press, 2017).

[14] Tufekci, "YouTube, the Great Radicalizer."

[15] Vaidhyanathan, *Antisocial Media*.

[16] Zeynep Tufekci, "YouTube Has a Video for That," *Scientific American*, April 2019.

[17] Aja Romano, "Reddit Just Banned One of Its Most Toxic Forums. But It Won't Touch The_Donald," *Vox*, November 13, 2017; Liam Stack, "Facebook Announces New Policy to Ban White Nationalist Content," *New York Times*, March 27, 2019; Megan Keller, "Dem Senator Defends Social Media Platforms Deleting Content: 'Not the Same as Government Censorship,'" *The Hill*, August 7, 2018; Adi Robertson, "Sen. Mark Warner Floats Major Tech Company Regulations That Don't Include Breakups," *The Verge*, July 30, 2018; Brian Barrett, "What Would Regulating Facebook Look Like?," *Wired*, March 21, 2018.

the participation of each member of a community in making the decisions that shape their lives. Minimizing citizens' role in selecting and evaluating sources of news and information—as well as managing which people and groups they encounter in that process—is therefore fundamentally undemocratic; it removes agency from citizens and places them under an external authority they cannot control. Instead, a more democratic solution to the problem of self-segregation must be one that empowers and incentivizes citizens—and the communities of which they are a part—to do this work for themselves, however difficult the work may be.

To identify that solution, I turn in this section to the work of American political theorist John Dewey to outline both the demands of democracy as a particular method of collective decision-making, as well as the environmental requirements needed to meet them. Writing at the turn of the twentieth century, Dewey devoted much of his decades-long career to the theory and practice of democratic education—to the problem of how to cultivate democratic citizens who are not only *capable* of engaging in the difficult work of cooperative decision-making, but also *willing* to do so.

Democracy, for Dewey, is a progressive ideal; specifically democratic communities must therefore work to expand opportunities for participation and improve conditions for all their members. And because democratic politics consists in a set of practices, this commitment to collectively improving a community's decisions and decision-making processes requires certain habits of its citizens. In particular, Dewey notes the importance of the "experimental habit of mind" that disposes citizens to participate in collective decision-making in an inclusive and expansive way.

Laws, norms, and other institutions can all help cultivate the experimental habit. But so, too, can the design of the built environment. As we have seen, the built environment can help us to identify the communities we belong to and generate the attachments that help sustain our efforts to care for those communities. In much the same way, the built environment can also facilitate the cultivation—or loss—of the experimental habit that helps us *improve* our communities; in order to practice this experimentalism, we need spaces that afford us the opportunity to do so. And this means spaces that are *flexible*—spaces that (1) reflect a variety of perspectives and experiences; and (2) are malleable, allowing citizens to exert control over their environments to suit their needs. Absent flexible spaces that provide opportunities to exercise the democratic habit of experimentation, citizens are more likely to lose their sense of open-mindedness and retreat into the comfort of the familiar. The result is that they are less equipped to engage in the specifically democratic work of improving and expanding their communities.

THE "METHOD OF DEMOCRACY": EXPERIMENTALISM

As the collective management of common affairs, democracy involves forming and maintaining communities over time. This not only requires the recognition that we share things in common with others, but also relies on an attachment to the resulting community and a sustained commitment to continue the work of caring for its interests in cooperation with one's peers. Yet not all self-sustaining communities should properly be called *democratic*. "A band of robbers has a common interest as respects its members," Dewey reminds us. "Gangs are marked by fraternal feeling, and narrow cliques by intense loyalty to their own codes."[18] Members of these groups might demonstrate ties of political friendship with one another; they can certainly engage in collective action and sustain that activity far into the future. Insofar as this is true, the band of robbers meets the criteria for a political community outlined in chapters 2 and 3. Yet we would not call this a *democratic* community because it fails to demonstrate a democratic commitment to inclusive improvement. Rather, these communities are "marked by exclusiveness, suspicion, and jealousy as to those without."[19] These exclusive groups may very well be political, but they are not properly called democratic.

What sets a specifically democratic community apart from other forms of social organization, then, is its additional commitment to *self-improvement.* A democratic community, Dewey tells us, is one "where progress, or readjustment, is an important consideration."[20] Moreover, this democratic commitment to progress, or improvement, is an inherently inclusive aim; it rests on a twofold assumption: that "all those who are affected by social institutions must have a share in producing and managing them"[21] and that each person is a member of many communities, all with different aims and interests.

Only when these multiple interests are "consciously communicated and shared," and the various groups involved have "varied and free points of contact with other modes of association,"[22] will democratic communities be able to engage in the activity "of consultation, of conference, of persuasion, of discussion, in the formation of public opinion, *which in the long run is self-corrective.*"[23]

[18] John Dewey, "Democracy and Education," in *John Dewey: The Middle Works, Vol. 9, 1899–1924*, ed. Jo Ann Boydston (Carbondale: Southern Illinois University Press, 1916), 88.

[19] Dewey, "Democracy and Education," 88.

[20] Dewey, "Democracy and Education," 92.

[21] John Dewey, "Democracy and Educational Administration," in *The Later Works of John Dewey, Volume 11: 1935–1937*, ed. Jo Ann Boydston (Carbondale: Southern Illinois University Press, 2008), 218.

[22] Dewey, "Democracy and Education," 89.

[23] John Dewey, "Creative Democracy—The Task Before Us," in *John Dewey: The Later Works, Vol. 14, 1939–1941*, ed. Jo Ann Boydston (Carbondale: Southern Illinois University Press, 2008), 227. Emphasis mine.

Only when all citizens fully participate—and only when such participation includes the most complete information possible, accounting for everyone's diverse array of interests—is a democratic community able to ensure that it is making the best decisions for itself.

Of course, this commitment to inclusivity and improvement is not without conflict; the contact between groups and the challenge that new information poses to the status quo is bound to generate disagreements. This is, however, beneficial for democratic decision-making. Indeed, the "method of democracy," Dewey tells us, is not to eradicate conflict but rather "to bring these conflicts out into the open where their special claims can be seen and appraised, where they can be discussed and judged in the light of more inclusive interests than are represented by either of them separately."[24] Only when citizens actively seek out new information, ideas, and experiences—and use them to secure "constantly widening participation"[25]—can we be confident that the collective decisions made are the right ones. When communities hold, by contrast, a "rigid adherence to their past actions,"[26] they cannot be sure their decisions are the best suited for their new circumstances. Instead, democratic decision-making must involve a constant reimagining of how to improve one's community, as well as a commitment to seeking out new information and interlocutors in order to do so.

But, as we know from decades of research, this commitment can be difficult for citizens to fulfill. We regularly engage in selective exposure when we seek out new information[27] and we deploy motivated reasoning when processing information and making arguments.[28] We often retreat into homogenous enclaves—both on- and offline—surrounding ourselves with people who are similar to us.[29] This is

[24] John Dewey, "Liberalism and Social Action," in *The Later Works of John Dewey, Volume 11: 1935–1937*, ed. Jo Ann Boydston (Carbondale: Southern Illinois University Press, 2008), 56.

[25] John Dewey, Boyd H. Bode, and William Heard Kilpatrick, "An Active, Flexible Personality," in *The Later Works of John Dewey, Volume 11: 1935–1937*, ed. Jo Ann Boydston (Carbondale: Southern Illinois University Press, 2008), 557.

[26] Dewey, "Democracy and Education," 92.

[27] Silvia Knobloch-Westerwick and Jingbo Meng, "Looking the Other Way: Selective Exposure to Attitude-Consistent and Counterattitudinal Political Information," *Communication Research* 36, no. 3 (2009): 426–48; Natalie Jomini Stroud, "Media Use and Political Predispositions: Revisiting the Concept of Selective Exposure," *Political Behavior* 30, no. 3 (2008): 341–66.

[28] Arie W. Kruglanski and Donna M. Webster, "Motivated Closing of the Mind: 'Seizing' and 'Freezing,'" *Psychological Review* 103, no. 2 (1996): 263–83; Ziva Kunda, "The Case for Motivated Reasoning," *Psychological Bulletin* 108, no. 3 (1990): 480–98; Charles S. Taber and Milton Lodge, "Motivated Skepticism in the Evaluation of Political Beliefs," *American Journal of Political Science* 50, no. 3 (2006): 755–69.

[29] Ryan D. Enos, *The Space between Us: Social Geography and Politics* (New York: Cambridge University Press, 2017); Lawrence, Sides, and Farrell, "Self-Segregation or Deliberation?"; Diana C. Mutz, *Hearing the Other Side: Deliberative Versus Participatory Democracy* (New York: Cambridge University Press, 2012).

why Dewey insists that the democratic commitment to progress, to improvement through "continuous readjustment,"[30] requires that citizens practice the "*experimental* habit of mind, that which regards ideas and principles as tentative methods of solving problems and organizing data."[31] More than just passive toleration, this experimental habit is an active practice; it involves a kind of curiosity and open-mindedness—a willingness to change one's mind—that leads citizens to both seek out and make use of a diverse array of information in order to improve their communities. And this democratic practice of experimentalism—like recognition and attachment before it—must be intentionally *cultivated*.

Institutions like laws and customs, as well as schools and communication technologies, can help to cultivate this experimental habit. Certainly, Dewey himself invested significant time and energy in developing techniques for democratic pedagogy to that end. But the built environment, as I have been arguing throughout, also exerts considerable influence over our habits, attitudes, and relationships—not only as individuals, but also and more importantly as members of communities. The built environment can, recall, help citizens recognize what interests they hold in common with others by way of boundaries that clarify what is shared and with whom. And the durability of the built environment can generate a sense of attachment and obligation, "[m]aking the individual a sharer or partner in the associated activity so that he feels its success as his success, its failure as his failure."[32] Within a built environment that is clearly bounded and durable, citizens can more easily identify the communities of which they are a part and form attachments that induce them to adjust their behavior to contribute to the aims and interests of the groups to which they belong.

Just as bounded and durable spaces can help citizens engage in these democratic practices of forming and sustaining communities, so too can characteristics of the built environment help citizens develop habits of improving these communities through the processes of democratic decision-making. In particular, here I highlight the role of *flexibility* in cultivating the experimental habit of mind democratic citizens require. Flexible spaces—spaces that both host a variety of perspectives and experiences and are malleable, able to be controlled by users—are environments in which citizens can actively practice the experimental habit required of democratic politics. Absent flexible spaces, even if citizens are open-minded, tolerant, and willing to participate in collaborative democratic work, they will ultimately lack the opportunities to engage in these practices.

30 Dewey, "Democracy and Education," 92.

31 Dewey, "The Bearings of Pragmatism upon Education," 188.

32 Dewey, "Democracy and Education," 18.

VARIETY: THE RAW MATERIAL OF DEMOCRATIC POLITICS

Democracy involves the ongoing participation of citizens "in forming and directing the activities" of their communities with an eye toward improving them.[33] This can only happen, however, if members of these groups are exposed to a variety of interests and information. With "more numerous and more varied points of contact," Dewey tells us, there are "a greater diversity of stimuli to which an individual has to respond; they consequently put a premium on variation in his action."[34] And it is this variation in action which provides the raw material for democratic decision-making. Without a diverse environment, it is less likely that citizens will adapt to meet new challenges and improve their collective decisions. This is because, as Dewey reminds us, "[d]iversity of stimulation means novelty, and novelty means challenge to thought."[35] Absent novel perspectives that can open new possible aims and ends or help revise the means to secure them, communities—however cohesive—will be "isolated" and "static."[36] Only by seeking out novelty, and thus continuing to challenge themselves, can citizens and their communities be sure their decisions and decision-making processes are the best possible.

Exposure to variety is thus vital to the work of democratic politics. Yet it can also be, as Dewey well recognizes, difficult to come by. This is why, towards the end of *The Public and Its Problems*, Dewey calls for the formation of a "Great Community" that would use new communication technologies to add "the elements of a variegated and many-hued experience"[37] and thus enrich local communities, ensuring that these spaces do not become provincial, however localized they may be.

But just as the communication channels of the Great Community can facilitate citizens' encounters with variety, so too can the design of the built environment. Indeed, Dewey himself notes the role of physical spaces like the school in "uniting and bringing together the exceedingly heterogeneous elements of our population."[38] By intentionally "mixing people up with each other,"[39] the spaces of the school are designed to provide students with a "richer, fuller and more

[33] John Dewey, *The Public and Its Problems: An Essay in Political Inquiry* (Chicago: Gateway Books, 1946), 147.

[34] Dewey, "Democracy and Education," 93.

[35] Dewey, "Democracy and Education," 90.

[36] Dewey, *The Public and Its Problems*, 216, 212.

[37] Dewey, *The Public and Its Problems*, 216.

[38] John Dewey, "The School as a Means of Developing a Social Consciousness and Social Ideals in Children," in *The Middle Works of John Dewey, Volume 15: 1923–1924*, ed. Jo Ann Boydston (Carbondale: Southern Illinois University Press, 2008), 150.

[39] John Dewey, "The School as Social Centre," in *The Middle Works of John Dewey, Volume 2, 1899–1924*, ed. Jo Ann Boydston (Carbondale, IL: Southern Illinois University Press, 2008), 90.

carefully selected and arranged environment" that would "afford the stimuli and conditions" necessary to cultivate the experimental habit of democratic citizens.[40] Designed to host a variety of people and experiences, Dewey envisions a school that provides a physical environment in which students come into contact with different groups and work to expand and improve their understanding through participation in collaborative problem-solving.

The importance of designing a built environment that supports variety is not just confined to formal spaces like the school, however. In her classic study of urban life, Jane Jacobs argues that a crucial requirement for vibrant cities is "a most intricate and close-grained diversity of uses that give each other constant mutual support, both economically and socially."[41] Consequently, she championed the design of mixed-use urban spaces that "serve more than one primary function; preferably more than two"[42] and thus invite "diversity among adjacent uses, and hence diversity among users and their schedules."[43] Only by designing heterogeneous spaces (see Figure 4.1), she argued, would cities see the

Figure 4.1 Rittenhouse Square (Philadelphia), one of Jane Jacobs's examples of a well-designed city park that facilitates multiple uses. Photograph: "Saturday in the Park" by Kevin Burkett, available at https://flic.kr/p/7M6gkx and licensed under CC BY-SA 2.0.

[40] Dewey, "The Bearings of Pragmatism upon Education," 186.

[41] Jane Jacobs, *The Death and Life of Great American Cities* (New York: Vintage Books, 1992), 14.

[42] Jacobs, *The Death and Life of Great American Cities*, 150.

[43] Jacobs, *The Death and Life of Great American Cities*, 97.

"liveliness and variety [that] attract more liveliness,"[44] since "only diverse surroundings have the practical power of inducing a natural, continuing flow of life and use."[45] Only by designing spaces that accommodate and invite a variety of users and experiences, as well as the diverse perspectives they bring, in other words, will cities continue to thrive. Absent this variety, with spaces designed for only one type of population or use, these same spaces would, Jacobs argued, invite the "deadness and monotony [that] repel life."[46]

Increasingly, however, we are seeing urban environments designed with features of "hostile" or "defensive architecture" intended to do precisely that—to reduce the number and type of uses any given space can host. Through mechanisms like anti-homeless spikes and "disciplining benches" that are divided into single-occupancy seats (see Figure 4.2), these spaces are "designed to actively exclude particular categories of person."[47] Rather than facilitate the variety that accompanies intentional mixed-use design, in other words, these architectural changes impose a single mode of accepted behavior; the result is that these spaces "lose their utility as spaces of social encounter, conversation and relaxation in favor of brief and individualized use, foreclosing the possibility for encounters with 'others' in the public realm."[48]

Figure 4.2 Examples of "defensive" or "hostile" architecture. These "anti-homeless" spikes (left) and "disciplining benches" (right) are designed to prevent people from lying down or lingering by making the surface uncomfortable. Left photograph by Kent Williams, available at https://flic.kr/p/nWg5MY and licensed under CC BY 2.0. Right photograph: "Seats, London" (2001), reproduced with permission from Nils Norman, available at www.dismalgarden.com.

[44] Jacobs, *The Death and Life of Great American Cities*, 99.

[45] Jacobs, *The Death and Life of Great American Cities*, 101.

[46] Jacobs, *The Death and Life of Great American Cities*, 99.

[47] Naomi Smith and Peter Walters, "Desire Lines and Defensive Architecture in Modern Urban Environments," *Urban Studies* 55, no. 13 (2018): 2983–84.

[48] Smith and Walters, "Desire Lines and Defensive Architecture," 2984.

Instead of inviting us to engage with members of the multiple groups that make up our larger community, in other words, spaces that lack variety cultivate "isolation and exclusiveness," which develops "wherever one group has interests 'of its own' which shut it out from full interaction with other groups, so that its prevailing purpose is the protection of what it has got, instead of a reorganization and progress through wider relationships."[49] In this kind of intentionally homogenized built environment, inhabitants are encouraged to protect the status quo. As a result, they are unlikely to engage in the experimental practices democracy requires—even if they wanted to. The raw material of variety is missing, rendering progress or improvement much more difficult to achieve.

MALLEABILITY: MAKING USE OF VARIETY

Dewey is by no means alone in recognizing the necessity of variety in democratic spaces. Contemporary democratic theorists have, for example, made strong cases for the "inclusion of multiple and plural voices, interests, concerns, and claims"[50] as well as the importance of diverse modes of discourse in public life.[51] Indeed, in highlighting the beneficial effects of a diverse environment, Dewey is making a psychological claim later echoed by thinkers like Gordon W. Allport and Robert D. Putnam: that social contact with a variety of groups under the right conditions can help to open minds and prevent stagnation.[52] Likewise, such claims underlie more recent calls by thinkers like Cass R. Sunstein to deploy algorithms that would introduce users of digital technologies to cross-cutting information that they might otherwise select out of.[53] By encountering a variety of new people, ideas, and experiences, these thinkers all argue, we are forced, in a manner, to alter our worldview, to acknowledge the limits of our singular experiences and adjust our account of the social effects of our behavior. Exposure to variety—encountering new ways of acting and organizing ourselves—is, in other words, a necessary condition for improving our communities. Without it, it is unlikely we would accurately identify the problems facing our communities, let alone solve them in an inclusive (and accurate) way.

[49] Dewey, "Democracy and Education," 91.

[50] Jane Mansbridge et al., "A Systemic Approach to Deliberative Democracy," in *Deliberative Systems: Deliberative Democracy at the Large Scale,* ed. John Parkinson and Jane J. Mansbridge (Cambridge, UK: Cambridge University Press, 2012), 12.

[51] Iris Marion Young, "Activist Challenges to Deliberative Democracy," *Political Theory* 29, no. 5 (2001): 670–90; Lynn M. Sanders, "Against Deliberation," *Political Theory* 25, no. 3 (1997): 347–76.

[52] G. W. Allport, *The Nature of Prejudice* (Cambridge, MA: Perseus Books, 1954); Robert D. Putnam, "Bowling Alone: America's Declining Social Capital," *Journal of Democracy* 6, no. 1 (1995): 65–78.

[53] Sunstein, *#Republic.*

Yet research also shows that the mere presence of variety alone will not necessarily lead us to develop the democratic habit of experimentalism that pushes us to respond to novelty in productive ways. Indeed, in many cases this exposure to new and different ideas "backfires," entrenching misperceptions and creating even deeper feelings of resentment, distrust, fear, and retreat.[54] Clearly, while variety is a necessary component in developing the experimental habit required to improve communities, it is insufficient for securing inclusive democratic practices.

This is because, Dewey reminds us, the habits that ground democratic practice are *active*. No "routine ways of acting,"[55] a habit, for Dewey, instead involves the "active control of the environment."[56] Habits, in other words, require conscious thought and action; they signal "an active preference and choice for the conditions involved in [their] exercise."[57] If citizens practice democratic habits, it means they are acting in a manner that demonstrates their commitment to readjusting their behavior in order to improve their community—to finding more opportunities for more people to participate in the processes of collective decision-making. Relying on the mere presence of variety, then, mistakes the nature of the experimental habit of mind; it involves more than mere exposure. Instead, variety must be consciously and meaningfully *used* if it is to have the behavioral effects we expect to see.

In addition to hosting a variety of experiences, then, for spaces of the built environment to be supportive of democratic politics, they must also be malleable enough to afford individuals the ability to exert control. They must provide opportunities for citizens to actively and consciously *use* the raw material of variety to improve their environment. Spaces that dictate how to behave will fail to cultivate active democratic habits. Instead, these spaces encourage citizens to passively obey external sources of authority—the antithesis of democratic participation. The presence of variety is meaningless, in other words, if we are not given opportunities to actively make use of that variety to "readjust" our environments in ways that improve our communities.

[54] David K. Sherman and Geoffrey L. Cohen, "The Psychology of Self-Defense: Self-Affirmation Theory," *Advances in Experimental Social Psychology* 38 (2006): 183–242; Enos, *The Space between Us*; Tanja Ellingsen, "Colorful Community or Ethnic Witches' Brew? Multiethnicity and Domestic Conflict during and after the Cold War," *Journal of Conflict Resolution* 44, no. 2 (2000): 228–49; Lincoln Quillian, "Prejudice as a Response to Perceived Group Threat: Population Composition and Anti-Immigrant and Racial Prejudice in Europe," *American Sociological Review* 60, no. 4 (1995): 586–611.

[55] Dewey, "Democracy and Education," 51.

[56] Dewey, "Democracy and Education," 54.

[57] Dewey, "Democracy and Education," 56.

Figure 4.3 Lecture hall, with fixed seats all oriented toward the instructor. Because of this unyielding design, students are unable to exert much, if any, control over their environment. Photograph: "Vikramshila V1 Auditorium 1" by Ambuj Saxena, available at https://flic.kr/p/Dd7vm and licensed under CC BY 2.0.

Consider a traditional lecture hall (see Figure 4.3). Though students may bring with them a variety of perspectives, the design of this classroom affords students no means of engaging with that variety in an authoritative way. The lecture hall, with its fixed seats oriented toward the lecturer, is "made 'for listening.'"[58] Rather than invite students to make use of the classroom resources—both their peers and the space itself—and take ownership of the material under consideration, the traditional lecture hall trains students to look to "the book or the teacher, [to] supply solutions ready-made."[59] By reducing the involvement of the students in the collective work of democratic problem-solving, the traditional lecture hall simply trains students to "slide along without an undue amount of friction."[60]

[58] John Dewey, "The School and Society," in *The Middle Works of John Dewey, Volume 1: 1899–1901*, ed. Jo Ann Boydston (Carbondale, IL: Southern Illinois University Press, 2008), 21.

[59] Dewey, "Democracy and Education," 163.

[60] Dewey, "The School and Society." Dewey's concern regarding the pedagogical impact of classroom layout is evident in his plans for the University of Chicago Lab School. For more, see Jennifer Forestal, "The Architecture of Political Spaces: Trolls, Digital Media, and Deweyan Democracy," *American Political Science Review* 111, no. 1 (2017): 149–61.

But if the traditional lecture hall exemplifies an inflexible space that "marks the dependency of one mind upon another,"[61] Dewey also gives us a model for a more flexible space—one that provides the environmental conditions required for democratic experimentation—in his discussion of the library.[62] The library, in Dewey's vision, provides an environment rich in variety; it hosts not only the experiences students bring to their investigations, but also the "accumulated knowledge" of books on the shelves. But in addition to this variety, the library is also a *malleable* space; it demands that students engage with the variety of intellectual material *on their own terms*. It is up to students, in other words, how they will frame the problems at hand by selecting certain precedents and bodies of literature to draw from. And it is left up to students to determine the best measures to address that problem by putting the accumulated knowledge of the past to new uses. The library, in other words, not only provides the "raw material" of a diverse environment, but it also situates that material in a space that cedes decision-making control to the students themselves. In so doing, it provides an environment within which students can actively develop the experimental habit required for democratic politics.

And we can see the impact of malleable spaces on developing the democratic habit of experimentalism in other environments as well. Workers' ability to control their workspaces, for example (see Figure 4.4)—including the ability to adjust the physical environment, to alter the layout of office floorplans, and to make use of available resources as they see fit—is positively associated with increased job satisfaction, increased group cohesiveness, more efficient job performance, and greater psychological well-being.[63] And scholars have shown that it is the combination of a flexible space—one that hosts a variety of experiences and is malleable, or open to worker alterations—and opportunities for workers

[61] Dewey, "The School and Society," 22.

[62] For a detailed discussion of Dewey's plans for his ideal school, which places the library at the center of the building because of its pedagogical importance, see Jason Kosnoski, "Artful Discussion: John Dewey's Classroom as a Model of Deliberative Association," *Political Theory* 33, no. 5 (2005): 654–77. See also John Dewey, "Individuality in Education," in *The Middle Works of John Dewey, Volume 15: 1899–1924*, ed. Jo Ann Boydston (Carbondale: Southern Illinois University Press, 2008), 170–79.

[63] So Young Lee and Jay L. Brand, "Effects of Control over Office Workspace on Perceptions of the Work Environment and Work Outcomes," *Journal of Environmental Psychology* 25, no. 3 (2005): 323–33; Margaret Anne McLaney and Joseph J. Hurrell Jr., "Control, Stress, and Job Satisfaction in Canadian Nurses," *Work and Stress: An International Journal of Work, Health, and Organisations* 2, no. 3 (1988): 217–24; Yueng-Hsiang Huang, Michelle M. Robertson, and Kou-I Chang, "The Role of Environmental Control on Environmental Satisfaction, Communication, and Psychological Stress: Effects of Office Ergonomics Training," *Environment and Behavior* 36, no. 5 (2004): 617–37.

Figure 4.4 Interior shots of the AT&T Foundry in Palo Alto, CA. Featuring moveable walls and furniture, the Foundry exemplifies a malleable space. Photographs by Sherman Takata.

Figure 4.5 Images of the Villa Verde housing project, designed by the architecture firm Elemental, in Constitución, Chile, an example of "sites-and-services" housing in which one half of the structure is provided (move-in ready) to residents, while the other half is to be built out by residents while they inhabit the space. Screencaptures from "DRON Villa Verde Constitución Región Maule" by CORMA CHILE, available at https://www.youtube.com/watch?v=nSsZrXkIM1k.

to practice managing that flexibility that leads to the most effective use of any given workspace.[64]

Likewise, "sites-and-services" housing programs (see Figure 4.5)—those in which a government prepares plots of land with only basic infrastructure (such as clean water and sanitation, waste disposal, and exterior walls and roofing) installed, leaving it the tenants' responsibility to "slowly improve or replace them over as many years as necessary"[65]—are another model of flexible environments. Because this approach to housing "has a high degree of, or the capability for, providing many different ways of achieving the same end,"[66] it provides residents with the raw material of variety. But it is also malleable, relying on the active participation of residents, who are responsible for determining their own goals and the best means to achieve them—both as individuals and as members of the community. These spaces, by providing both the raw material of variety as well as the malleability necessary for citizens to make use of that variety to actively manage their environments, not only enhance "buy-in" from residents and increase residents' satisfaction with their homes;[67] they also help citizens cultivate the active experimental habit required for democratic politics. Alongside boundaries and durability, then, spaces must also be flexible if they are to support democratic communities.

Flexibility in Digital Environments

Equipped with this understanding of the role of the built environment in citizens' development of democratic habits, we can now more easily see why traditional approaches to the problem of self-segregation in digital environments are incomplete. To date, scholars and practitioners alike have largely emphasized strategies for managing user behavior through increased moderation and regulation of digital content—external interventions that remove control from users in the name of protecting us from our own worst inclinations. Yet in taking this curatorial approach, these strategies all disempower users; like the traditional

[64] Michael J. O'Neill, "Work Space Adjustability, Storage, and Enclosure as Predictors of Employee Reactions and Performance," *Environment and Behavior* 26, no. 4 (1994): 504–26.

[65] Lisa R. Peattie, "Some Second Thoughts on Sites-and-Services," *Habitat International* 6, no. 1–2 (1982): 133.

[66] John F. C. Turner, "Housing as a Verb," in *Freedom to Build: Dweller Control of the Housing Process*, ed. John F. C. Turner and Robert Fichter (New York: Macmillan, 1972), 155.

[67] Vini Nathan, "Residents' Satisfaction with the Sites and Services Approach in Affordable Housing," *Housing and Society* 22, no. 3 (1995): 72. See also Sam Greenspan, "Half a House," 99% Invisible, 2016, https://99percentinvisible.org/episode/half-a-house/.

lecture hall, they train us to abdicate our role in actively making the decisions that govern our communities.

As we return to the question of how to democratize digital environments, then, we must keep the demands of democracy centered and ensure that solutions to the challenges posed by these technologies all work to expand opportunities for citizens to actively participate in managing the digital spaces that shape their lives. This means, as we have seen, designing environments that facilitate the collective practices of democratic politics—and, especially, the habit of experimentalism. This is as true in digital environments as it is in the schools and cities of the physical world. In this section, I use the criteria of flexible spaces outlined earlier—(1) a variety of experiences and (2) malleability, or citizens' control over their environments—and turn to the example of Reddit to show how we might build flexible digital spaces that cultivate the experimental habit of mind in their users.

After first showing how Reddit generally meets the criteria for a democratic space, I trace the developments of two subreddits —r/the_donald and r/TwoXChromosomes—to demonstrate how flexibility might also affect the development of specific communities on the platform. I find that while r/the_donald's choices to eschew variety ultimately led to the creation of an echo chamber that was integral to spreading extremist conspiracies like Pizzagate, r/TwoXChromosomes, while consciously inviting a variety of experiences, ultimately lacked malleability, failing to adequately cede users control over their environment. I conclude with suggestions for further democratizing the spaces of Reddit by making them more flexible and therefore more likely to develop users' experimental habits.

REDDIT: BOUNDED, DURABLE, AND FLEXIBLE

Created in June 2005 by Steve Huffman and Alexis Ohanian, Reddit is a popular platform on which users share pictures, links, and text posts that cover a wide range of topics. The site is divided into subreddits—smaller, user-created communities devoted to any number of shared interests. The self-ascribed "front page of the internet," Reddit is built around the idea that its over 52 million daily active users (self-described "redditors") are active participants in building and maintaining the site's 130,000+ active communities.[68] These communities, moreover, are each dedicated to a specific topic ranging from the mundane (r/movies) to the obscure (r/politicalphilosophy), the benign (r/mildlyinteresting), to the outlandish (r/monkslookingatbeer).[69]

[68] Jacob Kastrenakes, "Reddit Reveals Daily Active User Count for the First Time: 52 Million," *The Verge*, December 2020.

[69] All subreddits can be accessed the same way; they all share the same URL format: www.reddit.com/r/subreddit-name. Some subreddits, however, are "private"—meaning that users must be invited to join; otherwise they are barred from seeing that subreddit's posts.

And the site is wildly influential. Links posted to Reddit have raised the visibility of otherwise relatively obscure people and causes. In some cases, this "Reddit effect" can be beneficial, as when links posted to the platform helped then-US-congressional-candidate Rob Zerban raise $15,000 in a matter of days.[70] In other cases, Reddit's "hug of death" can cause major, albeit unintended, problems, such as in 2016 when redditors shared a link to a CodinGame website, and the resulting spike in traffic overwhelmed CodinGame's servers and ultimately crashed their site.[71]

Organized around membership in, and interactions between, a diverse array of subreddits, Reddit reflects precisely the kind of democratic Great Community that Dewey envisioned—a network of multiple, overlapping "local" communities. Subreddits are clearly bounded spaces; users can easily see when they leave one particular subreddit and enter another. And these clear boundaries make it immediately evident to redditors that they hold interests in common with others in the subreddits they visit. If, for example, you visit r/politicalphilosophy (see Figure 4.6), you know that everyone in that space is interested in "the discussion of political philosophies and theories." Moreover, because subreddits are durable and persist through time, they generate communal attachments in users.[72] These attachments are evident in redditors' behavior on the platform, including increased expressions of collective identity in users' posts[73] and, especially, the tailoring of posts to meet the unique rules and norms that govern each subreddit—norms that both differ between subreddits and make communicating within these specific communities easier (see Figure 4.7).[74]

[70] Alex Wilhelm, "How Reddit Turned One Congressional Candidate's Campaign Upside Down," *The Next Web*, January 16, 2012.

[71] Thibaud Jobert, "Story of a Reddit Hug of Death and Lessons Learned," *Medium: CodinGame*, September 27, 2016.

[72] In fact, "[b]ecause communities on Reddit are shared spaces that in many ways belong to the members of the community as much as the creator," there is no way to delete a subreddit. While a subreddit's creators can make it private and demod themselves, the subreddit and its contents will remain available to be requested in the future. Reddit administrators can, however, ban subreddits—though the subreddit itself persists as a digital space; it is simply made inaccessible to users. See Reddit, "How Do I Delete a Community I've Created?," *Reddit Help*, n.d., https://reddit.zendesk.com/hc/en-us/articles/360043044052-How-do-I-delete-a-community-I-ve-created-.

[73] William L. Hamilton et al., "Loyalty in Online Communities," in *Proceedings of the Eleventh International AAAI Conference on Web and Social Media* (Montréal, QC, 2017), 540–43.

[74] Benjamin D. Horne, Sibel Adah, and Sujoy Sikdar, "Identifying the Social Signals That Drive Online Discussions: A Case Study of Reddit Communities," in *Proceedings of the 26th International Conference on Computer Communication and Networks (ICCN)* (Piscataway, NJ: IEEE, 2017), 1–9; Eshwar Chandrasekharan et al., "The Internet's Hidden Rules: An Empirical Study of Reddit Norm Violations at Micro, Meso, and Macro Scales," in *Proceedings of the 2018 ACM on Human-Computer Interaction-CSCW* (New York: ACM Press, 2018), 32:1–25. We can see the kind of reputational concerns that I argue are developed out of durable bounded spaces at work in the level of caution that many redditors bring to their work. Often users will create different accounts in order to post in different subreddits—which recognizes the important distinctions between them.

Figure 4.6 Screenshot of the r/politicalphilosophy subreddit, a space "for the discussion of political philosophies and theories . . . or for just talking, seriously, about politics." Photograph by author.

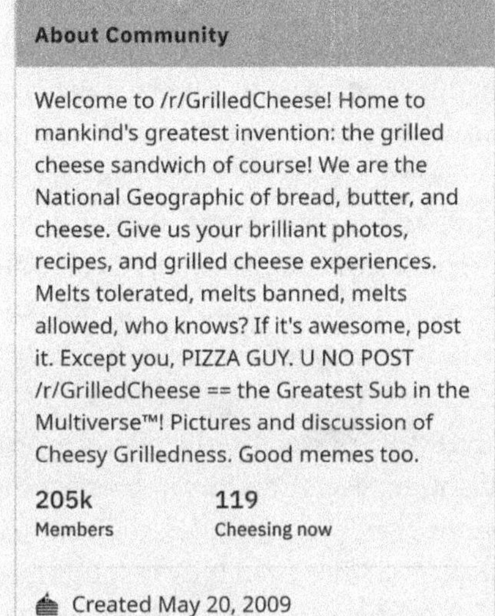

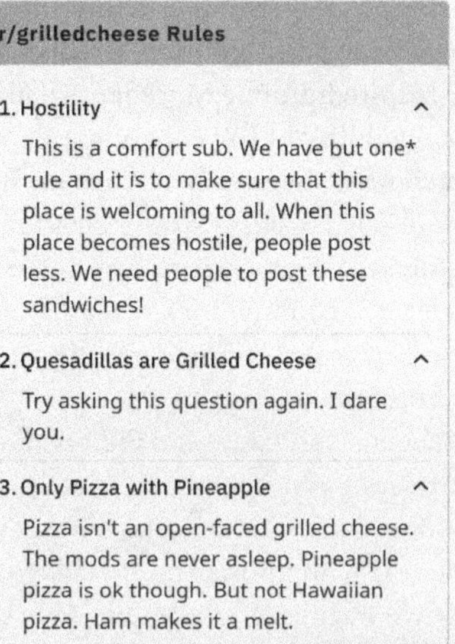

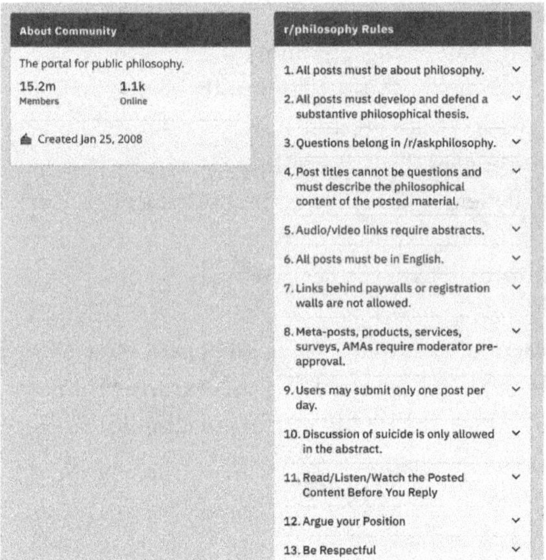

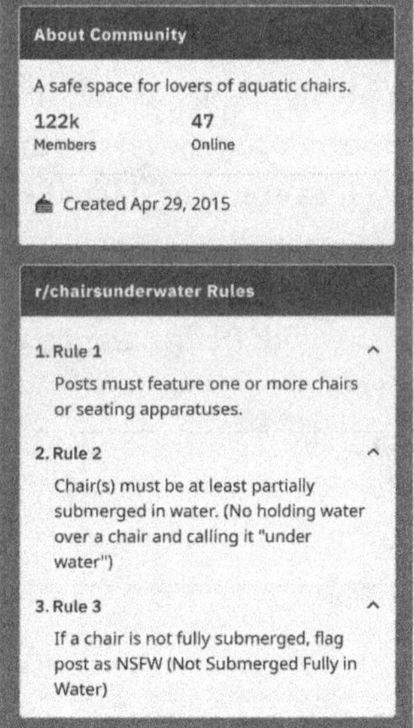

Figure 4.7 Sample of rules from different subreddits: r/grilledcheese (top), r/philosophy (bottom left), and r/chairsunderwater (bottom right). Due in large part to the subreddits' durability, subreddit communities tend to develop their own norms of discourse that help contribute to a unique communal identity. Photographs by author.

Reddit's subreddit structure thus provides an environment that facilitates the formation of political communities on the platform. Its clear boundaries help redditors easily identify interests they share with others. Likewise, the durability of those boundaries affords users the opportunity to form the attachments necessary to sustain those communities over time. And yet, as I have been arguing, these clear and durable boundaries are necessary but insufficient characteristics of democratic environments. Instead, specifically *democratic* communities must also work to improve themselves. Democratic spaces thus also require *flexibility*—a flexibility that is also evident in Reddit's architecture.

Though subreddits are the organizing principle of Reddit, the platform also introduces variety by deliberately highlighting users' multiple, overlapping memberships and interests. Redditors' "front page," for example, is a feed that collects the top posts and threads from the subreddits a redditor is subscribed to, encouraging users to engage with the many overlapping groups to which they belong (see Figure 4.8). This facilitates redditors' encounter with a variety of interests and experiences across the platform.[75]

Yet Reddit, as a whole, is also quite malleable; users are able to control a number of facets of Reddit's environment. Most significantly, users can create subreddits for any reason they choose; once created, moreover, subreddit communities exert considerable control over their space. There is a history of users redesigning Reddit's structural elements, like the comment sorting algorithm.[76] And there are a number of spaces where redditors continually engage in conversations with Reddit administrators to discuss the design and direction of the site as whole.[77]

By providing a built environment that helps users recognize their shared interests, generate attachments to their communities, and exercise collective control to improve those communities, the Reddit platform exemplifies a space

[75] Isaac Waller and Ashton Anderson, "Generalists and Specialists: Using Community Embeddings to Quantify Activity Diversity in Online Platforms," in *Proceedings of the 2019 World Wide Web Conference* (New York: ACM, 2019), 1954–64. In r/popular, the default view for logged-out users, selected posts are "the most shared, upvoted, and commented," while r/all features "the most active posts from all of Reddit." In either view, posts are sorted by "Hot," meaning they are randomly selected and normalized by "top posts" from each subreddit; as of 2018, however, logged-in users can also choose to sort by "Best," which personalizes the "Hot" sorting by selecting from more desired communities and filtering old posts. For a more detailed discussion of Reddit's algorithmic sorting and its implications for democratic politics, see chapter 5.

[76] Randall Munroe, "Reddit's New Comment Sorting System," *Reddit Blog*, October 15, 2009, http://www.redditblog.com/2009/10/reddits-new-comment-sorting-system.html.

[77] See, for example, r/TheoryOfReddit, r/meta, and r/redesign for examples of "meta" discussions about Reddit's functionality.

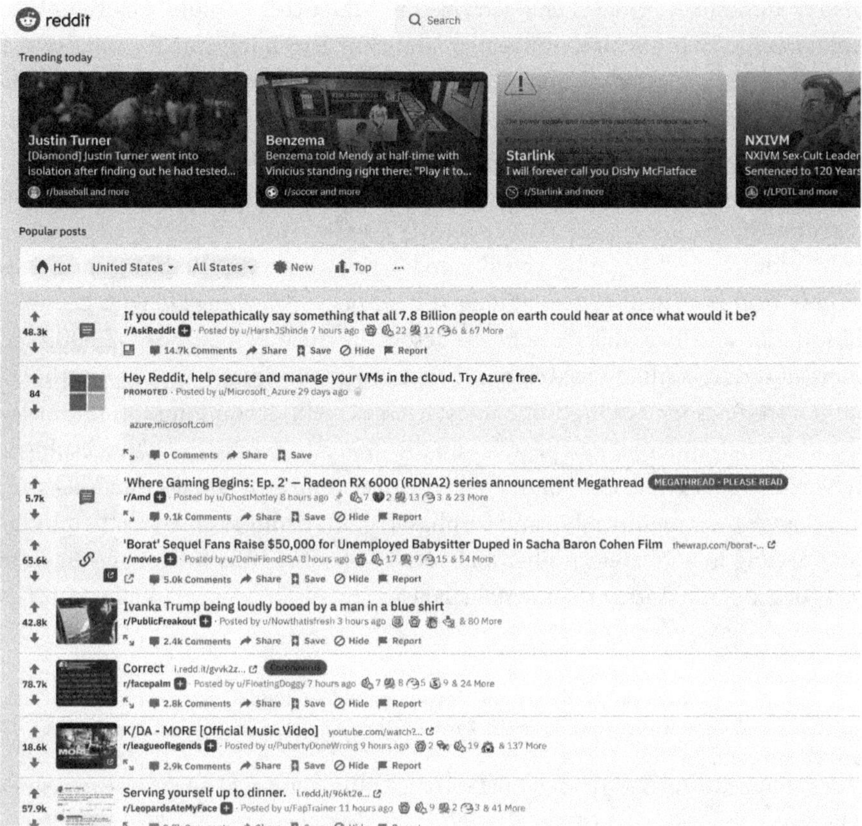

Figure 4.8 Example screenshot of Reddit's "Front Page" (for a user who is logged out, as pictured, this is r/popular), displaying top posts from a variety of subreddits. Photograph by author.

that affords users the opportunity to engage in democratic politics. Reddit can and does host subreddits that, for example, engage in "constructive, public discourse about the practices of democratic institutions";[78] share, discuss, and contextualize news and information regarding current events;[79] and support

[78] Michael Buozis, "Doxing or Deliberative Democracy? Evidence and Digital Affordances in the Serial Subreddit," *Convergence: The International Journal of Research into New Media Technologies* 25, no. 3 (2019): 357–73.

[79] Xinning Gui et al., "Multidimensional Risk Communication: Public Discourse on Risks during an Emerging Epidemic," in *Proceedings of the 2018 CHI Conference on Human Factors in Computing Systems* (New York: ACM Press, 2018), 1–14; Alex Leavitt and Joshua Clark, "Upvoting Hurricane Sandy: Event-Based News Production Processes on a Social News Site," in *Proceedings of the 32nd Annual ACM Conference on Human Factors in Computing Systems—CHI '14* (New York; Association for Computing Machinery, 2014), 1495–1504.

citizen journalism projects characterized by "nuanced, comprehensive debate and coverage."[80] It has also, unlike platforms like Facebook and Twitter, hosted significant instances of collective action, as when redditors organized protests aimed at Reddit's corporate governance[81] and, more recently, crafted an open letter calling for Reddit administrators to take immediate and concrete steps to ban toxic communities and make more proactive anti-racist changes to the platform.[82]

In addition to facilitating coordinated action, however, Reddit also invites contestation both within and among subreddits as they engage with the new information and ideas that disseminate across the site.[83] Not only does Reddit see inter-subreddit conflicts, as different communities disagree with one another,[84] but it also hosts *intra*-subreddit contestation as well, as communities internally negotiate their different perspectives on the interests they share.[85] The result is a dynamic, digital Great Community, where over time individual subreddits shift and change both membership and emphasis[86] and redditors diversify their interests, posting in a greater number and variety of subreddits the longer they are users of the site.[87] Rather than remain in echo chambers, subject to filter bubbles

[80] Scott S. D. Mitchell and Merlyna Lim, "Too Crowded for Crowdsourced Journalism: Reddit, Portability, and Citizen Participation in the Syrian Crisis," *Canadian Journal of Communication* 43 (2018): 399–419.

[81] J. Nathan Matias, "Going Dark: Social Factors in Collective Action Against Platform Operators in the Reddit Blackout," in *Proceedings of the 2016 CHI Conference on Human Factors in Computing Systems* (New York: ACM, 2016), 1138–51.

[82] Pro_creator, "We Have a Racist User Problem and Reddit Won't Take Action," *Reddit, r/Blackladies*, August 25, 2014, https://www.reddit.com/r/blackladies/comments/2ejg1b/we_have_a_racist_user_problem_and_reddit_wont/; DubTeeDub, "Open Letter to Steve Huffman and the Board of Directors of Reddit, Inc—If You Believe in Standing up to Hate and Supporting Black Lives, You Need to Act," *Reddit, r/AgainstHateSubreddits*, June 8, 2020, https://www.reddit.com/r/AgainstHateSubreddits/comments/gyyqem/open_letter_to_steve_huffman_and_the_board_of/; Kaitlyn Tiffany, "Reddit Is Finally Facing Its Legacy of Racism," *The Atlantic*, June 12, 2020.

[83] Jeremy R. Cole, Moojan Ghafurian, and David Reitter, "Is Word Adoption a Grassroots Process? An Analysis of Reddit Communities," *Lecture Notes in Computer Science (Including Subseries Lecture Notes in Artificial Intelligence and Lecture Notes in Bioinformatics)* 10354 LNCS (2017): 236–41.

[84] Srayan Datta and Eytan Adar, "Extracting Inter-Community Conflicts in Reddit," in *Proceedings of the Thirteenth International AAAI Conference on Web and Social Media* (Münich, Germany, 2019), 146–57.

[85] Bertan Buyukozturk, Shawn Gaulden, and Benjamin Dowd-Arrow, "Contestation on Reddit, Gamergate, and Movement Barriers," *Social Movement Studies* 17, no. 5 (2018): 592–609; Leavitt and Clark, "Upvoting Hurricane Sandy."

[86] Hussam Habib et al., "To Act or React? Investigating Proactive Strategies for Online Community Moderation," *Pre-Print, ArXiv*, 2019, https://arxiv.org/abs/1906.11932.

[87] Chenhao Tan and Lillian Lee, "All Who Wander: On the Prevalence and Characteristics of Multi-Community Engagement," in *Proceedings of the 24th International Conference on World Wide Web* (Geneva: International World Wide Web Conferences Steering Committee, 2015), 1056–66.

and closed communities, Reddit's design facilitates the kind of critical, diverse, and *collaborative* engagements that mark democratic politics.

But while Reddit as a whole affords democratic practices, this is not universally true of the individual subreddits on the platform. There are, of course, subreddits that do not engage in the experimental practices of self-correction and improvement that characterize democratic communities. Much of the activity on Reddit is non-objectionable, even ordinary—the r/funny subreddit has the most subscribers, for example, and the r/IamA subreddit, a community dedicated to Q&As, regularly hosts mainstream figures. But the site also often makes headlines for the racist, sexist, homophobic, and sometimes illegal activity that circulates within, and among, communities such as r/conspiracy, r/TheRedPill, r/the_donald, and, famously, r/pizzagate.[88] While these subreddits are a small subset of the overall Reddit ecosystem, they account for the majority of "alternative news sources" shared on the site[89] and often radicalize their long-time members.[90] Because these subreddits restrict and often ban users and information that might contradict or critique their stated purpose, the longtime members of these sites end up taking a dogmatic approach to their shared interests that is antithetical to democratic improvement. They are precisely the kinds of extremist echo chambers many scholars and critics warn of.

Yet the enormous variation between subreddits also provides an opportunity for more fine-grained analysis. Because Reddit is, as a whole, so malleable, subreddits have significant control over their subreddit environment. We can use the subsequent differences in subreddit design to explore precisely how the constituent elements of flexibility—variety and malleability—can be implemented in digital environments to either contribute to the democratic life of the platform, or else to undermine it. To that end, I compare r/the_donald with r/TwoXChromosomes to show how to best build flexible spaces and ensure the success of *democratic* communities in digital environments.

[88] In June 2020, Reddit banned more than 2,000 subreddits for violating the platform's content policy (of those 2,000, however, only 200 had more than 10 daily users). Among the banned subreddits was r/the_donald. Likewise, r/pizzagate was banned in 2016. As of August 2021, r/conspiracy remains openly accessible while r/TheRedPill is "quarantined"—meaning visitors to the subreddit must be registered redditors who confirm their desire to see "shocking or highly offensive content."

[89] Savvas Zannettou et al., "The Web Centipede: Understanding How Web Communities Influence Each Other through the Lens of Mainstream and Alternative News Sources," in *Proceedings of the 2017 Internet Measurement Conference* (London: ACM Press, 2017), 405–17.

[90] Mattia Samory and Tanushree Mitra, "Conspiracies Online: User Discussions in a Conspiracy Community Following Dramatic Events," in *Proceedings of the Twelfth International AAAI Conference on Web and Social Media (ICWSM 2018)* (Stanford, CA: AAAI Publications, 2018), 348.

POLICING BOUNDARIES: R/THE_DONALD

Consider r/the_donald, widely understood to be among the most notorious of Reddit's communities.[91] Created in 2015, the subreddit was dedicated to discussing then-presidential-candidate Donald Trump; it soon became so influential on Reddit that the platform changed its algorithm in 2016 to decrease the community's visibility on Reddit's front page.[92] And though r/the_donald was quarantined by Reddit administrators in June 2019, and banned a year later, it was until that point one of the more high-profile communities on the platform. But it was also an outlier in its extremist and insular behavior.

Despite its relatively benign origins as a subreddit for Trump supporters to share news, information, and opinions on the then-upcoming election, the community later evolved into "a disconcerting melting pot of posts that [ran] the gamut from InfoWars-style conspiracies, men's rights activist- and GamerGate-style real and faux outrage, memes and shitposts (basically, jokes that are only meant to be understood by those in the community), and, yes, Donald Trump news."[93] But this was not, I argue, necessarily inevitable. By tracing the evolution of r/the_donald, we can see how a series of structural decisions—namely, the subreddit's conscious choice to remove variety from its space—facilitated this transformation from candidate-centered political community to "online cesspit."[94]

Like all subreddits, r/the_donald was both durable and clearly bounded. Yet unlike most of Reddit's over 130,000 communities, r/the_donald rendered the space of its subreddit much less flexible than others on the platform—primarily by actively removing variety from the space. Using a combination of structural changes and aggressive moderation practices, r/the_donald entrenched its boundaries, ensuring the space was only open to specific kinds of information and individuals. The result was a community that resisted any new information that did not align with their existing perspectives. Absent this variety, the community became static, stagnant, and wholly at odds with the larger Reddit community of which it was ostensibly a part. The subreddit thus *became* less

[91] Jason Koebler, "How r/The_donald Became a Melting Pot of Frustration and Hate," *Motherboard*, July 12, 2016; Trevor Martin, "Dissecting Trump's Most Rabid Online Following," *FiveThirtyEight*, March 23, 2017; Romano, "Reddit Just Banned One of Its Most Toxic Forums"; Christine Lagorio-Chafkin, "Reddit and the God Emperor of the Internet," *New York Times*, November 19, 2016.

[92] Abby Ohlheiser, "Trump's Meme Brigade Took Over Reddit: Now Reddit Is Trying to Stop Them," *Washington Post*, June 17, 2016.

[93] Koebler, "How r/The_donald Became a Melting Pot of Frustration and Hate."

[94] Will Bedingfield, "Reddit Has Banned r/The_Donald. Who It Bans Next Matters More," *WIRED*, July 2020.

democratic, in part, because of its deliberate choices about how to design and manage the space that housed it.

In its original configuration, the boundaries of r/the_donald (like those of most subreddits) were quite permeable—anyone who knew the URL could visit the space and, importantly, were able to engage in the conversations taking place within it. Like most subreddits, then, r/the_donald began as a space that was open to variety. Indeed, r/the_donald began to noticeably diverge from other subreddits in *response* to this variety. Addressing the influx of new visitors from other politically oriented message boards—namely, r/politics (another subreddit) and 4Chan's /pol/ board (a non-Reddit site)—an r/the_donald moderator set the tone for how members of the community would respond:

> When /r/politics sends their people they aren't sending their best. They're losers, they're Reddit TOS violators, some of them I assume may be good people. . . . The 300+ new Trump-ites can stay. But those who came from an illegal brigade and manipulated votes . . . you have to go, sorry. If you wish to appeal your ban and repent we will consider allowing you back *legally*.[95]

Here, we see r/the_donald responding to the influx of new users by attempting to reduce the variety allowed in its space (only "new Trump-ites" could stay). And while moderators, like the one quoted here, threatened to expel and ban these new users and perspectives in order to do so, the subreddit also introduced *structural* changes designed to prevent a resurgence of this variety as well.

One prominent structural alteration was r/the_donald's change to Reddit's voting mechanism. Up- and down-voting, through which redditors signal their approval or disapproval of content posted to their subreddits, is a ubiquitous feature of the platform. The votes are factored in Reddit's algorithms, and content is sorted accordingly—posts and comments that receive too many downvotes disappear from view, while highly upvoted content is more likely to feature on users' front pages. In seeking to control the kinds of content shared in their space, however, r/the_donald *hid* the down-vote option from their subreddit; users could *only* upvote content, changing the structural features of the space to erase visible disagreement.[96] In addition, moderators "pinned" certain content to the top of the subreddit to display it more prominently for users and to encourage similar kinds of posts, again reinforcing the singular vision of the subreddit's interests.[97]

[95] NYPD-32, "The Great r/The_Donald Invasion," *Reddit, r/The_donald*, December 9, 2015, https://www.reddit.com/r/The_Donald/comments/3w0q4n/the_great_rthe_donald_invasion/.

[96] Fernando Alfonso III, "Reddit Punishes Pro-Trump Community r/The_donald for Threats, Other 'Rule-Breaking Behavior,'" *Forbes*, June 2019.

[97] Romano, "Reddit Just Banned One of Its Most Toxic Forums."

With these structural changes, r/the_donald implemented a kind of "defensive architecture" intended to send a clear signal to users that the subreddit was built for only a single type of use; divergent or dissenting opinions were not to be tolerated in their space.

As time went on, this rejection of alternative opinions and the people who voiced them became more explicit, leading to a subreddit community that was more and more closed-off and homogenized. Since, as Dewey reminds us, "[d]iversity of stimulation means novelty, and novelty means challenge to thought,"[98] it should perhaps be unsurprising that the subreddit's lack of novelty or challenge, and its corresponding insularity, led to a degradation of r/the_donald's members' ability to critically engage with the wider Reddit community. As the growing popularity of the subreddit led to more visitors from outside, the subreddit's method of addressing these new users became even more heavy-handed and their space more homogenous. The subreddit soon announced that "no one was allowed to question the direction of the subreddit"; anyone posting on the subreddit was told in no uncertain terms that they "must fit in or be banned."[99]

No longer even cloaked in language of "TOS violations" of the larger Reddit community—a claim that originally at least rhetorically connected r/the_donald to the more inclusive community of redditors—the subreddit explicitly disavowed the possibility of change based on new information or "challenge to thought" (see Figure 4.9). The subreddit, in other words, had become a self-consciously closed community—one that seemingly refused to engage in the habit of experimental self-improvement that is necessary for democratic politics. And the result of this refusal was, as Dewey warned, to "create the conditions of which the exploiters of sentiment and opinion only take advantage."[100] Rejecting any information or opinion that contradicted their own views, members of r/the_donald were all too ready to be swayed by the comforting narratives of conspiracy theories and misinformation campaigns—including, most prominently, the Pizzagate conspiracy.

EMBRACING VARIETY: R/TWOXCHROMOSOMES

The r/the_donald subreddit was notorious; it had a reputation, both on and off Reddit, as a controversial community.[101] Indeed, it was to r/the_donald

[98] Dewey, "Democracy and Education," 90.

[99] Koebler, "How r/The_donald Became a Melting Pot of Frustration and Hate."

[100] Dewey, *The Public and Its Problems*, 169.

[101] Koebler, "How r/The_donald Became a Melting Pot of Frustration and Hate"; Romano, "Reddit Just Banned One of Its Most Toxic Forums."

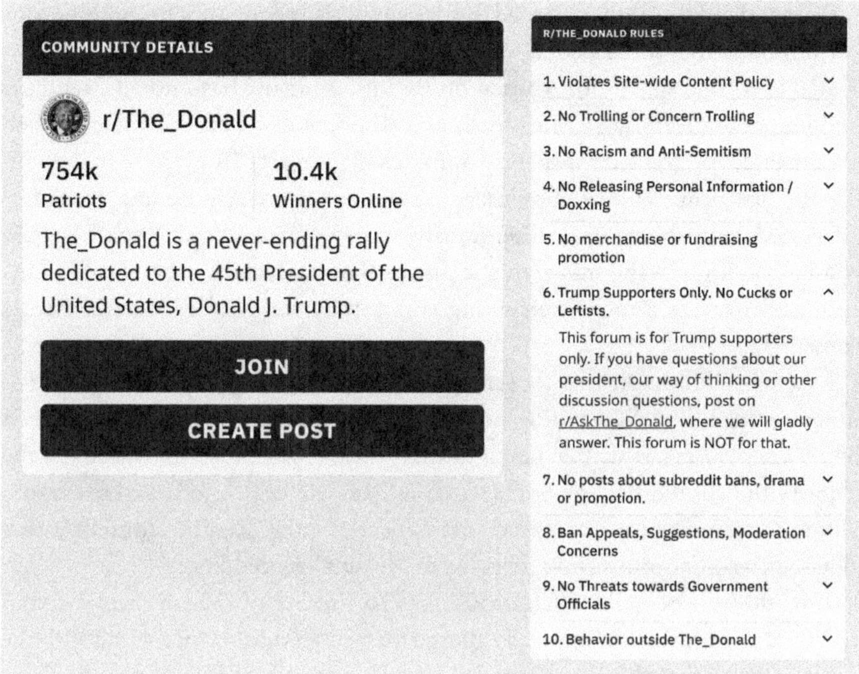

Figure 4.9 Rules of r/the_donald subreddit. Rule #6 ("Trump Supporters Only. No Cucks or Leftists.") reflects the community's lack of variety. Photograph by author.

that many commenters pointed as a prime example of how the internet supports and nourishes toxic environments. Yet this need not be the case. As we saw above, the toxicity of r/the_donald was, in large part, self-imposed; it was the result of self-consciously creating an inflexible space that did not afford variety. The subreddit was not *created* as an echo chamber, in other words; it *became* one as users reaffirmed and reinforced the site's boundaries, emphasized the subreddit's durability, and worked to remove any variety from their environment.

Because r/the_donald's toxic environment was the result of deliberate choices about how to manage their durable bounded space, however, it is possible to envision a more democratic alternative. We can imagine a similar situation in which an embattled, somewhat controversial, and relatively politicized subreddit faced the same challenge—how to deal with an influx of new members and new ideas—and made the opposite decision of r/the_donald. Instead of closing its boundaries and enforcing homogeneity, this more democratic alternative would retain the de facto flexibility of the general Reddit structure and embrace the variety of perspectives it affords. And we can see this alternative in the trajectory of r/TwoXChromosomes.

Founded in July 2009, r/TwoXChromosomes is "a subreddit for both serious and silly content, and intended for women's perspectives."[102] The subreddit was created as a "safe space" for women on Reddit. As many have noted, Reddit is predominantly used by (white) men; as a result, women on the site can often feel alienated or targeted for sharing opinions that diverge from those that dominate the platform.[103] Created by users in response to an "Ask Reddit" thread,[104] r/TwoXChromosomes was intentionally conceptualized as a space where women could resist the misogynistic norms that characterize many subreddits and instead create a more welcoming community for people who identify as women.[105]

As a subreddit dedicated to a marginalized—and relatively controversial—subject area, r/TwoXChromosomes, like r/the_donald, has had to address the influx of users with perspectives that differ from those espoused by the majority the subreddit's members. And, in May 2014, this influx of users into r/TwoXChromosomes increased dramatically after Reddit administrators added r/TwoXChromosomes to its list of "default" subreddits.

The addition of r/TwoXChromosomes to the list of defaults was a major structural change that dramatically altered the ways redditors interacted with the community. Rather than having to consciously seek out r/TwoXChromosomes in order to join its conversations, the addition of r/TwoXChromosomes as a default subreddit meant that all new redditors would be automatically subscribed to the community; its content would, by default, appear in their front-page feeds. As a result of this shift, the subreddit exploded with new users—it now boasts over 13 million members and hosts millions of pageviews per month.[106] Yet many of these new members, as is true of many default subreddits, did not share the "original" members' ideas about the aims of r/TwoXChromosomes and what constituted appropriate conduct in that space. Instead, as a default subreddit, r/TwoXChromosomes gained many new visitors who were uninterested in—or even hostile to—"women's perspectives."

[102] "FAQ," *Reddit,* r/TwoXChromosomes, n.d., https://www.reddit.com/r/TwoXChromosomes/wiki/faq.

[103] Hallie Workman, "Formation of Safe Spaces in Gendered Online Communities: Reddit and 'the Front Page of the Internet'" (Ft. Worth: Texas Christian University, 2014); Alex Goldman, "Making TwoXChromosomes a Default Subreddit Has Not Gone Over Well with Everyone," *WNYC on the Media Blog,* May 20, 2014.

[104] "Ask Reddit" is another subreddit (r/AskReddit) in which users post questions in order to solicit answers from their peers.

[105] Lauren Rae Orsini, "TwoXChromosomes, Reddit's Biggest Female-Focused Community, Turns 3," *The Daily Dot,* July 16, 2012.

[106] Alex Hern, "Reddit Women Protest at New Front-Page Position," *The Guardian,* May 13, 2014; "R/TwoXChromosomes," *Reddit,* n.d., https://www.reddit.com/r/TwoXChromosomes/.

With this influx of new members, the original r/TwoXChromosomes users were put into an uncomfortable position, forced to constantly engage with new users who did not necessarily agree with them, even on their most foundational beliefs. But rather than demand new users "fit in or be banned," as did r/the_donald's moderators, r/TwoXChromosomes retained the variety of their space, addressing conflict by bringing it out into the open through the "method of democracy." While r/TwoXChromosomes retained broad limits on debate—the subreddit explicitly states, for example, that it is "not the place to start debates just for the sake of debating"[107]—the community's moderators explicitly prioritized "open discussion and community"[108] and encouraged users to negotiate the resulting conflicts within the context of individual discussion threads (see Figure 4.10). By taking the subreddit default, then, r/TwoXChromosomes made a structural change to their space designed to encourage the "diversity of stimulation" that would pose a "challenge to thought"—with the goal of collectively improving the community for all of its members.

Yet, this increase in the subreddit's variety was not universally embraced by r/TwoXChromosomes members. Upon hearing the announcement that the subreddit would be added to the list of default subreddits, many members expressed frustration, anger, and outrage. "There were a few trolls and ignorant people on here before," said one r/TwoXChromosomes user in response to the change, "but most people on here were serious subscribers and there were enough of us to counteract them with downvotes and report. Not anymore. We can all say goodbye to a safe place on Reddit for women."[109] This disappointment was widespread in the community, with some users asking moderators to reverse the decision and remove r/TwoXChromosomes from the list of defaults and others calling for stricter moderation, including more banning.[110]

At the same time, however, the *moderators* of r/TwoXChromosomes—including the subreddit's founder—were largely resistant to implementing these suggested changes. Indeed, the initial decision to go default was largely moderator-driven. When first approached by Reddit administrators to be a default community, the moderators "had a backroom discussion about it"

[107] "FAQ," *Reddit*, r/TwoXChromosomes.

[108] Workman, "Formation of Safe Spaces in Gendered Online Communities."

[109] Hern, "Reddit Women Protest at New Front-Page Position."

[110] glycine, "Comment on 'To the Mods of 2X: A Question,'" *Reddit, r/TwoXChromosomes*, 2014, https://www.reddit.com/r/TwoXChromosomes/comments/25pfj8/to_the_mods_of_2x_a_question/chjl501/; U/[deleted], "TwoXChromosomes Is on TLDR, the Blog for NPR's Program, on the Media Talking about Becoming a Default Subreddit," *Reddit, r/TwoXChromosomes*, 2014, https://www.reddit.com/r/TwoXChromosomes/comments/25yvyc/twoxchromosomes_is_on_tldr_the_blog_for_nprs/; Goldman, "Making TwoXChromosomes a Default Subreddit Has Not Gone Over Well With Everyone."

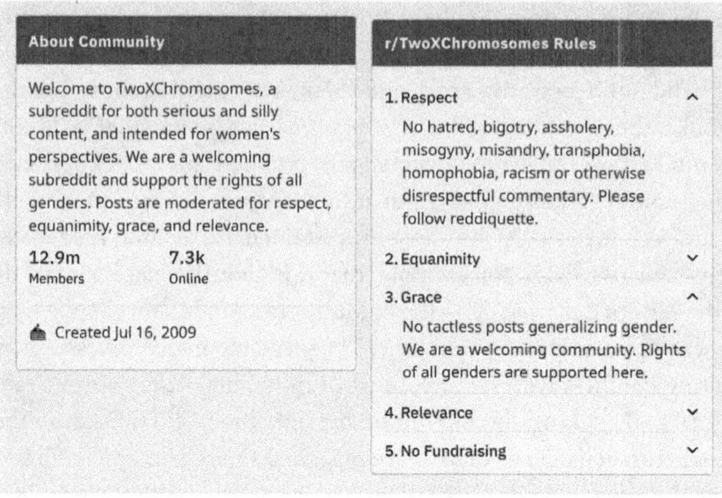

XY here; am I allowed to post?

All are welcome. It's not really about who you are, but about the quality of the discussion you'll generate. Absolutely feel free to comment. You should probably refrain from posting pictures of yourself and asking whether you're attractive.

Any question that starts with "Ladies of Reddit..." are welcome to post in the relationship community, relationship_advice askwomen, or AskFeminists, or even /r/AskReddit.

Please refrain from starting every comment here with "As a man" or similar. If it is really and truly relevant then by all means mention it, but remember we ladies don't mention that we're women on the rest of the site unless it matters. Just as we're often assumed to be men outside of 2xc and related communities you might be assumed to be a women here. And that's okay! All that matters is that we talk openly with each other.

Please also refrain from telling us what turns you on in most threads here, it's almost never relevant to the discussion. There are times when it *might* be, but please think long and hard (tee hee!) if this is one of those times before sharing that information.

I disagree with everything I've decided you stand for. Can I submit a post here telling you why you're wrong and debate the women of reddit?

No. This subreddit is a place for us to get together to chat about whatever is on our minds, not the place to start debates just for the sake of debating.
We welcome open discussion and we welcome anyone to join those discussions as long as they are participating in good faith. However, this is not /r/changemyview or /r/FeMRADebates. If you want to start a debate check out those subreddits.

Figure 4.10 Rules of r/TwoXChromosomes (top) as well as a selection from the subreddit's FAQs (bottom). Contrast with r/the_donald; r/TwoXChromosome's emphasis on variety appears in both Rule #3 ("We are a welcoming community.") as well as the FAQs' explicit welcoming of men and others who wish to join the discussions (as long as they are "participating in good faith"). Photographs by author.

and agreed to "try it out."[111] The decision was—as was the case with r/the_donald's decisions regarding the configuration of *their* space—very much in the hands of the moderators. And despite the negative reactions of some r/TwoXChromosomes users, the moderators seem to view the changes to r/TwoXChromosomes as a "net positive."[112] For example, in her reflections on the decision take the subreddit default, the r/TwoXChromosomes founder frames the benefits of increasing the variety of the subreddit in terms that echo Dewey's own democratic goals: "At this point," she said, "we're seeing a lot more positive things happen than negative things happen. People are having more gender related discussions and discussing the experiences of what it is to be a woman, and how weird and varied and diverse that is."[113] Despite resistance from r/TwoXChromosomes membership, it seems, the increase in the variety of experiences redditors can expect in the r/TwoXChromosomes space has led to the kind of diversifying and mutually enriching interactions that provide the foundation for democratic politics.

DEMOCRACY IN MODERATION?

Both r/the_donald and r/TwoXChromosomes are politically charged subreddits; both intentionally set themselves apart from the general Reddit community, whether in terms of content, tone, or both. As a result, both are often the target of "brigades," or "invasions" from hostile groups. Both r/the_donald and r/TwoXChromosomes often, in other words, face a dilemma familiar to democratic politics—how to build ties of political friendship between citizens and ensure the sustainability of the community in the face of unwelcome or hostile newcomers, while still remaining open to new ideas and experiences.

In comparing the responses of r/the_donald and r/TwoXChromosomes to this challenge, however, we can see two very distinct kinds of communities form in the spaces of the subreddits; these differences are, I am arguing, due in part to a series of choices each subreddit community made about the structural design of their environments—namely, how much variety to tolerate. When faced with the influx of anti-Trump comments, for example, r/the_donald reaffirmed its boundaries by changing certain structural elements—like removing downvotes and adding pinned posts—in order to enforce a singular vision of the community's interest. By agreeing to "go default," by contrast, r/TwoXChromosomes made a similarly structural change that nevertheless had the opposite effect—it

[111] Alex Goldman, "Being a Feminist on Reddit—The Defaulting of /r/TwoXChromosomes," *WNYC On The Media Blog*, May 19, 2014.

[112] Goldman, "Being a Feminist on Reddit."

[113] Goldman, "Being a Feminist on Reddit."

ensured a constant stream of new users bringing with them new, and often challenging, perspectives. And while r/TwoXChromosomes members complained about the decision, this choice nevertheless led to ongoing discussions in the subreddit about how, whether, and to what extent the members and moderators should police content.[114] That these kinds of conversations happened at all in the community indicates that r/TwoXChromosomes created a more varied and inclusive, and therefore more democratic, environment than r/the_donald, where similar collective contestations over the subreddit's direction did not take place.

At the same time, the decision-making that occurred around r/TwoXChromosomes's move to become a default subreddit was largely undertaken by the site's moderators. Indeed, moderators play an outsized role in determining the direction of the community in general. While r/TwoXChromosomes members do have some responsibility for "manag[ing] the boundaries of their community"[115] by flagging and downvoting posts "into oblivion"[116] or at the very least simply ignoring disruptive comments or attempts to incite debate,[117] they have very little power to actively exercise control over their environment.[118] Thus, while it may demonstrate a commitment to maintaining variety by creating "a system that has constantly changing boundaries,"[119] r/TwoXChromosomes nevertheless still operates in large part like the traditional lecture hall that, as Dewey reminds us, is inherently undemocratic: moderators, like teachers, set the terms of debate, while users, like students, can only respond to them.

[114] glycine, "Comment on 'To the Mods of 2X: A Question'"; Goldman, "Making TwoX Chromosomes a Default Subreddit Has Not Gone Over Well With Everyone."

[115] Jesse Betteridge, "Oppression in the Reddit Hivemind: Tracing Patterns of Misogyny in Electronic Public Spaces" (Burnaby, BC: Simon Fraser University, 2016), 83.

[116] Workman, "Formation of Safe Spaces in Gendered Online Communities." Downvoting a post "into oblivion" means comments are no longer automatically shown to users because of their low overall score.

[117] Betteridge, "Oppression in the Reddit Hivemind."

[118] Structurally shut out of the formal processes of decision-making that influenced the decision to go default, for example, r/TwoXChromosomes users were left with only limited opportunities to shape the direction of their community—namely, the ability to develop and maintain norms of discourse by creating posts and comments. The result was an increase in "graphic stories about health and body functions," which often occurred on the site as part of general sharing of experiences, but which members felt would be especially off-putting for "any misogynistic outside presence" (Betteridge, 108). Without an underlying structural change through which members could be empowered to exert control over the built environment to meet their community's needs, in other words, the only avenues open to user participation were to reinforce community norms and practices through their own posting practices—practices that were certainly less effective than the structural change to "go default," and that ultimately fell out of habit with users. Indeed, some users left the space entirely for newly established alternatives like r/TrollXChromosomes.

[119] Betteridge, "Oppression in the Reddit Hivemind," 115.

By limiting the number of options through which members of r/TwoXChromosomes can control their environment—and, instead, leaving outsized control over, especially, its structure in the hands of moderators—r/TwoXChromosomes is missing a key element of the flexibility necessary for a democratic space. Recall that, for Dewey, democratic habits require active cultivation; an environment that will facilitate democratic engagements must therefore be malleable, organizing users in such a way that they can actively take part in collectively managing and improving their environment. Both r/the_donald and r/TwoXChromosomes, with their overreliance on moderators, thus fail to fully meet the criteria of flexible spaces.

For both communities—and Reddit as a whole—moderators largely act as an elite group that controls the direction, tone, and general shape of the subreddits they serve. And while moderators often perform beneficial functions, such as the r/TwoXChromosomes moderators insisting on the variety of perspectives gained by going default, a platform that grants moderators more control over the space than "normal" users is one that is not as malleable as a democratic community requires; unable to actively practice the experimental habit of mind, the majority of users will end up losing it. And there is evidence that demonstrates this is indeed the case; research has shown, for example, that Reddit's up- and down-vote system, one of the few feedback mechanisms for lay users to direct their communities, is largely used by only a few dedicated users.[120] The majority of redditors, in other words, exercise no control over the environment in which they operate.

And yet, this need not be the case. As a number of studies have shown, there *are* systems of moderation that can be more successful at ensuring users practice habits of experimentation—changing their environment, holding others responsible for the changes they introduce, and being held to account for the same by one's peers.[121] On Slashdot, for example, moderation is distributed to a large group of the platform's users based on their reputation for good behavior on the site. As users prove that they embody the norms of the site, they are granted more power to direct it.[122] Rather than separate the actions of these moderators from those of the communities they shape, however—as was the

[120] Eric Gilbert, "Widespread Underprovision on Reddit," in *Proceedings of the 2013 Conference on Computer Supported Cooperative Work—CSCW '13*, (New York: ACM, 2013): 803–808.

[121] Lampe and Johnston, "Follow the (Slash) Dot"; Cliff Lampe et al., "Crowdsourcing Civility: A Natural Experiment Examining the Effects of Distributed Moderation in Online Forums," *Government Information Quarterly* 31, no. 2 (2014): 317–26.

[122] Lampe and Johnston, "Follow the (Slash) Dot." A similar model of distributed moderation was used on the Gawker Media websites both before and after they implemented the Kinja discussion system. See Forestal, "The Architecture of Political Spaces."

case with r/TwoXChromosomes—the actions of moderators on Slashdot are rated by other users of the site who also have positive reputations but who may not themselves yet be moderators. Moderation is therefore widespread, temporary, rotating, and overseen by the community.

By distributing moderation among all users and designing a system that allows all users to take a more active role in directing their communities, this kind of structural change works to increase a digital space's malleability. And by encouraging users' active engagement in the processes of collective decision-making and control over their environment, this kind of system further increases participation.[123] Redesigning platforms to include this kind of decentralized moderation thus reshapes the spaces in which it is used and puts the power of decision-making—and discipline—in the hands of community members; the result is that users are able to practice the experimental habit that Dewey highlights as crucial for the success of democratic politics. But this can only occur in spaces that are characterized by *both* elements of flexibility—not just a variety of experiences, but also the malleability that affords avenues for users to direct and change those experiences in response to their changing circumstances.

Constructing Digital Democracies

Democratic politics, as we have seen, requires both ties of political friendship as well as communal attachments; citizens must not only recognize one another as peers, but they must also make commitments to sustain those ties into the future. And these ties and commitments can be generated, at least in part, by designing spaces that are both clearly bounded and durable. By highlighting common interests and interlocutors, and facilitating affective attachments and repeated interactions, bounded, durable spaces create a firm foundation for communities to endure and thrive.

But as is by now clear, collective action is not necessarily democratic action; communities with deep and long-standing internal ties of solidarity can also be insular and stagnant, as well as hostile and aggressive to perceived outsiders. A specifically *democratic* community, then, requires its citizens to not only develop ties of political friendship and the communal attachments to sustain them, but also to practice the democratic habit of experimentation, and the openness and commitment to inclusion and improvement that experimentation

[123] When new users to the site were given moderator feedback, for example, Slashdot saw increased participation—regardless of whether that feedback was positive or negative. See Lampe et al., "Crowdsourcing Civility."

demands. Democracy, in other words, requires us to not only work with the neighbors we have, but also to remain open to—and even seek out—new and different people and perspectives as we engage in the processes of collective management of our common affairs.

And the development of these democratic habits is, as we have seen, influenced by the kinds of spaces in which citizens find themselves. Certain design elements in our environments, like affixing a "Do Not Enter" sign to a door, can reaffirm boundaries that may otherwise not seem intimidating. Removing that sign, or leaving the door open, is therefore a *spatial* change that helps to create environments that encourage experimentation by making the spaces more *flexible*. In order to afford this experimentalism, however, these flexible spaces must exhibit two distinct characteristics: they must (1) host a *variety* of perspectives and experiences and (2) be *malleable*, encouraging citizens' active participation in the work of managing the space. To the extent that spaces—like the traditional lecture hall or r/the_donald—disavow one or both of these characteristics, they will fail to provide an environment in which users can develop, practice, and refine the habits necessary for specifically democratic communities; instead, we might expect them to exhibit the stagnation and insularity of "echo chambers."

As we consider how best to build and maintain democratic communities in digital environments, then, it is clear that the spaces created with digital technologies must exhibit some balance of boundaries, durability, and flexibility. And yet, achieving this balance is much easier in theory than it is in practice. Notably, as many have pointed out, the current economic model that dominates the development and deployment of digital technologies—that of privately owned and managed, for-profit corporate endeavors—seems antithetical to the democratic outcomes we have been seeking. In the next chapter, however, I show these fears to be somewhat misdirected. Using the now fully developed framework of democratic space, I show how re-centering a focus on the built environment leads to new strategies for building digital democracies—alternatives that show questions of ownership to be somewhat secondary to the spatial characteristics of boundaries, durability, and flexibility.

5

Democracy for Profit?

Control, Community, and the Role of Algorithms

In March 2016, Twitter announced a major change to the way users encountered content on the platform. For most of Twitter's first decade in existence, users who logged on to the site saw every tweet and retweet from the users they followed in reverse-chronological order, meaning the most recent tweets appeared first. The result was that, upon logging in, users were presented with a barrage of uncurated tweets, "thrust into the middle of dozens of unrelated, often insider-y conversations, and the good stuff required tedious scrolling to unearth."[1] And while the reverse chronological feed was beloved by Twitter "power users"—the "insiders" effectively having conversations on the site—the format could be off-putting to new visitors. Unable to gain or retain a wide range of users, the company also failed to turn a profit; by 2016, it was losing hundreds of millions of dollars annually.[2]

After trying—unsuccessfully—to introduce a number of changes to the platform intended to boost user engagement, and thus increase profit, the company played their "last remaining card" and debuted algorithmic sorting in March 2016.[3] Instead of the strict reverse-chronology that characterized Twitter's original configuration, the updated feed presented users with the "best" tweets first—meaning that tweets were displayed not in chronological order but sorted according to the user's algorithmically determined personalized preferences. In calculating which tweets to display more prominently for each user, the new algorithm incorporated several factors, including "a tweet's overall engagement"

[1] Will Oremus, "Twitter's New Order: Inside the Changes That Could Save Its Business—and Reshape Civil Discourse," *Slate*, March 5, 2017.

[2] Rob Davies, "Twitter Loses Ad Revenue despite Gaining 2 Million Users and Trump 'Boost,'" *The Guardian*, February 9, 2017.

[3] Alex Kantrowitz, "An Algorithmic Feed May Be Twitter's Last Remaining Card to Play," *BuzzFeed News*, June 29, 2015.

Designing for Democracy. Jennifer Forestal, Oxford University Press. © Oxford University Press 2022.
DOI: 10.1093/oso/9780197568750.003.0005

(the number of clicks, retweets, and favorites it received) and how often users engaged with the tweet's author.[4]

Twitter's introduction of algorithmic sorting adjusted users' experiences on the platform in two distinct ways. First, by factoring in certain individual considerations—like the amount of time a user spent reading an author's tweets and what kinds of attachments (like links, photos, or videos) that user tended to engage with—the new Twitter algorithm personalized users' Twitter feeds, showing returning users content similar to that which they had previously shown interest in. Second, by incorporating into the algorithm's calculations factors like a tweet's overall engagement, aggregated from users across the site, the new change also made it more likely that all users signing on to Twitter would see *the same* content.

The results were somewhat contradictory: not only were individual users presented with personalized content, but they were also gathered with other Twitter users, made to "congregate" around certain high-profile users or viral tweets—such as those from then-US president Donald Trump.[5] In addition to showing users content they would likely find more familiar and engaging, then, Twitter's new algorithm also funneled users into a smaller number of conversations happening on the platform, sustaining those conversations for longer periods of time and breaking up the "insider-y conversations" that had once dominated the site by including wider audiences.[6]

Many Twitter users were deeply unhappy with this change; decrying the "death of Twitter" with hashtags like #RIPtwitter immediately following the announcement, users raised concerns that the introduction of a sorting algorithm would suppress important new stories (as, for example, the Facebook algorithm did with the 2014 Ferguson protests) or else artificially elevate certain kinds of content (like Donald Trump's tweets) over others.[7] But despite these criticisms, Twitter's sorting algorithm seems to have had the intended effect. Indeed, the company reported that "[e]very possible engagement and attention metric went up" after the introduction of the algorithm, making it "one of [Twitter's] most impactful product launches."[8] Even as critics pointed out the potentially devastating social and political effects of algorithmic sorting, in other

[4] Oremus, "Twitter's New Order."

[5] Oremus, "Twitter's New Order."

[6] Oremus, "Twitter's New Order." One effect of the switch to the algorithmic feed is that Twitter users are following *more* accounts, making their timelines more varied. See Will Oremus, "How Twitter Solved One of Its Oldest Problems," *Medium: OneZero*, September 6, 2019.

[7] Kantrowitz, "An Algorithmic Feed May Be Twitter's Last Remaining Card to Play"; Gail Sullivan, "How Facebook and Twitter Control What You See about Ferguson," *Washington Post*, August 19, 2014.

[8] Oremus, "Twitter's New Order."

words, user engagement metrics continued to improve after Twitter introduced it; in 2018, the site not only showed increases in user retention but also turned a profit for the first time in years.[9]

The controversy over Twitter's introduction of algorithmic sorting is not unique in its juxtaposition of social good versus profit motive; the debate over Twitter's algorithm exemplifies much of the rhetoric around the role of algorithms in the digital built environment more generally. By feeding users more of the content they crave, algorithms (and the data that make them work) are seemingly the secret to the staggering Silicon Valley profit margins.[10] At the same time, as "black boxes," with inner workings often obscured by proprietary claims of intellectual property or requisite expertise in technical knowledge, algorithms can work on users in mysterious and potentially problematic ways.[11] We know, for example, that algorithms play to some of our worst inclinations: the algorithms on Facebook have been linked to the spread of disinformation, while the YouTube algorithms have been shown to contribute to radicalization.[12] By amplifying feelings of fear, anger, and outrage, algorithms can be quite dangerous for democratic politics—even as these same emotions keep us returning to, and staying on, the social media platforms that fuel them.[13]

Due to the sheer amount of information online, however, it seems algorithms are unavoidable; in 2019, by one account, users shared over 41 million messages *per minute*.[14] As curators of this vast amount of content, algorithms make it possible for us to have meaningful experiences with digital content on a scale that is otherwise unmanageable. This is especially true of the algorithms that power social media platforms like Facebook and Twitter, where content curation is "essential, constitutional, definitional."[15] Because they can have such outsized effects on our behavior, then, finding the "proper" role for these social media algorithms is crucial for the success of digital democratic communities.

[9] Jacob Kastrenakes, "Twitter Lost Users in the US Again, but It Finally Made a Profit," *The Verge*, February 8, 2018; Jacob Kastrenakes, "Twitter's User Numbers Are Growing Again," *The Verge*, April 25, 2018.

[10] Steve Kovach, "Alphabet Had More than $70 Billion in Market Cap Wiped Out, and It Says YouTube Is One of the Problems," *CNBC*, April 30, 2019.

[11] Frank Pasquale, *The Black Box Society: The Secret Algorithms That Control Money and Information* (Cambridge, MA: Harvard University Press, 2015).

[12] Emily Dreyfuss and Issie Lapowsky, "Facebook Is Changing News Feed (Again) to Stop Fake News," *WIRED*, April 10, 2019; Kevin Roose, "The Making of a YouTube Radical," *New York Times*, June 8, 2019; Siva Vaidhyanathan, *Antisocial Media: How Facebook Disconnects Us and Undermines Democracy* (New York: Oxford University Press, 2018).

[13] Laura Hazard Owen, "One Year In, Facebook's Big Algorithm Change Has Spurred an Angry, Fox News–Dominated—and Very Engaged!—News Feed," *NiemanLab*, March 15, 2019.

[14] J. Clement, "Social Sharing—Statistics & Facts," *Statista*, August 27, 2019.

[15] Tarleton Gillespie, *Custodians of the Internet: Platforms, Content Moderation, and the Hidden Decisions That Shape Social Media* (New Haven: Yale University Press, 2018), 21.

In addressing this challenge, scholars and practitioners have largely framed their concerns in terms of ownership and control. It is (proprietary) corporate ownership, opaque decision-making, and suspect profit motive, according to this argument, that leads platforms like Twitter to design and deploy algorithms that prioritize engagement metrics over more "democratic" values. We know, in other words, that showing users more extreme videos can lead to radicalization—with potentially violent consequences. But, because these extreme videos also lead users to stay on YouTube for longer periods of time, we should not expect Google (the company that owns YouTube) to design the platform's algorithm otherwise.[16] As a result, scholars and practitioners often propose solutions that work to turn control of these algorithms over to users, whether by increasing transparency of the algorithms' inner workings or else by changing corporate ownership structures more generally. Only if these questions of design are accountable to "the people," variously defined, it seems, can we be sure that social media—and the algorithms that make them work—are supportive of democracy.

Certainly, placing more control in the hands of users is a more democratic approach to managing the effects of social media algorithms. These algorithms are, after all, objects we share; moreover, they structure our perceptions and our behavior, profoundly shaping our relationships with other users and with the communities that may or may not form in the spaces they create.[17] Insofar as algorithms have this powerful influence on our collective experiences, creating spaces that induce us to act in ways we otherwise might not, they *should* be subject to the collective control that characterizes democratic politics.

Moreover, there is a long history of skepticism regarding the privatization of the spaces of collective experience. Political theorists have, for example, shared similar anxieties regarding private control of the parks and public squares that can serve as sites of community life in the physical world.[18] In the same way, because

[16] Zeynep Tufekci, "YouTube, the Great Radicalizer," *New York Times*, March 10, 2018.

[17] Adam D. I. Kramer, Jamie E. Guillory, and Jeffrey T. Hancock, "Experimental Evidence of Massive-Scale Emotional Contagion through Social Networks," *PNAS* 111, no. 29 (2014): 8788–90; Tarleton Gillespie, "Algorithmically Recognizable: Santorum's Google Problem, and Google's Santorum Problem," *Information, Communication and Society* 20, no. 1 (2017): 63–80; Tarleton Gillespie, "The Relevance of Algorithms," in *Media Technologies: Essays on Communication, Materiality, and Society*, ed. Tarleton Gillespie, Pablo J. Boczkowski, and Kirsten A. Foot (Cambridge, MA: MIT Press, 2014), 167–94.

[18] Marcel Hénaff and Tracy B. Strong, eds., *Public Space and Democracy* (Minneapolis: University of Minnesota Press, 2001); Benjamin Barber, "Malled, Mauled, and Overhauled: Arresting Suburban Sprawl by Transforming Suburban Malls into Usable Civic Space," in *Public Space and Democracy*, ed. Marcel Hénaff and Tracy B. Strong (Minneapolis: University of Minnesota Press, 2001), 201–20; Margaret Kohn, *Brave New Neighborhoods: The Privatization of Public Space* (New York: Routledge, 2004); John Parkinson, *Democracy and Public Space* (Oxford: Oxford University Press, 2012).

it can make decision-making about our common spaces even more opaque to users, private ownership and control of social media algorithms also disempowers citizens in ways that are certainly problematic for democratic politics.

This emphasis on private ownership and control suggests a compelling reason why companies build the algorithms they do: we simply cannot expect profit-driven corporations to prioritize any other values. This may be true (though this, too, is debatable[19]), but it is also true that simply examining who builds and why is insufficient. Indeed, the focus on private ownership and control obscures other significant ways that social media algorithms can work to undermine democratic politics—ways unattached to questions of ownership. Moreover, commonly proposed solutions to the problem of privately owned and operated social media algorithms can often amplify these overlooked negative effects. To be clear: I am not arguing that framing the problem of these algorithms in terms of corporate ownership and control is necessarily *wrong*—merely that it is *incomplete*.

Instead, as I have been arguing throughout this book, in order to fully understand the democratic effects of social media algorithms, we also must examine *how* they are constructed and whether they afford the central democratic practices of recognition, attachment, and experimentalism. We must evaluate these algorithms, in other words, using the three criteria of democratic space I outlined over the previous chapters. Does the algorithm create spaces that are clearly bounded, durable, and flexible? Does it, as a result, help democratic communities form, sustain, and improve themselves?

When we do examine the democratic implications of social media algorithms using these criteria, it becomes clear that scholars and practitioners' emphasis on ownership and control betrays a singular focus on *flexibility*—and its constituent parts, variety and malleability. Our current discussions around digital algorithms, in other words, tend to prioritize questions of what kinds of content individual users can see and how much control they individually exert over their social media feeds; these discussions do not, however, balance these concerns with similar questions regarding the formation and maintenance of *communities* within these algorithmically generated spaces.

As a result, commonly proposed solutions to the problems raised by social media algorithms tend to suggest changes that may increase the flexibility of these algorithms but do little to help bolster the durable boundaries that are also required for democratic politics. Indeed, as we will see, some of these strategies for increasing user control may even *exacerbate* the problems of forming and

[19] See, for example, Abraham A. Singer, *The Form of the Firm: A Normative Political Theory of the Corporation* (New York: Oxford University Press, 2018).

sustaining communities by further individualizing users' online experiences. By taking an incomplete picture of the (un)democratic effects of social media algorithms, in other words, we may be undermining our own goals.

To more clearly diagnose the democratic challenge of algorithms, in this chapter I use the three characteristics of democratic space—clear boundaries, durability, and flexibility—to evaluate the algorithms of two major social media platforms: Facebook and Twitter. Prominent critiques of these algorithms highlight users' lack of control over their feeds; high-profile tools, like Gobo, designed to "fix" this problem work to increase the algorithms' flexibility by making them more malleable. But while solutions like Gobo are effective at improving social media algorithms' flexibility because they place more control in the hands of *individual* users, they are nevertheless insufficient for building democratic communities.

Instead, I argue that while Facebook and Twitter's algorithms could certainly be more flexible, the more pressing concern in both cases is the algorithms' lack of clear boundaries. Both Facebook EdgeRank (the algorithm that curates one's News Feed) and the Twitter sorting algorithm gather users in durable ways, but these structures are invisible to users. This invisibility undermines users' ability to recognize their communities and form the political friendships necessary for democratic politics. But this need not be the case. Using the examples of Reddit and Mastodon, I show how we might redesign Facebook and Twitter to "democratize" their algorithms in ways that not only increase user control over their digital environments and the algorithms that structure them, but also help to generate and sustain the *communities* required to exert this control democratically. Ultimately, I argue that while questions of ownership and control are important, we must place these considerations alongside concerns about the design of the platforms and their effects on communities if we are to build digital environments supportive of democratic politics.

Democratic Politics and the Challenge of Algorithms

Algorithms are a ubiquitous and integral element of the digital built environment. Indeed, algorithmic curation is, as Tarleton Gillespie argues, the central "product" that social media platforms like Facebook and Twitter provide.[20] Just as the streets and sidewalks of a city grid helps us navigate a large and complex

[20] Gillespie, *Custodians of the Internet*, 41.

urban environment, so too do algorithms help us make sense of the mass of otherwise undifferentiated content on digital platforms.

Yet algorithms, especially those structuring social media sites, are often blamed for the worst effects of digital technologies. It is algorithms, after all, that create the filter bubbles and cybercascades which help extremist views spread quickly and go unchallenged; and it is largely through algorithms that biases are codified in digital environments.[21] As a set of "rules" that tell a computer how to perform a task—like sorting through Facebook posts—algorithms carry the same potential for negative consequences as do other forms of rule-making. But because they build these rules into the material environment of social media, shaping our behavior on these platforms in significant—but often invisible—ways, algorithms are often the central architectural elements in contemporary discussions of digital technologies and democracy, and with good reason.

Most scholars and practitioners accept the necessity of algorithms; as a result, criticisms are often traced back to questions of *ownership*, and the corresponding control exerted by corporations over the algorithms they own. Platforms like Facebook and Twitter, critics argue, "are trapped inside a market-based system that forces them to keep growing."[22] These private companies, motivated by profit, are viewed as incapable of ceding control over their algorithms to users or taking similar actions that would risk losing revenue.[23] For all of these thinkers, the "combination of self-serving impulses: namely, profit motives, the structural incentives inherent to the company's business model, and the one-sided ideology of its founders and some executives,"[24] means that it is unlikely that users can trust that the algorithms structuring user experiences on Facebook, Twitter, and platforms like them will support democratic politics. Instead, these thinkers argue, we should expect that privately owned digital spaces will continue to incentivize users to act as consumers and products rather than as democratic citizens.

Because much of the criticism of algorithms is framed as a problem of private ownership and control, critics have, in recent years, advanced a number of strategies for wresting control over prominent algorithms away from for-profit

[21] Cass R. Sunstein, *#Republic: Divided Democracy in the Age of Social Media* (Princeton, NJ: Princeton University Press, 2017); Cathy O'Neil, *Weapons of Math Destruction: How Big Data Increases Inequality and Threatens Democracy* (New York: Crown Publishers, 2016); Safiya Umoja Noble, *Algorithms of Oppression: How Search Engines Reinforce Racism* (New York: NYU Press, 2018).

[22] Kevin Roose, "Can Social Media Be Saved?," *New York Times*, March 28, 2018.

[23] Jodi Dean, "Communicative Capitalism: Circulation and the Foreclosure of Politics," *Cultural Politics* 1, no. 1 (2005): 51–74; Jodi Dean, *Democracy and Other Neoliberal Fantasies: Communicative Capitalism and Left Politics* (Durham, NC: Duke University Press, 2009).

[24] Zeynep Tufekci, "Why Zuckerberg's 14-Year Apology Tour Hasn't Fixed Facebook," *WIRED*, April 6, 2018.

companies and giving that control directly to users. Many of these suggestions involve a fundamental shift in corporate governance structures. Some, like Max Read and Ethan Zuckerman, have proposed the creation of a "public social media platform" owned and managed by the (US) government or a nonprofit, public-interest organization.[25] Others have suggested turning companies like Twitter into user-owned cooperatives.[26] Still others take a less wholesale approach to reform, suggesting regulations that would mandate more transparency and give users more control over their data and how it is used, or building browser plug-ins that help users customize their social media experiences.[27] What all of these recommendations have in common is that they provide new tools—whether in the form of policies or software—that redistribute control over algorithms from private corporations to users (or the governments and groups who ostensibly represent them).

In this section, I examine one such innovation in detail to show how an emphasis on ownership and control alone is insufficient for developing robust democratic communities in algorithmically curated digital environments. Gobo is an open-source social media aggregator created by researchers at MIT; it is a tool designed for the purpose of not only introducing a wider variety of content into users' social media feeds, but also making the algorithms that curate those feeds more malleable—more open to user control. But while Gobo does provide users with more variety and afford them more control over what content they see from the various social media feeds it compiles, it does little to help users form and sustain *communities* on the platforms it draws from. Gobo, in other words—like similar interventions—privileges flexibility above the durable boundaries that are also necessary characteristics of digital democratic environments.

But, as we know from the previous three chapters, a built environment that supports democracy requires all three characteristics—not just an increase in flexibility, but also the presence of clear and durable boundaries that afford users the ability to form and sustain communities with others in those spaces. Thus, while Gobo may effectively diversify and increase user control over what information they see on the popular social media platforms it "fixes," it is not clear that the tool can address other, perhaps more significant, barriers to democratic

[25] Ethan Zuckerman, "The Case for a Taxpayer-Supported Version of Facebook," *The Atlantic*, May 7, 2017; Max Read, "Twitter Is a Mall, so It's Going to Regulate Itself Like a Mall," *New York Magazine*, January 13, 2016; Ethan Zuckerman, "The Case for Digital Public Infrastructure," *Knight First Amendment Institute at Columbia University*, January 17, 2020, https://knightcolumbia.org/content/the-case-for-digital-public-infrastructure.

[26] Nathan Schneider, "Here's My Plan to Save Twitter: Let's Buy It," *The Guardian*, September 29, 2016.

[27] Zeynep Tufekci, "We Already Know How to Protect Ourselves from Facebook," *New York Times*, April 9, 2018; Louise Matsakis, "How to Take Back Your Facebook News Feed," *WIRED*, February 7, 2018.

community-building in these same spaces. As I will show, the algorithms that generate both the Facebook and Twitter feeds, while they gather users in durable ways, ultimately lack the clear boundaries that facilitate users' recognition of themselves as members of communities. And this lack of clear boundaries will not be fixed by an intervention like Gobo—or any other tool intended primarily to empower individual users. Rather, Gobo and other strategies like it may in fact be exacerbating this problem.

GOBO AND THE PROBLEM OF PRIORITIZING FLEXIBILITY

Originally created by a team at the MIT Media Lab's Center for Civic Media, Gobo (gobo.social) is "a social media aggregator with filters you control."[28] Intended as a "provocation" meant to "encourage platforms like Facebook to give their users more control over what they see," Gobo is a tool that allows users to directly manipulate the algorithms that govern their social media feeds and thus to see or hide content they otherwise might not due to automatic algorithmic suppression or amplification.[29] The goal of Gobo is thus to prioritize "personal control" and to be "plural in purpose";[30] it is one prominent example of a tool that "would let people control what they read on online platforms—helping them live up to their aspirations"[31] by navigating an increased variety of content from multiple platforms while ultimately maintaining control over their experiences. As a space that prioritizes variety and malleability, then, Gobo is designed to be a preeminently *flexible* environment.[32]

Importantly, Gobo is not a platform where users go to post and share content directly. Rather, Gobo "aggregates distributed feeds from users' multiple social media accounts and lets the users decide which ones to see."[33] Upon signing up for Gobo, users connect their individual accounts from supported platforms—as of 2021, that list included Facebook, Twitter, and Mastodon—and Gobo pulls content from these accounts and compiles it into a single feed on gobo.social (see Figure 5.1). The purpose of Gobo, then, is not to replace

[28] Ethan Zuckerman, "Who Filters Your News? Why We Built Gobo.Social," *Medium: MIT Media Lab*, November 16, 2017.

[29] Ethan Zuckerman, "Facebook Only Cares about Facebook," *The Atlantic*, January 27, 2018.

[30] Anna Woorim Chung, "Gobo: Your Social Media, Your Rules," *Civic Media Blog*, June 3, 2019.

[31] Zuckerman, "Facebook Only Cares about Facebook."

[32] In July 2020, the Gobo team announced that the research project was ending. While the (first version of the) tool is still available at gobo.social (as of August 2021), it is no longer updated regularly and is not affiliated with MIT or the Center for Civic Media.

[33] Rahul Bhargava et al., "Gobo: A System for Exploring User Control of Invisible Algorithms in Social Media," in *Proceedings of the 2019 Conference on Computer Supported Cooperative Work and Social Computing* (Austin, TX: ACM, 2019), 151–155.

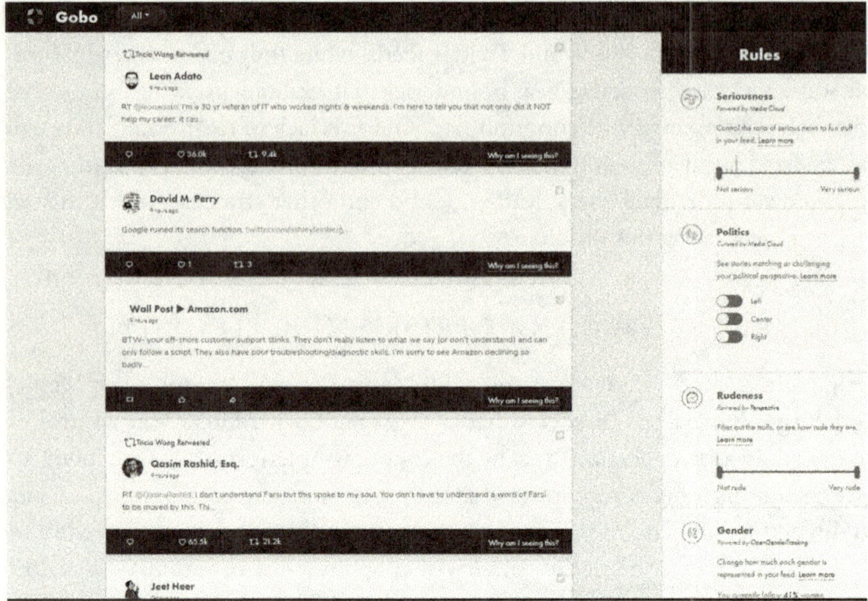

Figure 5.1 Example of the Gobo feed, with posts from both Twitter and Facebook visible. Photograph by author.

Facebook or Twitter; instead, it is intended to increase the "transparency and accountability of invisible algorithms"[34] powering these popular platforms. In so doing, Gobo is designed to increase the malleability of prominent algorithms—to afford users more control over their digital environments—with the goal of also introducing more variety into the spaces that are created.

As a tool for users to take a more active role in shaping their online experiences by exerting control over the digital spaces in which they find themselves, Gobo's main emphasis is on increasing the malleability of popular algorithms. It does so by providing users with "meta and micro level controls" they can use to override the Facebook or Twitter algorithms and filter content from those platforms to suit their own preferences.[35] Unlike the "top-secret black box" algorithms that power Facebook and Twitter, then, Gobo's developers "made it an open box where you can reach in and set the sliders and experiment."[36] To that end, Gobo provides users with a number of filters, called "rules," with which to sort and display content (see Figure 5.2). Using these sliders, Gobo users directly control the content they see, both "'filtering-out' i.e. hiding content

[34] Bhargava et al., "Gobo."

[35] Bhargava et al., "Gobo."

[36] Ethan Zuckerman, quoted in Rachel Metz, "Social Networks Are Broken. This Man Wants to Fix Them.," *MIT Technology Review*, February 9, 2018.

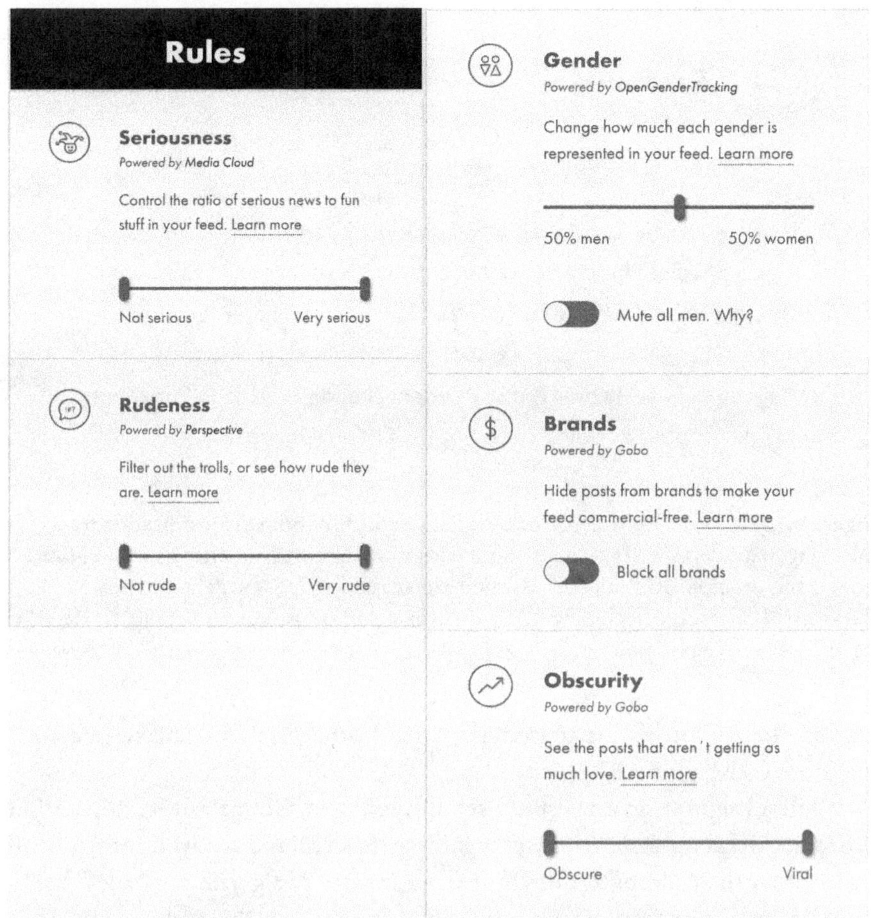

Figure 5.2 Examples of Gobo's rules, including "Seriousness," "Rudeness," "Gender," "Brands," and "Obscurity." For each rule, users can experiment with controlling the content they see in their feeds. Photograph by author.

from the feed and 'filtering-in' i.e. adding content from accounts they do not already follow."[37]

With the "obscurity" rule, for example, users are presented with a sliding scale. Users can, at one extreme, choose to see only content that has a certain number of shares or likes—posts that go "viral." At the other extreme, users can choose to see only those posts with very few shares or likes—adding variety to their feed by displaying content that may have been suppressed by, for example, an algorithm like Facebook's that privileges virality. Similar rules exist for tone (e.g., seriousness, rudeness), gender, politics, and brands; for each of these

[37] Bhargava et al., "Gobo."

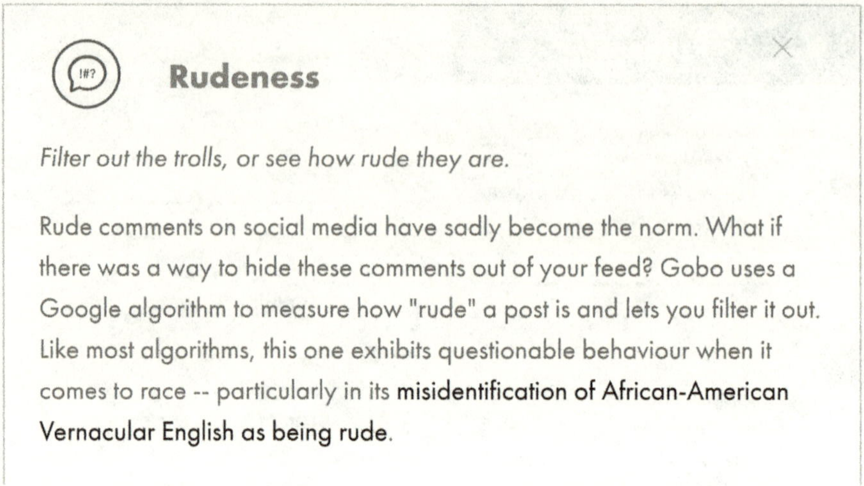

Rudeness

Filter out the trolls, or see how rude they are.

Rude comments on social media have sadly become the norm. What if there was a way to hide these comments out of your feed? Gobo uses a Google algorithm to measure how "rude" a post is and lets you filter it out. Like most algorithms, this one exhibits questionable behaviour when it comes to race -- particularly in its misidentification of African-American Vernacular English as being rude.

Figure 5.3 For each of its rules, Gobo explains to the user both the justification for including that rule, as well as details about what it will and will not filter and *how*. Notice how, in this example of "Rudeness," Gobo's explanation includes insight into how "rudeness" is measured, including its biases against African-American Vernacular English (AAVE). Photograph by author.

"rules," Gobo explains the underlying logic so that users can make informed decisions (see Figure 5.3).

While all algorithms consist of a set of rules, then, Gobo's novel intervention is to place decision-making power regarding these rules directly in the hands of *users*, rather than computers or companies. Instead of algorithmic "rules" being set by private corporations who seek to keep users on these platforms for as long as possible, Gobo encourages users to take a more active role in curating their online experiences by directly selecting these rules, seeing the results, and experimenting with different combinations. By creating algorithmic environments that users are more easily able to control, then, Gobo effectively works to increase the *malleability* of these algorithms.

In providing users with a way to directly control what content they see, however, Gobo is also designed to induce users to increase the *variety* of content they are exposed to. For each post that appears on one's feed, Gobo explains why the displayed content was selected; it describes "how each rule interpreted the post and reasons why it was included in the feed . . . [as well as] the mechanism and tools used to power each rule."[38] More important, for each configuration of rules a user sets, Gobo also shows users how many posts are hidden and what rule caused them to be hidden (see Figure 5.4). By rendering visible content which is

[38] Bhargava et al., "Gobo."

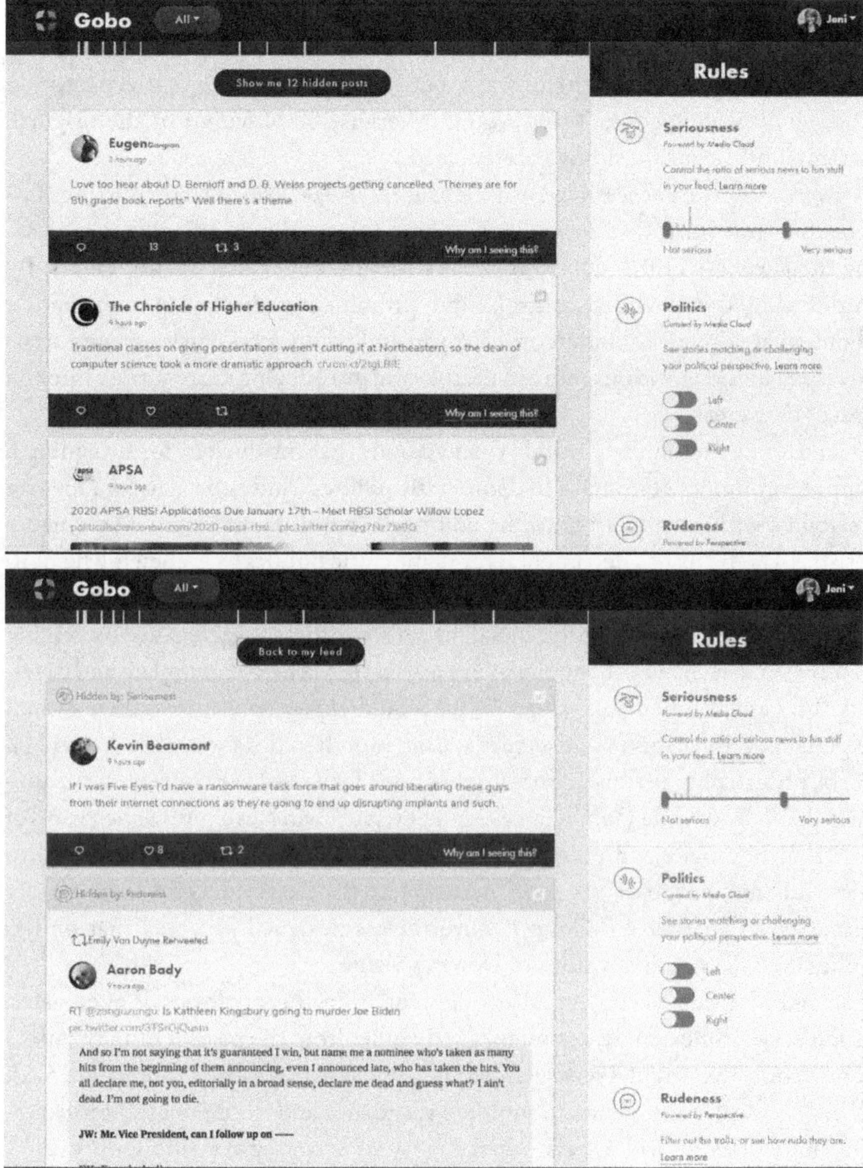

Figure 5.4 Example of how Gobo reveals previously hidden posts. The top image is the screen displayed once a user sets certain rules in place; notice how the resulting feed displays the number of posts "hidden" at the top of the screen. Clicking on the "Show me 12 hidden posts" button will reveal to users what content was hidden by the configuration of rules they set (see bottom image). Photographs by author.

otherwise invisible in their Facebook and Twitter feeds, Gobo not only reveals important information that helps users exert control over their environment in more informed and meaningful ways, but it also reintroduces variety into the feed, by displaying content that would otherwise be obscured by the original, automatically algorithmically curated, feed.

By making more accessible both the causes ("rules") and effects (missing content) of algorithmic decision-making, Gobo is exceedingly effective at increasing the *flexibility* of the algorithms that structure our digital environments. By introducing user-friendly controls and prominently displaying information about what content is hidden or displayed and why, Gobo illustrates one strategy for making algorithms more malleable and introducing more variety into the spaces they create.

And yet, as we know, flexibility is necessary but insufficient for designing a built environment conducive to democratic politics. And a too-narrow focus on flexibility, without attending to the additional requisite environmental characteristics, can be just as detrimental for democratic politics as eschewing flexibility entirely. We can see this at work with Gobo. Gobo is exceedingly effective at improving the flexibility of the social media algorithms it aggregates. By placing control in users' hands, the tool makes it easier for users to manipulate and diversify their environments in ways that we would expect to improve their overall experiences. But Gobo is an *individualistic* tool. It cedes control to individual users, prioritizing "*personal* control" over one's feeds and the content that populates them. And while Gobo's development team advocates a pluralistic vision of digital technologies, with multiple, decentralized platforms that would "exist to serve different purposes"[39]—akin, in theory, to the Deweyan Great Community discussed in chapter 4—Gobo is nevertheless designed in a way that undermines the *collective* dimensions of Dewey's vision.

Notably, Gobo decontextualizes content from the platforms it aggregates. Gobo erases, for example, comments and replies from the posts it displays; users can see only the original posts that would appear in one's feeds (see Figure 5.5). While a tweet might generate multiple responses and quote tweets, for example, none of these will appear when the tweet is aggregated into Gobo. Thus, while individual users can exert more control over what they see, they lose the ability to interact *with others* in response to that content without leaving Gobo and returning to the original platform—where the post may not appear due to the original algorithmic rules.[40] Gobo, in other words, is focused primarily on

[39] Chung, "Gobo."

[40] This spatial displacement of original posts and the comments they generate is exacerbated by a similar temporal displacement; because Gobo pulls content from external sites, it often lags behind what users would see if they logged into, for example, Facebook directly.

Figure 5.5 Tweet on Gobo (top) compared to the same tweet on Twitter (bottom). Notice how the tweet's engagement—its number of "likes" and "replies"—is visible on Gobo, but without the content. The conversations that unfold in response to the original tweet (visible in the bottom image) do not appear when the tweet is imported into the space of Gobo. Photographs by author.

changing how individual users manage what original posts they see; in so doing, however, it draws users out of the collective engagements that occur with and around that content.

Though it dramatically and effectively increases users' ability to experiment with and improve their individual online experiences, in other words, Gobo ultimately fails to address the other two fundamental practices of democratic politics: forming and sustaining *communities*. Indeed, by drawing users away from the communities (however latent) on these original platforms, Gobo's emphasis on individual control undermines the possibilities for the kind of *collective* action that marks democratic politics. By individualizing control and decontextualizing content, Gobo fixes one problem (the lack of user control) while exacerbating another (the lack of community).

FACEBOOK, TWITTER, AND THE LACK OF COMMUNITY

By emphasizing "personal control" and "plurality of purpose," Gobo addresses concerns over algorithms by focusing on their flexibility. The problem, as the Gobo team frames it, is the lack of transparency around corporate algorithmic decision-making and the corresponding lack of control users can exert over the algorithms that structure their social media experiences. Their solution, then, is to increase the flexibility of these algorithms by empowering users with more information and decision-making capability—to make the algorithms more malleable so that users can increase the variety of content they see.

This is, as I have been arguing, a laudable goal. But it is insufficient for ensuring that algorithms help support democratic politics, and for two reasons. First, by focusing solely on flexibility, Gobo and similar strategies that emphasize users' control over content overlook other necessary elements of democratic politics—namely, forming and sustaining democratic communities in these digital spaces. Second, and following, approaches like Gobo's are often centered on *individual* users—they focus on personal control rather than the collective action that characterizes democratic politics. And, as a result of this focus on individual control, scholars and practitioners have largely overlooked another challenge that algorithms pose for practicing democratic politics in digital spaces: that of forming communities in the first place.

As the collective management of common affairs, however, democratic politics is a *communal* activity. Solutions like Gobo that focus on increasing individual control are thus working on the wrong level of analysis. Citizens, as we know, must first recognize themselves as members of a community (and, later, develop attachments to it) if they are to engage in the cooperative work of democratic politics. Any evaluation of the democratic potential of algorithms like those of Facebook or Twitter must, therefore, not only address their effects on individual users but must also reckon with their ability (or lack thereof) to afford the kind of recognition that grounds political friendships and, ultimately, sustains collective action. To the extent that algorithms fail to help facilitate this recognition, we can rightfully say that they undermine democracy just as much as if users lack control over them.

Yet the algorithms powering some of our most prominent platforms—like those of Facebook and Twitter—do precisely that. There can be no doubt that these algorithms act as durable structures which gather users together; in effect, the algorithms for each platform select the "audience" for each piece of content shared on the site. Yet, crucially, users are unable to recognize themselves as members of those audiences—the boundaries around these communities of interest are invisible to their members.

The algorithms behind both Facebook and Twitter work to personalize users' feeds in similar ways; they each select and display content like that content users have already shown interest in. As a result, these algorithms provide every user with a unique configuration of content; they do little, however, to signal to users what they have in common with others on the platform. Facebook and Twitter users cannot, for example, see who else sees the content they do, except in looking at those who have "liked," commented, or otherwise visibly engaged with it. And this is true not only of others' content, but also of one's own. Though Twitter, for example, does share metrics for the "reach" of one's tweet (e.g., showing the total number of "impressions" and "engagements"), it is impossible for any user to identify precisely *which* other users the sorting algorithm has selected to be part of their audiences (see Figure 5.6).[41]

For both platforms, though users see content they have shown interest in, and though they see that content and the users producing it repeatedly, users have no sense of who else shares their interests. Though the Facebook and Twitter algorithms do gather users into communities of interest, in other words, they do so based on a set of criteria that are opaque to end-users; missing are the clear boundaries necessary to remind users of their entanglements with others by highlighting the shared interests that form the foundation of political friendships.

It is important to note, however, that while users cannot easily identify and communicate as members of communities of interest on Facebook and Twitter, there can be no doubt that these communities exist. Indeed, both companies' profit models are based on advertisers paying handsomely for the

[41] Facebook shares similar information with users regarding the advertisements that appear in one's feed (e.g., the "Why Am I Seeing This Ad?" button); it also used to show users why they were seeing certain content from other users—but as of the 2020 Facebook redesign, this is no longer an option. Moreover, even when Facebook did make it easy for users to see *why* certain content appeared in their Feeds, it still failed to signal to users *who else* saw that same content.

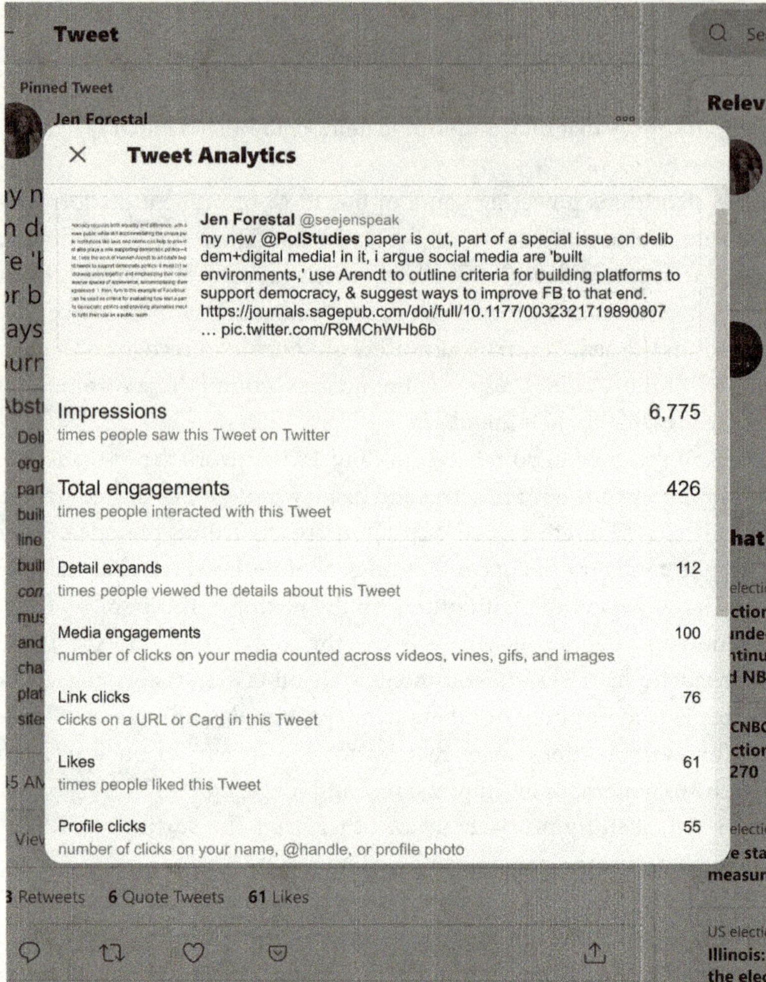

Figure 5.6 Example of "Tweet Analytics," which reveals a tweet's engagement metrics to that tweet's author. Notice how the author can see *how many* users saw, clicked, and liked the tweet, but they cannot see *who*. Photograph by author.

opportunity to identify and sell to the latent communities that are present in these spaces. Advertisers on Facebook, for example, can target groups as specific as "Individuals that are frequent transactor at lower cost department or dollar store," "Hungarian sausages," and "Breastfeeding in Public"[42]—while members

[42] Julia Angwin, Madeleine Varner, and Ariana Tobin, "Facebook Enabled Advertisers to Reach 'Jew Haters,'" *ProPublica*, September 14, 2017; Ariana Tobin and Jeremy B. Merrill, "Facebook Is Letting Job Advertisers Target Only Men," *ProPublica*, September 18, 2018; Julia Angwin, Surya Mattu, and Terry Parris Jr., "Facebook Doesn't Tell Users Everything It Really Knows about Them," *ProPublica*, December 27, 2016.

of these groups are prevented from knowing who else, or even how many others, share their interests and are thus shown the same content.

The result is that while all Facebook and Twitter users ostensibly share a common experience—in that Facebook and Twitter work the same way for (and on) us all—the platforms nevertheless fail to facilitate our *recognition* that the content we see in these spaces is shared with others. And in obscuring our recognition of the interests we share, these invisible boundaries decrease the salience of the collective consequences of one's activity on the platform. Instead, users are more likely to think of their actions in these digital spaces in isolation and are less likely to act collectively to manage their consequences.

Indeed, we can see these effects in users' behavior—or lack thereof. Almost two-thirds of users leave decisions about their collective interests up to Facebook rather than taking that responsibility upon themselves.[43] Likewise, most users express uncertainty or ignorance about Twitter's decision-making structures.[44] Because they cannot easily identify others they share interests with on these platforms, individual Facebook and Twitter users are ill-equipped to identify, discuss, and direct the effects of the algorithms that structure their experiences on the platforms.[45] Instead, users of both platforms are induced to focus on their own narrow individual concerns.

By designing algorithms that gather users with invisible boundaries, Facebook and Twitter organize their users in ways that largely obscure their memberships in—and obligations toward—the different communities that exist on the platform; instead, users are made responsible for curating their own *personalized* experience on the sites. These platforms are all designed, in other words, to facilitate users' individualism—encouraging users to withdraw into their own interests and eschew the wider communities of which they are a part.[46] By making it difficult for citizens to recognize their membership in any number of communities on the site, in other words, the algorithms that organize Facebook and Twitter render the collective action of democratic politics all but impossible.[47]

[43] Aaron Smith, "Many Facebook Users Don't Understand How the Site's News Feed Works," *Pew Research Center*, September 5, 2018.

[44] Nicholas Proferes, "Information Flow Solipsism in an Exploratory Study of Beliefs about Twitter," *Social Media + Society* 3, no. 1 (2017): 1–17.

[45] See also Jennifer Forestal, "Constructing Digital Democracies: Facebook, Arendt, and the Politics of Design," *Political Studies* 69, no. 1 (2021): 26–44.

[46] Will Oremus, "Who Controls Your Facebook Feed," *Slate*, January 3, 2016.

[47] Moreover, there is evidence that users are seeking to fill precisely this gap. Indeed, on Twitter, when users do attempt to exert "control over algorithmic processes," they are doing so in order to "draw boundaries around the communities they are building." See Jenna Burrell et al., "When Users Control the Algorithms: Values Expressed in Practices on the Twitter Platform," in *Proceedings of the 2019 ACM on Human-Computer Interaction* (New York: ACM, 2019), 1–20.

And yet, as should now be clear, this loss of collective control is not solely a problem of flexibility. Indeed, both Facebook and Twitter have made moves in recent years to give individual users more control over what they see, by choosing between, for example, different kinds of algorithmic sorting options.[48] Yet these changes do little to address the underlying challenge for the possibility of *democratic* politics on these platforms. Democracy is, as I have been arguing, about exerting collective control over shared objects and interests. But the Facebook and Twitter algorithms prevent the formation of these collectives in the first place; there is no "community" that can exert this control.

Moreover, there is no reason to think that making these platforms public—of turning over control to users—would in itself do anything to address the lack of visible boundaries, and the corresponding lack of community, in these spaces. Instead, increasing the flexibility of Facebook or Twitter without also imposing clearer boundaries might have the effect of exacerbating users' individualism. As was the case with Gobo, this kind of solution would work to increase *individual* user control without implementing the structures required to ensure that control is *collectively* exercised.

More than private ownership or corporate control, then, it is the design of these algorithmically generated spaces to which we must attend when evaluating their democratic potential. Indeed, by evaluating Facebook and Twitter holistically—with all three characteristics of a democratic built environment in mind—it becomes clear that an analytic focus on user control tends to overemphasize the role of flexibility in these spaces. The result is an incomplete diagnosis of the democratic dangers posed by the algorithms powering Facebook and Twitter, as well as a somewhat problematic overestimation of the effectiveness of solutions like Gobo.

But if increasing user control alone is not necessarily a productive strategy for building democratic spaces, then how should we proceed? In the next section, I turn to two models of democratic space, Reddit and Mastodon, to discuss strategies for constructing algorithms (and social media platforms more generally) that may be more supportive of democratic communities. Using these platforms as examples of how to balance all three elements of democratic space, I then suggest changes that Facebook and Twitter might introduce to make their platforms more supportive of democratic politics.

[48] Emily Dreyfuss, "Twitter's Chronological Timeline Will Save Us from Ourselves," *WIRED*, September 18, 2018; Jon Porter, "Twitter Is Making It Easier to Toggle between Latest and Top Tweets," *The Verge*, November 1, 2018.

Democratizing Algorithms

The algorithms powering Facebook and Twitter excel at creating environments that keep individual users engaged on these platforms for longer periods of time—thus generating revenue for the companies who own them. But, as many have argued, this engagement often comes at the cost of our social and political well-being. Highlighting the opacity of algorithmic decision-making, and the ways that algorithms disempower—even dominate—users, scholars and practitioners have suggested mechanisms, like Gobo, for improving these algorithms by providing tools with which users can (re)assert control over their online experiences.

In narrowing our focus to user control (and the question of ownership, which often serves as its proxy), however, these recommendations approach the democratic implications of algorithmic design primarily from the perspective of flexibility; algorithms are, in this view, evaluated for their democratic potential based on the diversity of the content they show (their variety) or the amount of control users can exert over that display (their malleability). These are important considerations, to be sure. But they do not exhaust the needs of democratic politics. Indeed, as we have seen, when we take a holistic view of democracy's environmental requirements, it becomes clear that Facebook and Twitter's algorithms' lack of flexibility is not the only—or perhaps even the most pressing—barrier to the possibility of democratic politics on these platforms. As they largely work to isolate users from one another by obscuring the boundaries that draw users together and structure their behavior, these algorithms ultimately make it difficult for users to recognize themselves and their peers as members of a shared community and thus form the political friendships that ground democratic action.

But what is the alternative, if not increasing individual user control by way of interventions like Gobo? Given the integral role of algorithms in structuring our online experiences—making it possible, for example, to sort through the vast amounts of content posted online each day—it seems unlikely that we can jettison them entirely. The challenge, then, is to design social media platforms with algorithms that can continue to provide users with a way of making sense of staggering amounts of content while also supporting the core practices of democratic politics: the collective work of forming, sustaining, and improving communities.

In this section, I discuss two such examples of well-designed democratic platforms in order to identify strategies Facebook and Twitter might use to improve their own spaces. As we will see, Reddit and Mastodon negotiate the criteria of democratic space differently; they nevertheless both exhibit all three characteristics of a built environment supportive of democratic politics. Because Reddit was discussed in more detail in chapter 4, I will generally confine the discussion here to Reddit's use of algorithms. The second example, Mastodon (an open-source Twitter-like platform), I discuss more broadly. While Mastodon does not, by default, use a sorting algorithm—instead it generally displays content in reverse-chronological order—it is characterized by a federated structure that nonetheless helps users sort through content in a meaningful way. By examining both, then, we can gain deeper insight into how to build (algorithmically powered) digital democratic spaces.

These examples are not exhaustive; there are any number of ways developers can build democratic environments using digital tools. In providing this analysis, then, I seek to highlight how a holistic view—thinking of how to support democratic *communities*, not just increasing individual control—might shift our thinking regarding a contemporary problem like algorithms and how to manage them. I conclude with a discussion of how Facebook and Twitter might incorporate insights from Reddit and Mastodon to democratize their platforms while still retaining their (corporate-controlled) use of sorting algorithms.

REDDIT: FOR-PROFIT DEMOCRATIC SPACE

Reddit, as discussed in chapter 4, exhibits all three characteristics of a democratic built environment. Subreddits provide clear boundaries that demarcate the limits of each community on the platform. The result is that, at any given time, the spaces of Reddit signal to users both what they share (the topic of interest) and with whom they share it (the other members of the subreddit). Moreover, these subreddits persist; once created, it is difficult to erase a subreddit from existence. As a result of this durability, it is easier for redditors to form attachments to their specific subreddit communities as well as the wider Reddit community as a whole.

Given its clear and durable boundaries, we would expect Reddit to be a space that would support the formation of enduring and self-conscious communities. And there is evidence that it has precisely this effect. Unlike Facebook or Twitter, regular users of Reddit have a clear collective identity. Self-styled "redditors," a name explicitly designating their membership in the platform's community, these users also regularly engage in instances of collective action. Redditors have, for example, a number of annual gift exchanges, in which strangers—over 200,000 last year alone—share their addresses and send gifts to one another.[49]

[49] "Eight Things to Know about Redditgifts," *redditgifts*, n.d., https://www.redditgifts.com/about/; Greg Kumparak, "Reddit Acquires Fan-Made Secret Santa Site, RedditGifts," *TechCrunch*, August 23, 2011; Rachel Feltman, "How Redditgifts Is Making Money on Altruism," *Quartz*, July 12, 2013.

They have held competitions between subreddits to raise money for charity[50] and organized themselves to work together to, for instance, ensure a button is pushed every 60 seconds[51] or to design a (hate-symbol-free!) collage on a blank canvas.[52] And this collective action also extends to more obviously political issues. Redditors have effectively coordinated efforts at politically motivated trolling,[53] hosted collective protests aimed at Reddit's corporate governance,[54] organized boycotts in response to concerns over US policies like SOPA/PIPA,[55] and collectively called for Reddit administrators to take more concrete action to address concerns of racism and hate speech on the platform.[56]

And Reddit's algorithm reinforces this collective identity and action. Like Twitter and Facebook, Reddit uses an algorithm to gather and sort content for its "front page"—the home screen for any given Reddit user. Like the Facebook and Twitter feeds, the Reddit front page is personalized; users see content tailored specifically to them. Unlike Facebook and Twitter, however, Reddit's front page is *not individualized*. Instead, the content populating redditors' feeds is always presented in the collective context of the subreddits they subscribe to.

When a user logs in to Reddit, their front page is generated by an algorithm that displays one post from 100 subreddits randomly selected from a user's

[50] Plet Levy, "Christians and Atheists Square Off in Online Battle to Raise Money for Charity," *HuffPost*, December 16, 2010.

[51] Joshua Bleiberg and Darrell M. West, "Have You Pressed the Button?," *Brookings TechTank Blog*, April 27, 2015; Timothy B. Lee, "The Button: The Fascinating Social Experiment Driving Reddit Crazy," *Vox*, April 14, 2015.

[52] Andrew Marantz, "Reddit and the Struggle to Detoxify the Internet," *New Yorker*, March 19, 2018; Clayton Purdom, "Reddit Gave Its Users Something to Fight Over besides Anime and Cucks," *The AV Club*, April 3, 2017; Sam Machkovech, "Did Reddit's April Fool's Gag Solve the Issue of Online Hate Speech?," *Ars Technica*, April 3, 2017.

[53] Claudia Flores-Saviaga, Brian C. Keegan, and Saiph Savage, "Mobilizing the Trump Train: Understanding Collective Action in a Political Trolling Community," in *Proceedings of the 12th International Conference on Web and Social Media (ICWSM 2018)* (Stanford, CA: AAAI 2018), 82–91.

[54] J. Nathan Matias, "Going Dark: Social Factors in Collective Action Against Platform Operators in the Reddit Blackout," in *Proceedings of the 2016 CHI Conference on Human Factors in Computing Systems* (New York: ACM, 2016), 1138–51.

[55] Richard Mills and Adam Fish, "A Computational Study of How and Why Reddit.Com Was an Effective Platform in the Campaign against SOPA," in *Proceedings of the 2015 International Conference on Social Computing and Social Media* (Cham: Springer, 2015), 229–41.

[56] Kaitlyn Tiffany, "Reddit Is Finally Facing Its Legacy of Racism," *The Atlantic*, June 12, 2020; DubTeeDub, "Open Letter to Steve Huffman and the Board of Directors of Reddit, Inc—If You Believe in Standing Up to Hate and Supporting Black Lives, You Need to Act," *Reddit, r/AgainstHateSubreddits*, June 8, 2020, https://www.reddit.com/r/AgainstHateSubreddits/comments/gyyqem/open_letter_to_steve_huffman_and_the_board_of/; Pro_creator, "We Have a Racist User Problem and Reddit Won't Take Action," *Reddit, r/Blackladies*, August 25, 2014, https://www.reddit.com/r/blackladies/comments/2ejg1b/we_have_a_racist_user_problem_and_reddit_wont/.

Figure 5.7 Example screenshot of Reddit's "Front Page" (sorted by "Hot"). Notice how each post's collective context is made prominent in the display: the subreddit's name is shown first, and in bold, while the handle of the individual user who posted is secondary (in an unbolded, lighter gray font). Photograph by author.

subscriptions.[57] While each user's feed might be different, then, since each user subscribes to their own selection of subreddits and the algorithm will randomly select from that set, the subreddit structure always remains prominent. This collective context is reinforced by the front page display; while it is populated by individual posts, these posts always feature the name of the subreddit more prominently than that of the individual users who posted (see Figure 5.7). This foregrounding of subreddits renders visible the clear boundaries that help users recognize themselves—and content on their "front pages"—as belonging to a community, even with the use of a personalized algorithm.

[57] Reddit, "Some of My Subreddits Keep Disappearing. Why?," *Reddit Help*, n.d., https://www.reddithelp.com/en/categories/using-reddit/frontpage-and-subscriptions/some-my-subreddits-keep-disappearing-why.

Importantly, however, Reddit is not just a communal space; it is also a *democratic* one. In addition to clear and durable boundaries, as we saw in chapter 4, Reddit also exhibits extraordinary flexibility. With hundreds of thousands of subreddits, the site provides a variety of experiences for users;[58] each subreddit, moreover, can reshape the rules and design of that subreddit to fit their communal needs. And this flexibility is also evident in Reddit's algorithm. Though all visitors to Reddit are presented with an algorithmically curated front page, there are multiple ways to view this content. Users who have logged into the site are presented with a front page populated by the algorithmically generated selection of subreddits described earlier. For new and logged-out users, however, r/popular is default; any post that collects enough votes—from almost any subreddit on the platform—will appear visible to all users in r/popular.[59] But all users—logged in or not—can also choose to view content on Reddit via r/all, which displays content from all subreddits, with or without a subscription.[60] Moreover, for each of these aggregations (r/all, r/popular, and the customized front page), redditors can choose how they would like to see that content sorted. Selecting "hot," "new," "top," or "rising," for example, would each configure content on one's front page differently—and users can easily toggle back and forth between these choices (see Figure 5.8).[61]

[58] "Reddit by the Numbers," *Reddit*, 2018, https://www.redditinc.com/. The site boasted 138,000 communities as of November 2017.

[59] simbawulf, "Introducing r/Popular," *Reddit, r/Announcements*, February 15, 2017, https://www.reddit.com/r/announcements/comments/5u9pl5/introducing_rpopular/. Unlike r/all, certain subreddits are filtered out of r/popular, including "NSWF and 18+ communities," "communities that have opted out of r/all," and "a handful of subreddits that users consistently filter out of their r/all page." "Consistently filtered" subreddits include "for example, subreddits that are large and dedicated to specific games . . . as well as specific sports, and narrowly focused politically related subreddits, etc." See simbawulf, "Comment on 'Introducing r/Popular,'" *Reddit, r/Announcements*, February 15, 2017, https://www.reddit.com/r/announcements/comments/5u9pl5/introducing_rpopular/ddsczx1/.

[60] simbawulf, "Introducing r/Popular."

[61] These options have different "rules" for what content is displayed. "Top" shows users posts with high scores based on upvotes and comments; "rising" does the same but looks only at posts from within a short period of time. "Controversial" shows users posts based on their ratio of up- and downvotes, while "hot" "takes the log10 of the score and weighs it against 12-hour periods. Ie. to keep the same place a post must increase its score by ×10 every 12 hours." See yawkat, "Comment on 'How Does "Hot" vs "Best" vs "controversial" vs "Rising" Work? Is the Algorithm Known, and Does It Depend on Engagement with a Sub, as Opposed to Simply Whether You Are Apart of It or Not?,'" *Reddit, r/TheoryofReddit*, May 17, 2019, https://www.reddit.com/r/TheoryOfReddit/comments/bpmd3x/how_does_hot_vs_best_vscontroversial_vs_rising/envijlj/.

With more sorting options than what is provided by Facebook and Twitter, redditors are able to exert a greater amount of control over the kind of content that populates their feeds than are users of these other platforms. And while decisions about Reddit's design, including the inner working of its algorithms, are increasingly opaque, this need not be the case.[62] Indeed, Reddit was, for almost a decade, open-source, meaning that anyone could see the underlying structure of the algorithm.[63] And even today Reddit employees maintain an open dialogue with redditors, through spaces like r/changelog ("Official information from Reddit, Inc. on minor updates and bug fixes applied to Reddit"), r/announcements ("Official announcements from Reddit, Inc."), r/modnews

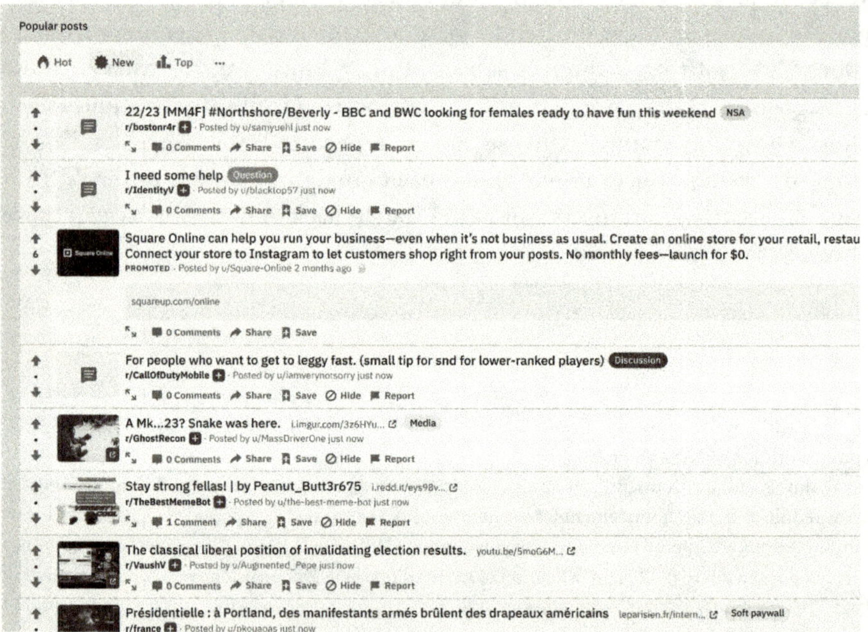

Figure 5.8 Examples of different algorithmic sorting options for Reddit's "Front Page." Toggling between the "Hot" (See Figure 5.7), "New" (above), "Top" (top, opposing page), and "Rising" (bottom, opposing page) sorting options will present users with different content. Photographs by author.

[62] Arielle Pardes, "The Inside Story of Reddit's Redesign," *WIRED*, April 2, 2018.

[63] Shuffman56, "Reddit Goes Open Source," *Reddit Blog*, June 17, 2008, https://redditblog.com/2008/06/17/reddit-goes-open-source/; Keyser Sosa, "An Update on the State of the Reddit/RedditandReddit/Reddit-Mobile Repositories," *Reddit, r/Changelog*, September 1, 2017, https://www.reddit.com/r/changelog/comments/6xfyfg/an_update_on_the_state_of_the_redditreddit_and/.

Figure 5.8 Continued

("An official community for announcements from Reddit, Inc. pertaining to moderation"), and r/ideasfortheadmins ("This subreddit is for **reddit-wide ideas for improvement**"). In each of these spaces, we see engaged discussion with redditors regarding the decisions that shape their experiences on the platform—a collective engagement that has no parallel on Facebook or Twitter.

Crucially, however, we cannot fully explain Reddit's democratic potential by focusing solely on its ownership structure. Like Facebook and Twitter, Reddit is privately owned (though not publicly traded); it is currently funded by over twenty private investors, from investment firms to individuals.[64] Yet the platform hosts more robust democratic engagements than do Facebook or Twitter, despite their similar ownership structures. And while Reddit has, in recent years, made moves that might undermine its flexibility by taking control away from users, it nevertheless continues to host robust communities that are more actively engaged in collectively managing their environments than are users on other major social media platforms. The effects of this more democratic environment are evident, in other words, as redditors have vocally, collectively, and effectively pushed back against Reddit's top-down decisions in ways that are unparalleled on Facebook and Twitter. This is, I argue, due in no small part to Reddit's design; the site is marked by clear boundaries, durable spaces, and flexibility, and the platform's algorithm reflects these characteristics as well. This design, more than the platform's ownership structure, is what supports democratic politics in its spaces.

MASTODON: DECENTRALIZED DEMOCRACIES

Reddit is one model of a democratic digital environment. But it is not the only one; indeed, Reddit's democratic value is often obscured by its reputation as a "cesspool."[65] Instead, when scholars and practitioners discuss democratic social media, the platform that is often invoked is Mastodon.[66] Mastodon is one of the most successful open-source social networking sites

[64] Kurt Wagner, "Reddit Raised $200 Million in Funding and Is Now Valued at $1.8 Billion," *Recode*, July 31, 2017; Aparajita Saxena, "Reddit Valued at $3 Billion after Raising $300 Million in Latest Funding Round," *Reuters*, February 11, 2019. Co-founder and CEO Steve Huffman is largely in charge of major decisions regarding the company's direction.

[65] Bryan Clark, "Study Reveals Reddit Isn't as Big a Cesspool as You Thought. But It's Still a Cesspool," *The Next Web*, March 20, 2018.

[66] Margaret Rhodes, "Like Twitter but Hate the Trolls? Try Mastodon," *WIRED*, April 13, 2017; Casey Newton, "Mastodon.Social Is an Open-Source Twitter Competitor That's Growing like Crazy," *The Verge*, 2017; Roose, "Can Social Media Be Saved?"; Laurel Wamsley, "As Facebook Shows Its Flaws, What Might a Better Social Network Look Like?," *NPR: The Two-Way*, May 1, 2018.

existing today, with over two million users registered since the site was created in 2016.[67]

Functionally, Mastodon works much like Twitter, with users sharing brief 500-character messages, called "toots," with those users who follow them—as well as anyone who sees a "boost" (the Mastodon version of a "retweet") of that toot.[68] But Mastodon is quite distinct from Twitter in one major structural way: instead of a single, centralized platform, Mastodon is federated. Whereas all users on Twitter are registered on the same platform, in other words, users who register for Mastodon must select a specific "instance" when they sign up; one's toots are then, by default, visible to all members of that instance as well as to one's followers (though this does depend on the settings of one's chosen instance).[69] The result is that Mastodon looks more like

> clusters of independent nodes—Mombook and Athletebook and Gamerbook—all of which could be plugged into the umbrella network when it made sense. Rather than requiring a one-size-fits-all set of policies that apply to billions of users, these nodes could be designed to reflect users' priorities. (A network for privacy hawks and one for open-sharing maximalists could have different data-retention rules, and a network for L.G.B.T. users and one for evangelical pastors could have different hate speech rules.)[70]

Despite this separation, however, users on different instances can easily follow one another. The result is that content is not "trapped" in one instance or another, but can still be widely circulated among all those who use Mastodon, regardless of what instance they are formally members of.[71]

This federated structure, with its multiple "instances," means that Mastodon—unlike Twitter—has clear and durable boundaries. When registering for the site, users are asked to select the instance they wish to join and

[67] Roose, "Can Social Media Be Saved?"

[68] Megan Farokhmanesh, "A Beginner's Guide to Mastodon, the Hot New Open-Source Twitter Clone," *The Verge*, April 1, 2017; Roose, "Can Social Media Be Saved?"; Wamsley, "As Facebook Shows Its Flaws, What Might a Better Social Network Look Like?"

[69] Users can, however, change the privacy settings of their toots (though this varies by instance). In mastodon.social, the largest instance, toots can be restricted to one's followers only, as well as made visible only to users who are mentioned in that toot.

[70] Roose, "Can Social Media Be Saved?"

[71] Wamsley, "As Facebook Shows Its Flaws, What Might a Better Social Network Look Like?"

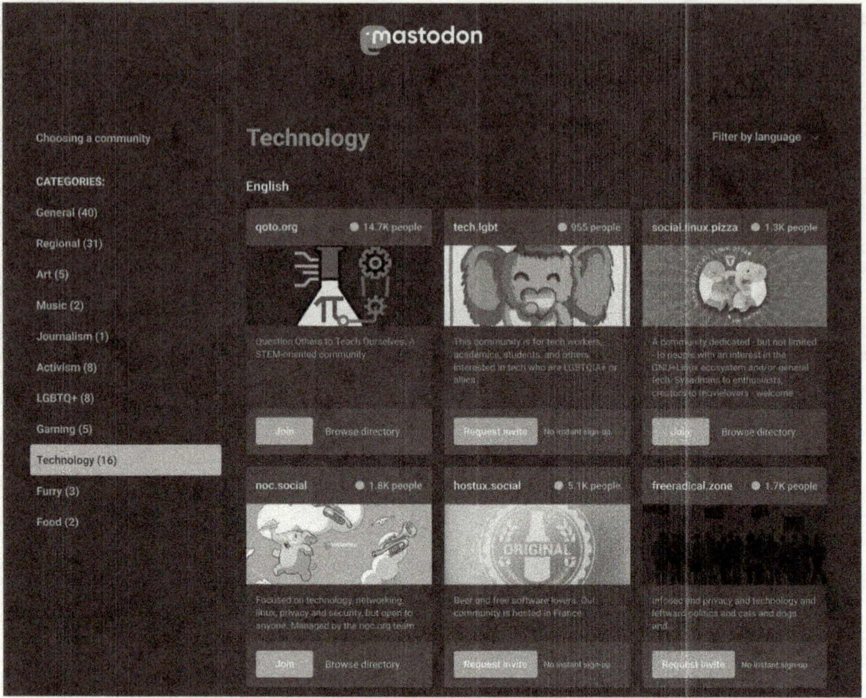

Figure 5.9 Examples of instances users can choose to join when signing up for Mastodon. Like subreddits, Mastodon's instances provide clear, durable boundaries that help to highlight what interests or sensibilities members share. Photograph by author.

thus invest in—a decision Mastodon facilitates by showing users a variety of instances to choose from, based on interest or language (see Figure 5.9).[72] The result is that all users in a specific instance have selected to be there for a reason; by virtue of the instance's clear boundaries, moreover, users are able to recognize that they share common interests or sensibilities with other members of that instance. Much like Reddit's subreddits, the federated structure of Mastodon means users can more easily identify what they share and with whom. And these instances are durable; unlike Twitter's hashtags, they outlast individual uses and users. Indeed, instances are a major structural component of the platform that shape user behavior in perceptible and lasting ways;[73] users on Mastodon are, for example, more likely to engage in the repeated interactions

[72] "The Mastodon Project," *Mastodon*, accessed July 12, 2018, https://joinmastodon.org/.

[73] Matteo Zignani et al., "The Footprints of a 'Mastodon': How a Decentralized Architecture Influences Online Social Relationships," in *Proceedings of the 2019 IEEE Conference on Computer Communications Workshops* (Piscataway, NJ: IEEE, 2019), 472–77.

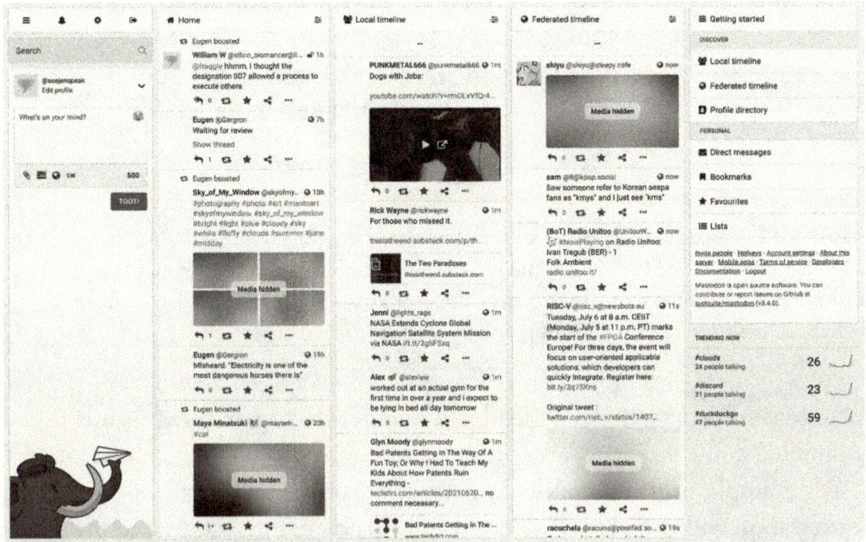

Figure 5.10 Screenshot of Mastodon homepage. Notice how users can simultaneously see three different feeds: "Home" (content from accounts the user follows), "Local timeline" (content from one's instance), and "Federated timeline" (public content from users on other Mastodon instances who are connected to one's home instance). Photograph by author.

that sustain ties of political friendship and generate communal attachments than are users on Twitter.[74]

These durable boundaries are also evident in Mastodon's content feed. Unlike Facebook, Twitter, and Reddit, Mastodon does not use a sorting algorithm to populate a user's feed. Instead, the platform defaults to presenting content in reverse-chronological order. But each user can toggle between three different feeds; alongside one's "Home" feed (displaying content from accounts a user follows), there is an instance-specific, or "local," timeline as well as a "federated" timeline that gathers public content from users connected to your instance, regardless of what instance they are members of (see Figure 5.10). Instead of sorting content by way of an individualized algorithm,

[74] Miao Liu, Robert W. Gehl, and Diana Zulli, "Rethinking the 'Social' in 'Social Media': Insights into Topology, Abstraction, and Scale on the Mastodon Social Network," *New Media and Society* 22, no. 7 (2020): 1188–205. Sarah Jeong's experiences on Mastodon also illustrate the kind of behaviors we would expect to see: a new user to the site violated the norms of the instance; after much backlash, the norm violator was reined in by other users' responses, rather than doubling down on their original disruption. See Sarah Jeong, "Mastodon Is Like Twitter without Nazis, So Why Are We Not Using It?," *Vice: Motherboard*, April 4, 2017.

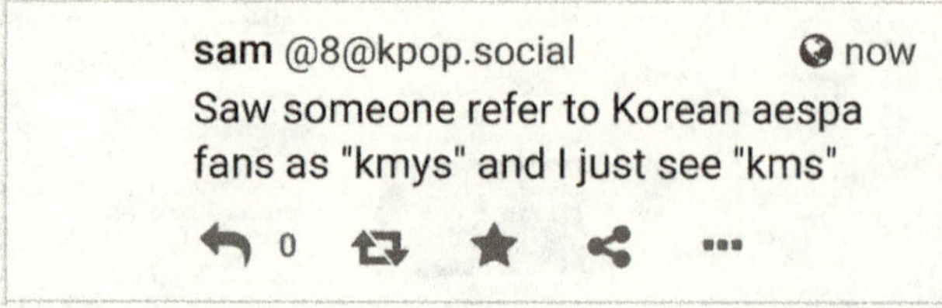

Figure 5.11 Example of a post in a user's Federated timeline. Notice that in the federated timeline, the instance name is part of the user's handle, following the pattern @username@instancename. In this case, the user's instance is kpop.social, an instance dedicated to K-pop fandom. Photograph by author.

then, Mastodon structures its feed in a manner that again foregrounds users' communal contexts.

For example, toots in one's local instance are presented as part of an ongoing conversation within one's self-selected community of interest. And in the federated timeline, users' toots are identified by their own instance of origin, included as part of any user's handle (see Figure 5.11). Like Reddit, and unlike Twitter, Mastodon's front page feed is therefore structured in a way that highlights the collective context of any given content. The prominent display of a post's subreddit or instance of origin clarifies its communal boundaries and reminds users that this is content they share with a readily identifiable community of peers. And, just as we would expect from a clearly bounded space, there is evidence that Mastodon hosts more reciprocal connections than does Twitter; whereas Twitter relationships are, for the most part, unidirectional (meaning users follow more users than they are followed by), Mastodon users, on average, have as many followers as people they follow.[75]

In addition to the durable boundaries of Mastodon's federated structure, the platform is also quite flexible. For one, it hosts a variety of content, with over 1,200 instances, all dedicated to their own topic, and with their own rules, norms, and expectations.[76] And because users can follow and share content across instances, there are multiple opportunities for users to see new information and have new experiences. Indeed, "despite the decentralized and fragmented architecture, Mastodon users keep connected to the core of the network and are able to search for friendships in other instances."[77] Like Twitter, then,

[75] Matteo Zignani, Sabrina Gaito, and Gian Paolo Rossi, "Follow the 'Mastodon': Structure and Evolution of a Decentralized Online Social Network," in *Proceedings of the Twelfth International AAAI Conference on Web and Social Media (ICWSM 2018)* (n.p.: AAAI Publications, 2018), 541–50.

[76] Thekinrar, "Mastodon Instances," https://instances.social/list/advanced, accessed June 29, 2021.

[77] Zignani, Gaito, and Rossi, "Follow the 'Mastodon.'"

one of Mastodon's strengths is its ability to provide users with heterogenous experiences—it hosts the breadth of information and serendipitous interactions that are the hallmark of a diverse and democratic space.

Alongside this variety, moreover, Mastodon is also more malleable than Facebook, Twitter, or even Reddit. Just as redditors and Twitter users, in the beginning, were able to exert more influence over the sites' functionalities, so too are Mastodon's users still able to continue reshaping their instances. Within these "individually moderated communities,"[78] users are able to set the rules for discourse as well as make major design decisions; the absence of a "quote-boost" ("quote tweets," in Twitter parlance), for example, and the restrictions on searches are both major design choices that were collectively made and defended by users.[79]

And because Mastodon is open-source, there are increased opportunities for users to be involved in these kinds of foundational design decisions, such as "the internal details of interface design, networking algorithms, and software-to-hardware relationships."[80] As a result, Mastodon users are deeply involved in the maintenance of their space—in terms of both site governance and architectural decisions. With its immense variety and incentives for users to actively participate in collectively managing their environment, Mastodon is therefore *more* flexible than either Facebook or Twitter; it "turns the site's technical development, platform design, and governance into social enterprises."[81] It is unsurprising, then, that many proponents laud its democratic nature.

Importantly, however, this democratic potential is not derived solely from the platform's emphasis on user control—the feature that is most widely remarked upon by commentators. Instead, as should by now be clear, it is Mastodon's federated structure that facilitates the formation and maintenance of *communities* on the platform and thus makes it possible for users to exert that control democratically—not as individuals, but collectively, with their peers. Mastodon's democratic potential, in other words, is derived from *balancing* the three characteristics of a democratic built environment: clear boundaries, durability, and flexibility. And this balance is evident not just in the federated structure, generally, but also in how it presents content to users by organizing their feeds.

[78] Rhodes, "Like Twitter but Hate the Trolls?"

[79] Jeong, "Mastodon Is Like Twitter without Nazis, So Why Are We Not Using It?"

[80] Liu, Gehl, and Zulli, "Rethinking the 'Social' in 'Social Media.'"

[81] Liu, Gehl, and Zulli, "Rethinking the 'Social' in 'Social Media.'"

DEMOCRATIZING FACEBOOK AND TWITTER

Both Reddit and Mastodon, despite their different ownership structures and design details, exhibit all three characteristics of a democratic built environment. Moreover, while Reddit uses an algorithm to sort content and Mastodon does not, both platforms organize information for users in ways that highlight the *communal* context within which that content is shared with others. As a result, both platforms are better positioned to support the kind of democratic communities and practices that are currently absent from Facebook and Twitter.

But turning to Reddit and Mastodon as exemplars of democratic spaces—despite their structural differences and the corresponding differences in the communities they host—can also suggest strategies for redesigning more prominent platforms like Facebook and Twitter to be more supportive of democratic politics. This need not, as we can see from the example of Reddit, mean giving up private ownership or eliminating algorithmic sorting altogether. It does, however, require solutions that facilitate *collective* control rather than the individualized solutions of tools like Gobo. In order for platforms like Facebook and Twitter to support democratic politics, in other words, they must remind users of the collective context of content—creating spaces where users can recognize themselves, and act, as members of communities of interest to manage the content they see, the algorithms that curate it, and the effects of both.

Recall that both Reddit and Mastodon organized their feeds in terms of communities. Though the posts and toots were made by individual users, in both cases they were presented to audiences with the author's subreddit or instance prominently displayed. On both platforms, then, users viewing that content were immediately reminded of the post's collective context; the prominent display of the originating subreddit or instance cues users to both the other users seeing that content (members of the subreddit or instance) as well as that community's shared interest (the subreddit or instance's focus). Rather than encourage users to think of content—both their own and others'—in isolation, then, as Facebook and Twitter do, Reddit and Mastodon's highlighting of content's originating subreddit and instance serves to reify boundaries in users' feeds and remind those users of their membership in site-wide communities. By rendering these boundaries visible, in other words, the platforms make it easier for communities to form and sustain themselves in these spaces—and to work together to improve their collective experiences.

In order to democratize the environments of Facebook and Twitter, then, one first step would be to afford similar practices by introducing boundaries into their users' feeds. Facebook currently does this with Facebook Groups, as discussed in chapter 2; Twitter has introduced a similar innovation with "Topics" (see Figure 5.12)—like the proposed "Rooms" and "Groups" discussed in chapter 3.

Figure 5.12 Example of Twitter Topics as both separate location within Twitter (left) and embedded in one's feed (right). In both cases, the collective context of the included tweets is made more salient to users. Images from Casey Newton, "Twitter Is Rolling Out Topics, a Way to Follow Subjects Automatically in the Timeline," *The Verge*, November 6, 2019, available at https://www.theverge.com/2019/11/6/20948547/twitter-topics-launch-sports-gaming-entertainment-test.

In both cases, content from a Group or Topic is labeled as such in one's feed, reminding users that they are not alone in seeing that content—they are instead seeing it as part of a community, with a shared interest in what they see and how.

Yet in the case of Twitter Topics, users are not made aware of who else shares those interests. Likewise, the bulk of content in Facebook users' feeds does not originate with Groups; for this non-Group content, users cannot see who else is (or is not) seeing those same posts. In both cases, then, while Facebook and Twitter might send *some* signals to users that the content they see is based in shared interests, the platforms' designs still obscure the other users with whom those interests are shared. This makes it difficult for users to exert collective control—if members of a community cannot identify one another, it is little wonder they will not gather to act.

One way to facilitate this recognition, then, is to render the boundaries of each post's audience clearer to those within in. Just as redditors can see who else is a member of their subreddit, Facebook might make visible to users who else can see the posts they do. Likewise, just as Mastodon users can see those in their instance, Twitter might reveal other followers of each Topic a user is subscribed to.[82]

Of course, simply rendering visible these existing boundaries, and thus facilitating users' recognition of themselves as a member of a community, is insufficient to exercise democratic control over the algorithms that curate our social media experiences. The resulting communities must also have durable spaces where they are able to encounter one another repeatedly, form attachments, and work collectively to manage their shared environments.

Again, recall the subreddits and instances of Reddit and Mastodon. These spaces are more than simply markers of community; they are also durable spaces to which users can return time and again in order to share, discuss, and decide on issues of concern. It is within these durable subreddits and instances that redditors and Mastodon users make decisions about what content best reflects their community and how that content should be presented. It was within a subreddit, for example, that redditors were able to discuss—and advocate for changes to—the Reddit sorting algorithm when it was overrun by posts from r/the_donald in 2016.[83] And it is within each individual instance that Mastodon users negotiate the norms governing banning, blocking, and otherwise moderating content in that space.[84]

Such durable spaces are largely absent from Facebook and Twitter. While users can see the advertising groups they belong to, or the reasons why they see certain content, they cannot see who else falls in these groups. And, with the exception of Facebook Groups, users lack entirely the durable spaces in

[82] In November 2020, Twitter announced plans to start testing a new feature similar to the app Clubhouse. With this new feature, Twitter users can "create 'spaces' for voice-based conversations right on Twitter" (Peters). Notably, for our purposes, users in these Spaces are "able to see who is a part of the room and who is talking at any given time," thereby giving them the potential to serve as clearly bounded spaces within the platform. While Spaces have clear boundaries, however, they ultimately lack the requisite durability. Spaces exist only as long as they are in use: "once ended, they will no longer be available publicly on Twitter." See Jay Peters, "Twitter to Introduce Clubhouse-like Voice Chat Rooms in Testing Later This Year," *The Verge*, November 17, 2020; "About Spaces on Twitter," Twitter, n.d., https://help.twitter.com/en/using-twitter/spaces.

[83] Spez, "Let's All Have a Town Hall about r/All," *Reddit, r/Announcements*, June 16, 2016, https://www.reddit.com/r/announcements/comments/4oedco/lets_all_have_a_town_hall_about_rall/. "Spez" is the username of Reddit CEO Steve Huffman.

[84] Liu, Gehl, and Zulli, "Rethinking the 'Social' in 'Social Media.'"

which to interact repeatedly with other community members, even if they could see those members' names. But creating these spaces—for example, turning Facebook's advertising categories into the more durable spaces of Groups—might allow these latent communities a space within which they could share, compare, and discuss their experiences with content on the platform, facilitating the political friendships and communal attachments required to ultimately exert democratic control. By rendering visible one's membership in the existing, but latent, communities on these platforms and creating durable spaces for those audience members to encounter one another repeatedly, these changes are better designed to support collective control rather than to exacerbate the individualism currently driving experiences on these platforms.

These changes are by no means the only possibilities available for democratizing Facebook and Twitter; they are also accompanied by trade-offs, like privacy, that will also have to be negotiated by the communities involved. What they suggest, however, are ways that Facebook and Twitter might redesign their platforms to support not just users' control over the content they see, but also the formation and sustainability of the *communities* that should rightly exert that control. Algorithms on these platforms already sort users into communities of interest. In this, Facebook and Twitter are no different from Reddit and Mastodon. What the former miss, and the latter provide, then, are the clear boundaries that render these communities visible to users and the durable spaces within which they can form attachments necessary to, ultimately, exert collective control over their environments and the algorithms that create them. The suggestions outlined here may not, in the end, be the most effective; they are, however, a good place to start.

Designing for Digital Democracy

Debates over the democratic potential of digital technologies often focus on the role of algorithms, and for good reason. Algorithms structure our online experiences, shape our search results, curate our news feeds, and recommend friends to follow, videos to watch, and objects to buy. And with terabytes of information uploaded to social media platforms each day, algorithms are indispensable in helping us make sense of our digital lives. But they can also be quite dangerous. Algorithms can amplify our worst behaviors by entrenching our biases, fueling our (mostly) negative emotions, and radicalizing us. By feeding us more content we enjoy, algorithms often encourage us to passively receive information rather than take an active role in managing our environments. As such, algorithms—as they are currently deployed—do much to undermine the possibilities for democratic politics.

Responding to this state of affairs, scholars and critics have turned their attention to diagnosing—and improving—algorithms for democracy. But, to date, this conversation has largely taken place within the framework of ownership and control. Algorithms that are "bad" for our democratic lives excel, it turns out, at increasing user engagement and thus generating profit. So long as algorithms are owned and controlled by private, for-profit corporations, so this line of thinking goes, it is naïve to expect anything different from them. In order to prevent algorithms from undermining democracy, then, the solutions seem clear: turn control over to users.

This inclination is a good one. Of course placing control over common objects in the hands of those who share in their effects is more democratic than leaving decision-making up to a few corporate executives who are accountable only to investors. But this approach—focusing solely, or even primarily, on increasing the *flexibility* of algorithms—ignores perhaps the fundamental principle of democratic politics: it is a collective endeavor. Democratic control, in other words, requires the existence of democratic *communities*. Right now, at least on platforms like Facebook and Twitter, these communities remain latent. And solutions like Gobo, designed to increase individual user control, have successfully wrested that control away from corporations without thinking about how to draw out and support the (existing) communities which must take their place.

As we consider how best to design algorithms—and the social media platforms they power—to support democratic politics, we must approach the problem holistically, keeping in mind all three core practices of democracy. We must, in other words, design flexible spaces that balance the need for user control with clearly visible and durable boundaries that help to form and sustain the communities that will, ultimately, exert that control. To focus on control, without the corresponding care for building and maintaining communities, risks undermining the possibility for democratic politics just as much as does eschewing concerns of control entirely.

Reddit and Mastodon provide us with two possible models for designing democratic digital spaces—for balancing the characteristics of boundaries, durability, and flexibility that facilitate the collective work of democratic politics. Sites like Facebook and Twitter, then, might draw lessons from these two platforms and consider how to reorganize their feeds to highlight the collective context of content and to provide durable spaces for these various communities to discuss, critique, and challenge how that content is presented. But these solutions, like the platforms they are modeled after, are not perfect. Like democracy itself, these strategies exhibit a number of tensions: the problems of managing trolls and other bad actors, of compelling norms of "good" behavior from users, and of addressing other important considerations like privacy, to name a few.

In offering these suggestions, then, I am not arguing that all social media platforms should be redesigned in the same way; indeed, Reddit and Mastodon look and feel quite different from one another—and that variety is immensely valuable. Instead, as they have in this chapter, these platforms should serve as inspiration, motivating us to consider the possibilities—both available and imagined—of building digital technologies that start from the premise of community and center the collective work of democratic politics. We can, undoubtedly, improve on these examples. But if we are to improve at all, it is crucial that we start by framing the problem in terms of democracy, with *all* its facets in mind. Questions of ownership and control alone are insufficient; the design of the platforms, and the communities they support, matters too.

6

"Make No Little Plans"

Designing the Future of Democracy

The society of the modern world which I have sought to delineate, and which I seek to judge, has but just come into existence. Time has not yet shaped it into perfect form.

—Alexis de Tocqueville, *Democracy in America*, Vol. 2

In November 2019, the *New York Times* published an opinion piece by science journalist and author Annalee Newitz. Entitled "A Better Internet Is Waiting for Us," the piece followed Newitz as they "spoke to experts in media history, tech designers, science fiction writers and activists for social justice" in order to "imagine a different reality" where "future companies designed media to facilitate democracy right from the beginning."[1] Suggestions offered by these experts varied. Some drew from existing digital practices, like the community curation of Black Twitter, while others imagined a whole new ecosystem of "slow media," in which moderators and editors would review content before it was visible to users. Perhaps expectedly, most of these alternatives centered on new uses and manifestations of digital technologies, including AI-generated rules and virtual-reality worlds. But Newitz concluded their piece by gesturing to the role of the digital built environment in this "better internet." "After the social media age is over," they argued, "we'll have the opportunity to rebuild our damaged public sphere by creating digital public places that imitate actual town halls, concert venues, and pedestrian-friendly sidewalks."[2]

Starting the work of democratizing digital technologies by focusing on rebuilding digital public places is, as I have been arguing throughout this book, a powerful strategy. But in order to successfully construct these digital public

[1] Annalee Newitz, "A Better Internet Is Waiting for Us," *New York Times*, November 30, 2019.

[2] Newitz, "A Better Internet Is Waiting for Us."

Designing for Democracy. Jennifer Forestal, Oxford University Press. © Oxford University Press 2022.
DOI: 10.1093/oso/9780197568750.003.0006

places—to design them in ways that "facilitate democracy"—we need blueprints. After all, the town halls, concert venues, and pedestrian-friendly sidewalks that Newitz groups together in their piece function quite differently from one another. Moreover, they may not all be as supportive of democratic politics as we might think.[3] If we are to successfully rebuild the digital public sphere, and create the "better internet" that is waiting for us, then we need a clearer understanding of precisely how to design spaces that support it.

Providing these blueprints has been the project of this book. Taking a participatory approach to democratic politics, understood as the collective management of common affairs, I argued, first, that democracy is not an activity confined to the formal apparatus of government. It is, rather, a form of collective decision-making that should extend into all the spheres of our lives we share with others. And, as the work of collective problem-solving, democracy requires three conditions: communities must form, they must sustain themselves, and they must work to improve over time. To secure these conditions, citizens must continually engage in three corresponding practices: we must (1) *recognize* ourselves as part of communities, thereby calling them into existence; (2) form *attachments* to those communities and our fellow members, helping to maintain them; and (3) cultivate *experimental habits* to ensure that both our decisions and decision-making processes become better and more inclusive over time.

In order to build an environment that supports these democratic practices, then, I argued that we must design spaces that balance three characteristics: they must (1) have *boundaries*; (2) be *durable*; and (3) be *flexible*. Boundaries help citizens recognize what they share and with whom they share it; they help communities form. Durable spaces facilitate affective attachments that sustain citizens' engagement with the ongoing (and often frustrating) work of collective problem-solving. And flexible spaces provide the requisite resources and opportunities to improve communities by practicing experimental habits. Taken together, these characteristics create a built environment that affords citizens the ability to engage in the practices that ground democratic politics. Boundaries, durability, and flexibility are, in other words, the defining characteristics of "democratic spaces."

Having identified these requisite design characteristics, we are better positioned to begin the work of rebuilding our digital public places in ways that facilitate democracy. Yet, as should be clear from the various examples used throughout this book, this work need not—and *should* not—wait until "after the social media age is over," as Newitz's article implies. Rather, we can and should start this work immediately, by evaluating the digital environments within which

[3] For example, the town hall, as Jane J. Mansbridge has shown, often replicates hierarchical positions of power in ways that run counter to the democratic values of equality and inclusion. See Jane J. Mansbridge, *Beyond Adversary Democracy* (Chicago: University of Chicago Press, 1983).

we find ourselves and working to democratize them, to make them more hospitable to democratic practices. This is likely to be a long and difficult task, with more than a few obstacles standing in our way. But such is the work of democracy.

However, accepting that there will be challenges does not mean we must be unprepared to meet them. Indeed, developing a clear sense of precisely what stands in our way can help us to anticipate and, perhaps, overcome these challenges more effectively. To that end, this final chapter offers some concluding thoughts on the possibilities and limits of democratizing digital technologies by redesigning them. First, I highlight once more the value of approaching this task as a question of the design of the built environment, rather than, as do many of Newitz's interlocutors, a question of curatorial practices or technological advances. The reasons for starting with the built environment are twofold. For one, using the conceptual framework of democratic space provides us with more nuanced evaluations of existing digital platforms like Facebook, Twitter, and Reddit as well as technological tools like Gobo. But it also, second, provides a wider perspective on the broader relationship between digital technologies and democracy; the language of democratic space reframes our underlying assumptions about the spaces we inhabit, highlighting points of continuity between physical and digital environments as well as the democratic challenges unique to each.

And yet, building democratic digital environments is—like many proposals made by democratic theorists—perhaps easier said than done. I conclude the book, then, by taking up some common concerns and criticisms that this project of democratization often invites. In particular, I address the troublingly authoritarian impulses of architecture—and the lack of faith in citizens that leads us to cede the work of building to others in the first place—as well as the "proper" role of experts in any project of democratization. Ultimately, these concluding thoughts are, like many of the recommendations in this book, my best suggestions for how we might start this collective undertaking. Like any instance of collective action, however, constructing democratic spaces is work the outcomes of which we cannot predict in advance. But that is no reason not to begin it now. The only way we will end up with more democratic spaces, after all, is if we start building them.

Starting with the Built Environment

In the process of "reimagining what it means to build public spaces where people seek common ground," many of the suggestions Newitz collects in their article center on directly regulating behavior around digital technologies—whether the behavior of technology firms or of users themselves. Citing concerns with companies' single-minded pursuit of profit and unchecked collection of user data, as well as the torrential amount of content users upload and circulate daily, Newitz's experts suggest "an intense emphasis on the value of curation"[4] and "limits on how quickly content circulates" as strategies for improving digital technologies for democracy.[5] Behind all of these recommendations is the goal to "set up rules that limit undesirable outcomes."[6] Alternatively, as some experts suggested to Newitz, we might see a turn away from digital environments entirely. Rather than improve digital spaces, we might revise our expectations such that authentic interactions would, as Newitz puts it, instead "hinge on that low-tech practice known as meeting face to face."[7] By imposing the right rules, or altering social norms, these experts all argue, we can once again "maintain and create the digital public spaces we actually want."[8]

That imagining a better internet largely takes the form of altered rules and norms is unsurprising. As we have seen, the turn to these formal and informal institutions is a common one, both in contemporary discussions of digital technologies' democratic potential as well as in political theorists' investigations into cultivating and sustaining democratic practices more generally. But while they may be effective, these institutional approaches are not exhaustive; indeed, as I have been arguing, the design of the built environment can have just as much—if not more—influence over citizens' attitudes, behaviors, and relationships as can these more traditional manifestations of power. When designed correctly, the built environment affords citizens opportunities to engage in the democratic practices of recognition, attachment, and experimentalism. But it can just as easily foreclose these practices and render democratic politics more difficult.

Throughout this book, I have shown how taking a spatial approach—an approach centered on the role of the built environment—can help us to identify the underlying structural incentives for user behavior on individual digital platforms like Facebook, Twitter, and Reddit. Rather than focus on user behaviors in isolation, in other words, the environmental approach I develop here can help to explain *why* we see users engaging—or failing to engage—in certain patterns of action on these platforms. In so doing, a spatial focus highlights structural changes that we can make to help augment the rules and norms that many scholars recommend to make digital technologies work for democracy. This environmental approach can also help us reassess how, and whether, certain existing tools, like Gobo, will actually achieve the more democratic outcomes they aspire to.

[4] John Scalzi, science fiction writer, quoted in Newitz, "A Better Internet Is Waiting for Us."
[5] Newitz, "A Better Internet Is Waiting for Us."
[6] Newitz, "A Better Internet Is Waiting for Us."
[7] Newitz, "A Better Internet Is Waiting for Us."
[8] Newitz, "A Better Internet Is Waiting for Us."

But taking this environmental approach to democratizing digital technologies is helpful for more than simply evaluating and improving single platforms or tools. It also gives us a conceptual framework with which to place these new technologies into a wider context, highlighting the points of continuity and rupture as we shift the medium we use to build our political environments. In each of the book's chapters, I have drawn important comparisons between physical and digital environments. But they are, of course, different. For one, "[p]hysical architecture," as James Grimmelmann notes, "shares neither software's level of precision nor its nearly costless replication."[9] The shift in the medium of our built environment, in other words—from bricks, say, to computer code—makes a difference for the kinds of problems we are likely to run into as we work to build, maintain, and improve democratic communities and the environments that host them.

Notably, bricks and mortar—building blocks typical of the physical built environment—lend themselves to durability. The economics of building and destroying spaces in physical environments are such that changing physical spaces is often difficult, time-consuming, and obvious to inhabitants. As a result, we tend to take the characteristic of durability for granted in physical environments. Because of their building medium, in other words, it is more likely that the spaces of the physical built environment will endure than not—and, if they do not endure and are instead altered or destroyed, such changes or disappearances will be noticeable to citizens and thus subject to discussion and contestation.

As a result of this physical property of our traditional building materials, those invested in democratizing the spaces of the built environment often focus attention on these spaces' *flexibility*. Many political theorists, for example, are rightly quite skeptical of the idea that durable boundaries are required for democratic communities. And this is because it is easier, in physical environments, to build spaces that passively exclude by means of such boundaries. As a result, as Susan Bickford argues, physical spaces like cities and suburbs "should be fuzzy and multilayered."[10] Likewise, Iris Marion Young suggests a model of a democratic city as a "place of many places." Invoking Jane Jacobs's insistence on multiuse urban spaces, Young envisions a city in which citizens would "[w]alk around the corner, or over a few blocks, and . . . encounter a different spatial mood, a new play of sight and sound, and new interactive movement."[11] In our traditional

[9] James Grimmelmann, "Regulation by Software," *Yale Law Journal* 114 (2005): 1719–58.

[10] Susan Bickford, "Constructing Inequality: City Spaces and the Architecture of Citizenship," *Political Theory* 28, no. 3 (2000): 369.

[11] Iris Marion Young, *Justice and the Politics of Difference* (Princeton, NJ: Princeton University Press, 1990), 240.

projects of democratizing physical (and social) spaces, in other words, thinkers have largely focused their efforts around increasing those spaces' flexibility.

But, as should now be clear, when we shift to digital environments our calculations must change. Increasingly, the spaces created by digital technologies are introducing an unprecedented lack of boundaries and durability into the built environments in which we find ourselves. In contrast to brick, code lends itself to flexibility; as Lawrence Lessig notes, code is subject only to the restrictions we set for ourselves—the laws of physics no longer apply.[12] As a result, as we saw in chapters 2, 3, and 5, boundaries and durability are often much more difficult to come by. Indeed, digital platforms are often premised on novelty and change; these spaces can be altered or even disappear in the blink of an eye from the perspective of users. This was evident in Google's decision to discontinue—and remove—Google Reader, in Facebook's initial introduction of the News Feed and its subsequent changes to the EdgeRank algorithm, and in Yahoo's continued destruction of long-standing online communities like Geocities and Yahoo Answers.[13] And while users can (and often do) register their disapproval after the fact, these alterations are often made without their knowledge or input—and they are very rarely reversed.[14]

Taking the environmental approach I have outlined in this book, we are better able to identify and explain this shift from physical to digital—and to deal with its consequences for the possibilities of democratic politics. Using the framework of democratic space, it becomes clear why, for example, different social media platforms see different forms and levels of collective action among users; the digital built environment, like that of the physical world, can be designed to afford certain behaviors and not others. But the language of democratic space also helps us see more clearly why the traditional emphasis on rendering spaces more flexible, which works so well in physical environments and which motivates a project like Gobo, might end up creating digital spaces that remain unsupportive of democratic communities—despite the best intentions of their creators.

[12] Of course, there are physical constraints to computer programming. Computer hardware, as well as physical cables, servers, routers, exchange points, and so on, are all required for any digital space to exist, let alone function in its intended ways. These are important considerations, but they fall outside the scope of my argument in this book.

[13] Mat Honan, "RIP: Google Reader Meets Its Inevitable End," *WIRED*, March 13, 2013; Christina Bonnington, "Why Google Reader Really Got the Axe," *WIRED*, June 6, 2013; Issie Lapowsky, "15 Moments That Defined Facebook's First 15 Years," *WIRED*, February 4, 2019; Katie Notopoulos, "RIP Yahoo Answers: It Died as It Lived, Needlessly and Stupidly," *BuzzFeed News*, April 5, 2021.

[14] Pamela Statz, "Facebook Faces Backlash," *WIRED*, September 6, 2006.

What the conceptual frame of democratic space provides us with, in other words, is a vocabulary with which to explore points of continuity and change between different spaces—both within physical and digital environments, as well as between the two media. The characteristics I have identified here—boundaries, durability, and flexibility—should always be present in spaces intended to support democratic politics. But these characteristics will manifest differently in different environments and the spaces they generate. How these characteristics are negotiated in any given space will depend on the associated community's goals and its members. But the conceptual framework of democratic space presented here highlights some of the challenges and assumptions we must (re)consider as we collectively undertake the work of democratization. In so doing, it redirects our efforts—highlighting those aspects of democratic politics we have taken for granted in physical spaces, while also opening new possibilities for creating, sustaining, and improving democratic communities in both our existing digital environments as well as those yet to be imagined.

Addressing Common Challenges

Of course, as I have cautioned from the beginning, simply building the "right" spaces is not a panacea. But the idea that we can design our way out of the challenges of democratic politics is not uncommon. Indeed, this kind of logic is evident in both architectural projects in the physical environment as well as technocratic proclamations coming out of Silicon Valley. And while architects like Louis Sullivan and Frank Lloyd Wright understood themselves as creating an "architecture of democracy,"[15] there is very clearly an anti-democratic impulse at work in architectural "solutions" to social and political problems—though its underlying logic is perhaps understandable. People, it is often said, cannot be trusted to secure the proper conditions for democracy on their own; one need

[15] Frank Lloyd Wright, *An Organic Architecture: The Architecture of Democracy* (Cambridge, MA: MIT Press, 1970). In his commitment to developing a "democratic" architectural style, Wright was following in the steps of his "lieber Meister" Louis Sullivan. Though Sullivan does not draw explicitly on the language of democracy in his own published work, he nevertheless owned a copy of—and had obviously read and made notes in—John Dewey's *Reconstruction of Philosophy*. In particular, he marked a passage in which Dewey connects the liberation of human capacities with the unleashing of art. See Hugh D. Duncan, *Culture and Democracy: The Struggle for Form in Society and Architecture in Chicago and the Middle West during the Life and Times of Louis H. Sullivan* (Totowa, NJ: Bedminster Press, 1965). Sullivan's copy of *Reconstruction in Philosophy* is available as part of the University of Minnesota Elmer L. Andersen Library's William Gray Purcell papers collection; special thanks to Cheryll Fong, Assistant Curator of Archives & Special Collections, for her help tracking it down, scanning its pages, and emailing them to me in spring 2015.

only look to the proliferation of gated communities and other exclusive—but wildly popular—architectures to see how citizens continually choose non-democratic environments for themselves when given the option. If we cannot trust citizens to make the "right" choices on their own, it seems, the only alternative is for experts—whether architects or software developers—to make those choices for them.

These two related concerns—the likelihood of citizens' "opting-out" of democratic environments and the anti-democratic implications of architectural solutions more generally—are common ones. And we must therefore be attentive to them as we consider the work of democratizing digital technologies. But these concerns are also not unique to the environmental approach to democratization I outline in this book. Indeed, both anxieties—of the capacity of citizens and the reliance on experts—are long-standing questions for democracy more generally. In these final pages, then, I briefly take each up in turn and show how we might reconsider these challenges in light of digital technologies and democratic spaces.

DEMOCRACY, FAITH, AND HUMAN NATURE

Often when I present this work, the argument—that we should strive for a more participatory democratic society and build digital spaces that support that goal—is met with skepticism: should we really place such faith in citizens? The members of r/TwoXChromosomes were, after all, quite reluctant to introduce variety into their space; it was the moderators' (unilateral and unpopular) decision to take the subreddit "default" that ultimately led to a more flexible environment. And there are countless digital communities—like anti-vaxxer Groups on Facebook or r/TheRedPill on Reddit[16]—where it seems that the majority of members have decided (democratically!) to marginalize and exclude others. With the proliferation of examples such as these, observers argue, it can be difficult to convincingly make the case that the solution to digital technologies' democratic failings is to put more power and control in the hands of users.

[16] r/TheRedPill is a prominent "men's rights" subreddit, characterized by extreme misogyny and ties to white supremacist views. Though currently "quarantined" by Reddit, meaning it is only visible to registered redditors—and only after they have confirmed their intention to see its content—the subreddit is still active and has been tied to offline political organizing. See Shawn P. Van Valkenburgh, "Digesting the Red Pill: Masculinity and Neoliberalism in the Manosphere," *Men and Masculinities* 24, no. 1 (2018): 1–20; Julia DeCook, "How Deep Does the Rabbit Hole Go? The 'Wonderland' of r/TheRedPill and Its Ties to White Supremacy," *B2o: An Online Journal* 4, no. 2 (2019); Pierce Alexander Dignam and Deana A. Rohlinger, "Misogynistic Men Online: How the Red Pill Helped Elect Trump," *Signs: Journal of Women in Culture and Society* 44, no. 3 (2019): 589–612.

But the idea that citizens are ill-equipped to meet the admittedly high demands of participatory democratic theory is not a new one. In 1925, Walter Lippmann lamented the "unattainable ideal" that posits a democratic citizen with "an unlimited quantity of public spirit, interest, curiosity, and effort."[17] And the result of this unattainable ideal, E. E. Schattschneider argued in 1960, is that we continually "try to whip the public into doing things it does not want to do, is unable to do, and has too much sense to do."[18] And these criticisms continue today. As recently as 2016, Christopher H. Achen and Larry M. Bartels noted that "real people are not much like the citizens imagined" by participatory democratic theorists, whose ideas are based in "unrealistic expectations about human nature."[19] There is, it seems, no evidence to support—and much evidence to refute—the argument, reflected in this book, that cultivating democratic practices in citizens is a practical goal. And it would seem that this remains true in digital environments. Even when we do see successful instances of digital collective action—for example, in the coordinated and sustained campaigns of harassment and trolling conducted by Gamergaters, Anonymous, and 4Chan users—they are often not exactly exemplars of democratic participation.[20]

These are, of course, valid concerns. Certainly, the behaviors that often lead observers to voice this skepticism—like apathy, trolling, extremism, and harassment—are problematic from the perspective of participatory democracy. But this is not a reason to throw up our hands and admit defeat. Democracy, as John Dewey reminds us, is a project fundamentally grounded in faith: a belief that "the habit of amicable cooperation—which may include, as in sport, rivalry and competition—is itself a priceless addition to life"[21] and a corresponding "faith in the capacity of human beings for intelligent judgment and action *if proper conditions are furnished.*"[22] For democracy to succeed, in other words, we must not only believe it to be a worthwhile goal, but also have faith that citizens are, *under the right conditions*, capable of this work and invested in seeing it through.

Of course, as both Dewey and I recognize, securing these conditions is no easy feat. But to think of human behavior as static and unchanging—as

[17] Walter Lippmann, *The Phantom Public* (New Brunswick, NJ: Transaction Publishers, 1993), 24.

[18] E. E. Schattschneider, *The Semisovereign People: A Realist's View of Democracy in America* (Boston: Wadsworth, 1960), 131.

[19] Christopher H. Achen and Larry M. Bartels, *Democracy for Realists: Why Elections Do Not Produce Responsive Government* (Princeton, NJ: Princeton University Press, 2016), 299, 301.

[20] David Karpf, "The Internet and Engaged Citizenship" (Cambridge, MA: Commission on the Practice of Democratic Citizenship, 2019).

[21] John Dewey, "Creative Democracy—The Task before Us," in *John Dewey: The Later Works, Vol. 14, 1939–1941*, ed. Jo Ann Boydston (Carbondale: Southern Illinois University Press, 2008), 228.

[22] Dewey, "Creative Democracy," 227. Emphasis mine.

Lippmann, Schattschneider, and Achen and Bartels seem to argue it is—is a claim contradicted by decades of research, including the examples used throughout this book. Humans regularly change their behavioral patterns in response to new ideas and, importantly, new environments. The project of democratization, then, is one that works to secure the conditions under which humans can flourish and their democratic capacities—heretofore unrealized, perhaps—can become commonplace habits.

The kind of radical remaking of our built environments that I propose in this book intends to do precisely that—to shift our behaviors, to train us in new practices, and to inculcate new habits. In short, the goal is to democratize our spaces and the communities they house in order to realize political capacities that now lay underutilized. This work is bound to seem disruptive, even impossible. Indeed, "[t]hat the new project is contrary to some traits of human nature *as they exist at the time* is certain," Dewey argued in response to criticisms of his own project of democratization. "For the proposed policy is openly one for a change; therefore of course it goes against those particular habits which have been formed by the very conditions it is proposed to alter."[23] That our current digital environments predominantly play host to targeted harassment (e.g., Gamergate on Twitter) or dangerous misinformation campaigns (e.g., anti-vaxxers on Facebook) should not, then, be surprising. The environmental conditions that currently characterize these digital spaces are, as I have shown, not conducive to supporting the practices we know to be necessary for democratic politics. But that does not mean these habits cannot be changed; and, as I have been arguing, there are good reasons to begin by changing the design of the digital environments that facilitate them.

Importantly, in advocating for attention to the role of the built environment, I am not working to supplant efforts to reshape behavior through traditional mechanisms like laws, education, and norms. We can, and should, also consider how to implement community guidelines and terms of service, moderation practices, external measures of accountability and regulation, and digital literacy programs that will help support us in the ongoing work of forming and practicing the habits of democratic citizens. And yet, the success of these institutions can be augmented by having them overlay spaces that are built for the same ends. Without built environments that foster the practices and values of democracy, it is much less likely that we will cultivate them. And if we design the spaces correctly, we will at least have hospitable environments for the rest of the work that needs to be done. Spaces that are designed in ways that

[23] John Dewey, "'Contrary to Human Nature,'" in *The Later Works of John Dewey, Volume 14: 1939–1941*, ed. Jo Ann Boydston (Carbondale: Southern Illinois University Press, 2008), 258. Emphasis in original.

balance these three architectural characteristics—boundaries, durability, and flexibility—will be more likely to support robust democratic communities. In the absence of one or more of these design elements, however, it will be much more difficult for citizens to engage in the kinds of practices that we know sustain democratic communities, regardless of the rules, norms, or training that they receive.

ARCHITECTURE, EXPERTS, AND THE PROJECT OF DEMOCRATIZATION

In addition to skepticism regarding citizens' capacities, my arguments outlining the characteristics required for environments to be "properly" supportive of democratic politics often invite another line of criticism—that the spatial approach, as one that dictates the terms of democratic environments to their inhabitants, is itself quite undemocratic. Indeed, James C. Scott has described the work of architecture and urban planning as taking "a God's-eye view, or the view of an absolute ruler."[24] And this kind of technocratic logic is prevalent not just in architecture, but also in discussions of digital technologies and democracy. As David Karpf calls it, this "Field of Dreams Fallacy" has led many to start "from the premise that, if you build a good enough platform, you can radically increase political participation."[25] The similarly technocratic impulses of architecture and technology promise simple, easy solutions to some of our messiest problems; it is easy to see why they are so attractive.

But this architectural logic also seems removed from (and placed above) the political fray, imposing a unilateral vision for communities that is at odds with the participatory picture of democratic politics-as-collective-problem-solving that forms the foundation of this book. And, indeed, that is the case. "Social advance," wrote Jane Addams in 1922, "depends as much upon the process through which it is secured as upon the result itself."[26] In order to successfully build democratic communities, we must commit to doing so using democratic practices and processes. The challenges of political life cannot be solved solely through appeals to experts; in the work of democratizing digital technologies, *citizens* should be at the center of the decisions around what to build and how.

[24] James C. Scott, *Seeing Like a State: How Certain Schemes to Improve the Human Condition Have Failed* (New Haven: Yale University Press, 1998), 57.

[25] Karpf, "The Internet and Engaged Citizenship." Of course, these largely fail. At the "Civic Tech Graveyard" (www.civictech.guide/graveyard), Micah Sifry and Matt Stempeck have kept track of over seventy failed "civic technology" startups. See Micah L. Sifry, "Learning from the Civic Tech Graveyard," *Civicist*, October 1, 2018, https://civichall.org/civicist/civic-tech-graveyard/.

[26] Jane Addams, *Peace and Bread in Time of War* (New York: Macmillan, 1922), 133.

This is not to say, however, that there is *no* room for experts in the work of building democratically. We cannot expect communities to tackle complex problems without the kind of technical knowledge and skill provided by experts; this is a recipe for wasted time and energy as each community would be forced to "reinvent the wheel." But neither can we allow experts to dictate solutions, ready-made, to the communities with whom they are ostensibly working. Rather, a democratic approach to building necessitates a *collaboration* between experts and citizens—one where technical knowledge and expertise are understood as a communal resource (experts are, after all, community members themselves) and thus directed by, and for, community ends.

Happily, models for this kind of democratic collaboration already exist. The Citizens and Technology (CAT) Lab at Cornell University, led by J. Nathan Matias, is one such example; the Lab is run by scholars who work closely with online communities, like those on Reddit and Wikipedia, to improve their environments through rigorous scientific experimentation. CAT Lab partners with members of a community to help them identify problems—like strengthening community ties, preventing online harassment, and supporting free expression for marginalized groups[27]—generate possible solutions, and collect the information required for those communities to make their own informed decisions on how to address them.

In 2018, for example, the moderators of the subreddit r/feminism worked in collaboration with Matias and the CAT Lab team (then called CivilServant) to design a project that examined "ways to help commenters feel more welcome on the sub"[28] (see Figure 6.1). Working with the moderators and members of r/feminism, the Lab designed and deployed a two-year study that surveyed members about the reasons they stayed silent within the subreddit and designed a structural intervention (a private welcome message sent to new users) intended to increase newcomer participation in that space. The Lab then shared and discussed the results of the study with r/feminism (as well as other subreddits, like r/TheoryOfReddit, whose members might be interested in the results),

[27] J. Nathan Matias, Tyler Simko, and Marianne Reddan, "Study Results: Reducing the Silencing Role of Harassment in Online Feminism Discussions," *CAT Lab*, June 2020, https://citizensandtech.org/2020/06/reducing-harassment-impacts-in-feminism-online/. J. Nathan Matias et al., "Volunteers Thanked Thousands of Wikipedia Editors to Learn the Effects of Receiving Thanks," *CAT Lab*, June 2020, https://citizensandtech.org/2020/06/effects-of-saying-thanks-on-wikipedia/.; J. Nathan Matias, "Preventing Harassment and Increasing Group Participation through Social Norms in 2,190 Online Science Discussions," *PNAS: Proceedings of the National Academy of Sciences of the United States of America* 116, no. 20 (2019): 9785–89; J. Nathan Matias, "Do Downvote Buttons Cause Unruly Online Behavior?," *CAT Lab*, January 2018, https://civilservant.io/do_downvotes_cause_bad_behavior_jan_2018.html.

[28] Thats_not_marxist, "We Are Working with CivilServant to Better Your Sub Experience," *Reddit, r/Feminism*, April 2018, https://www.reddit.com/r/Feminism/comments/8cozom/we_are_working_with_civilservant_to_better_your/.

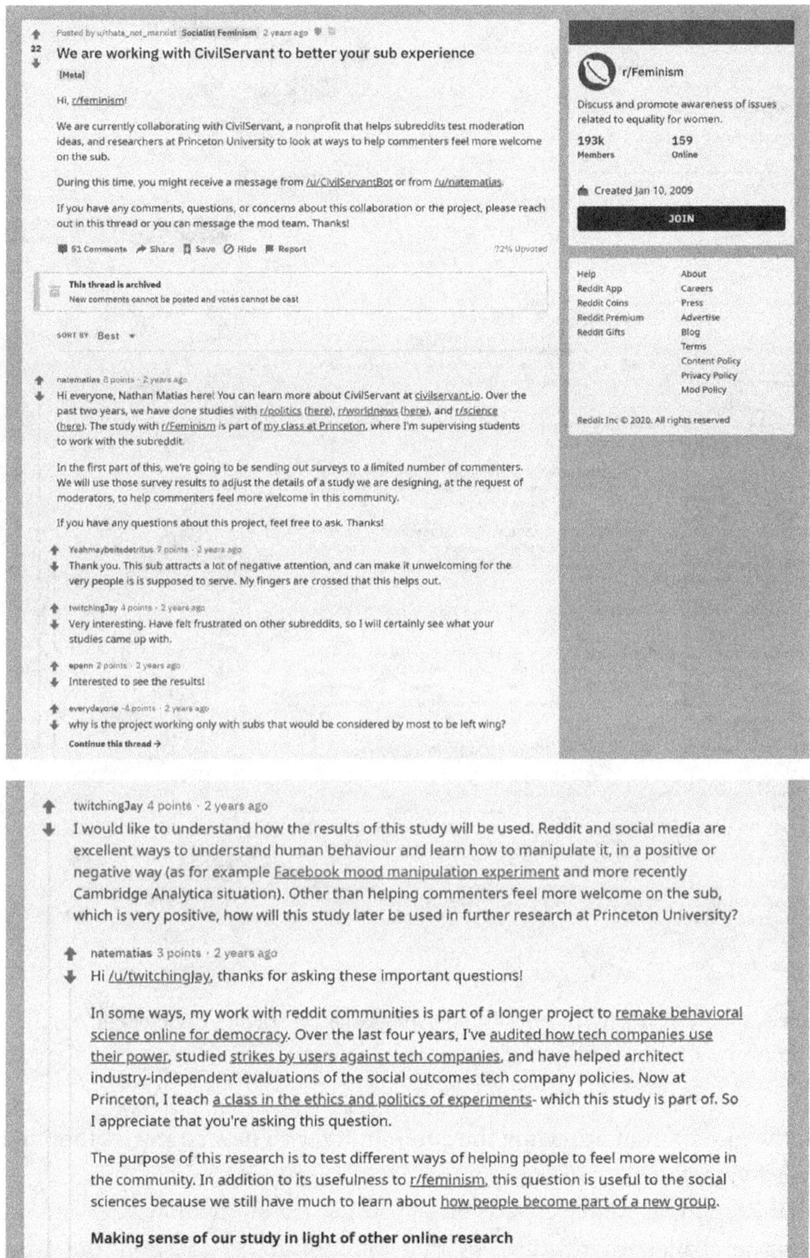

Figure 6.1 Screenshots of the r/feminism moderators' initial announcement of their collaboration with CivilServant/CAT Lab (top) and the ensuing discussion (bottom). Many of the comments, like those pictured, feature study lead J. Nathan Matias (natematias) discussing the project in more detail with r/feminism members. Photographs by author.

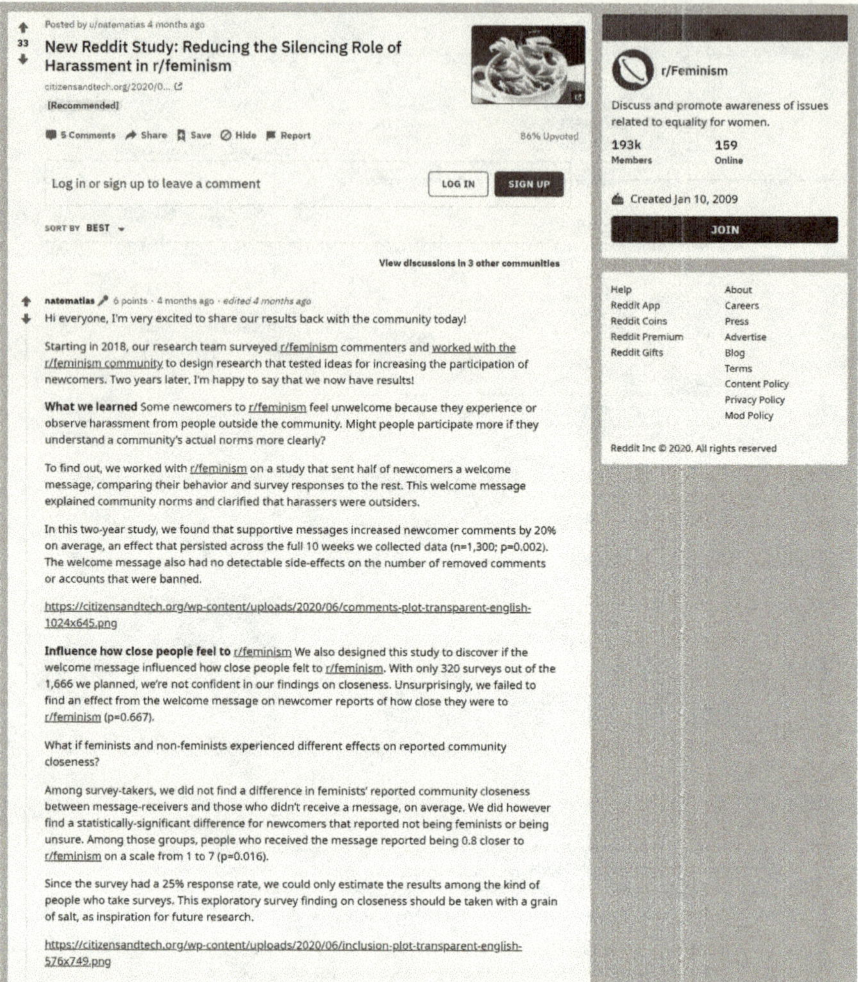

Figure 6.2 Screenshot of study lead J. Nathan Matias's reporting CivilServant/CAT Lab's study results in r/feminism. Photograph by author.

with the intention of providing the community with new strategies they could deploy to meet their goals (see Figures 6.2, 6.3, and 6.4).[29]

In this example, we see experts bringing their technical knowledge and skills to bear on challenges identified by the communities in question; the experts involved, in other words, are not *imposing* solutions so much as providing a

[29] Natematias, "New Reddit Study: Reducing the Silencing Role of Harassment in r/Feminism," *Reddit, r/Feminism,* June 2020, https://www.reddit.com/r/Feminism/comments/hfmtg5/new_reddit_study_reducing_the_silencing_role_of/; Natematias, "Study Results: Reducing the Silencing Role of Harassment in r/Feminism," *Reddit, r/TheoryofReddit,* June 2020, https://www.reddit.com/r/TheoryOfReddit/comments/hfo0l7/study_results_reducing_the_silencing_role_of/.

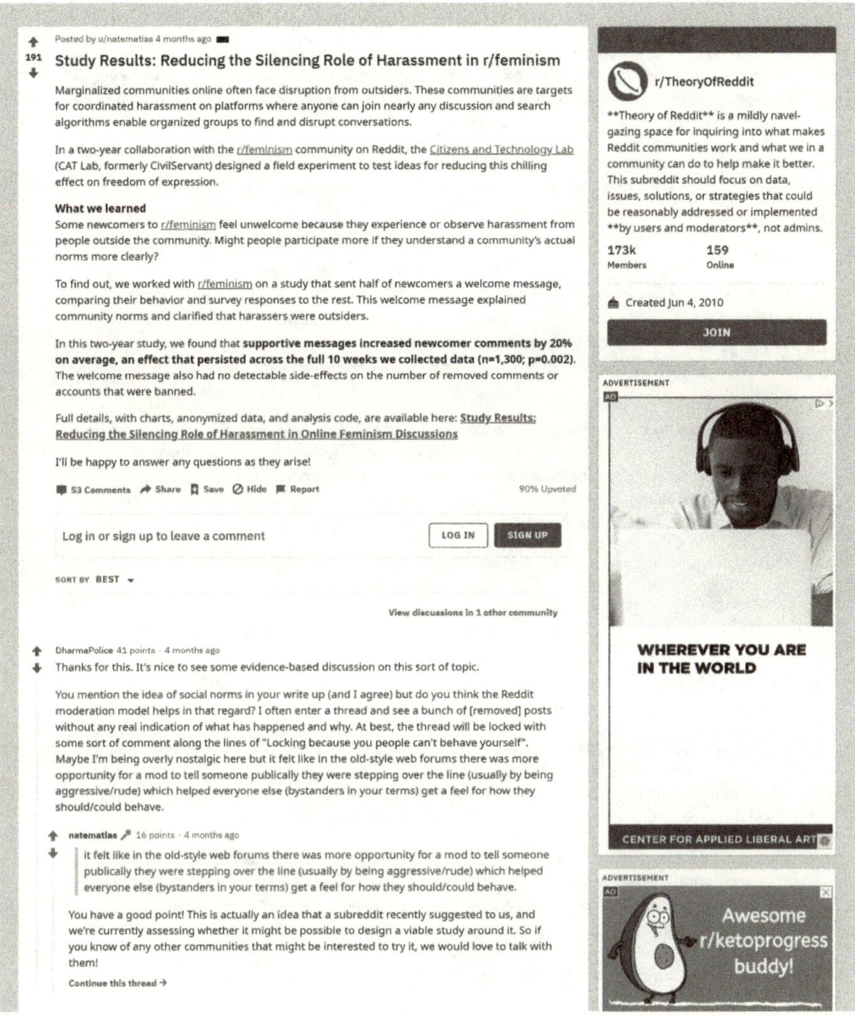

Figure 6.3 Screenshot of study lead J. Nathan Matias sharing results and responding to questions from r/TheoryOfReddit community members regarding the r/feminism study. Photographs by author.

framework to help communities clarify the problem, identify and test solutions, and collect the necessary data to make an informed decision. Deciding upon—and implementing—a specific course of action, however, is work for the community to do itself.

It is in that same spirit—as both a democratic theorist and democratic citizen—that I present the characteristics of democratic space outlined here: not as an authoritarian dictate, but as a set of conceptual tools—a vocabulary with which we can begin to collectively engage in the work of constructing environments for our various communities. Indeed, we should not interpret the

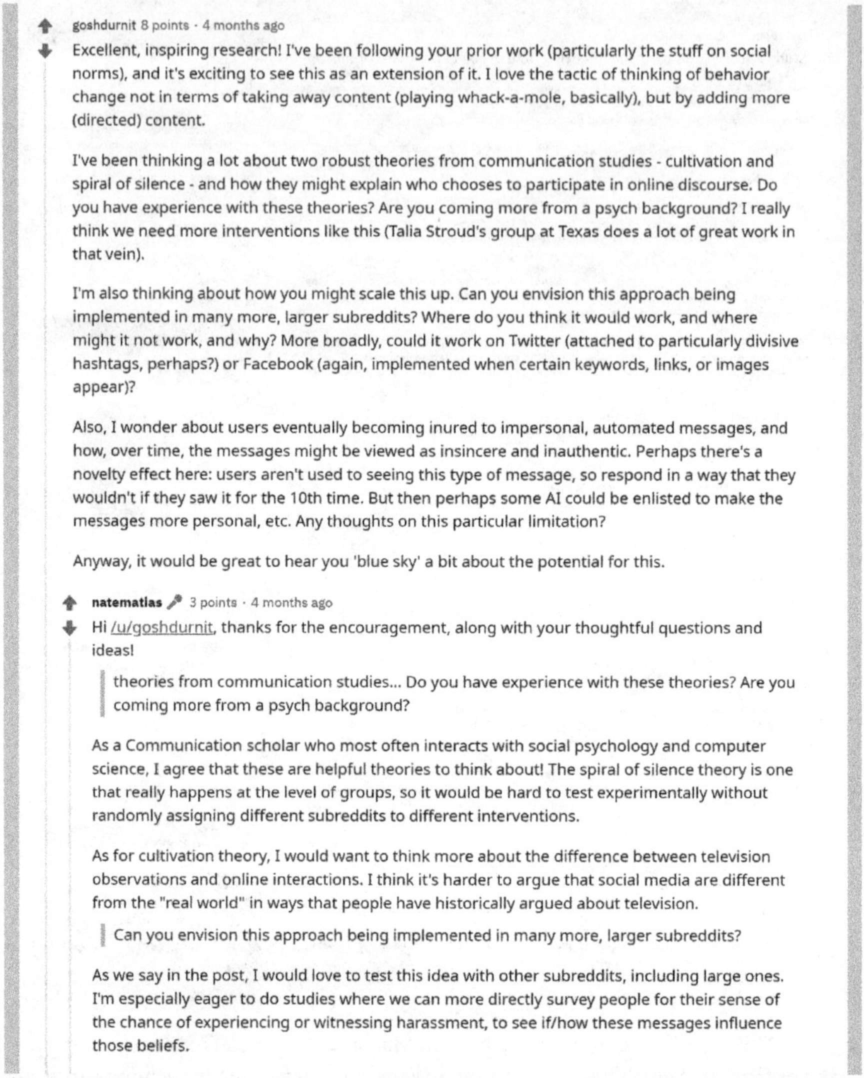

goshdurnit 8 points · 4 months ago

Excellent, inspiring research! I've been following your prior work (particularly the stuff on social norms), and it's exciting to see this as an extension of it. I love the tactic of thinking of behavior change not in terms of taking away content (playing whack-a-mole, basically), but by adding more (directed) content.

I've been thinking a lot about two robust theories from communication studies - cultivation and spiral of silence - and how they might explain who chooses to participate in online discourse. Do you have experience with these theories? Are you coming more from a psych background? I really think we need more interventions like this (Talia Stroud's group at Texas does a lot of great work in that vein).

I'm also thinking about how you might scale this up. Can you envision this approach being implemented in many more, larger subreddits? Where do you think it would work, and where might it not work, and why? More broadly, could it work on Twitter (attached to particularly divisive hashtags, perhaps?) or Facebook (again, implemented when certain keywords, links, or images appear)?

Also, I wonder about users eventually becoming inured to impersonal, automated messages, and how, over time, the messages might be viewed as insincere and inauthentic. Perhaps there's a novelty effect here: users aren't used to seeing this type of message, so respond in a way that they wouldn't if they saw it for the 10th time. But then perhaps some AI could be enlisted to make the messages more personal, etc. Any thoughts on this particular limitation?

Anyway, it would be great to hear you 'blue sky' a bit about the potential for this.

natematias 3 points · 4 months ago

Hi /u/goshdurnit, thanks for the encouragement, along with your thoughtful questions and ideas!

> theories from communication studies... Do you have experience with these theories? Are you coming more from a psych background?

As a Communication scholar who most often interacts with social psychology and computer science, I agree that these are helpful theories to think about! The spiral of silence theory is one that really happens at the level of groups, so it would be hard to test experimentally without randomly assigning different subreddits to different interventions.

As for cultivation theory, I would want to think more about the difference between television observations and online interactions. I think it's harder to argue that social media are different from the "real world" in ways that people have historically argued about television.

> Can you envision this approach being implemented in many more, larger subreddits?

As we say in the post, I would love to test this idea with other subreddits, including large ones. I'm especially eager to do studies where we can more directly survey people for their sense of the chance of experiencing or witnessing harassment, to see if/how these messages influence those beliefs.

Figure 6.4 Screenshot of study lead J. Nathan Matias answering questions and engaging in discussion with a r/TheoryOfReddit community member regarding the r/feminism study. Photograph by author.

framework of democratic space I outline here as a one-size-fits-all solution to designing democratic spaces; it most emphatically is not. For one, such a solution does not exist.

Compare the physical sites of the town halls and sidewalks in Newitz's example with Reddit and Wikipedia in digital environments. All these spaces exhibit the characteristics of boundaries, durability, and flexibility. But they negotiate these characteristics quite differently. Despite their structural similarities, subreddits and town halls look and feel different (so, for that matter, do town halls, sidewalks, and concert venues, as well as Wikipedia and Reddit). In each case, while the walls and lines of code might perform the same function, their forms are quite distinct. And these differences in form have an impact on the kinds of communities they support and the activities they engage in collectively. And this is to be expected—even encouraged. Because democratic politics is the collective management of common affairs, and because those affairs will be different for each community, communities should develop their own specific processes through which to make decisions and meet their aims. The spaces supporting this work should therefore differ as well.

The language of democratic space, then, provides a broad set of characteristics that citizens and communities can use to reconceptualize the challenges they face and identify new strategies to address them. It is an (admittedly technical) starting point for the work of democratizing digital technologies—but it is the communities themselves who must ultimately use this framework to carry out the work itself. Without buy-in from citizens, after all, changes—even democratically minded ones—can lead to the disintegration of communities as members become alienated and, ultimately, abandon the space, and community, entirely.[30]

Building (for) the Future

Importantly, the kinds of collaborations between experts and citizens necessary to "fix" digital technologies for democracy—like all democratic processes—must be self-reflective, open to change with an eye toward improvement. Democracy, after all, rests on experimentation. The project of democratizing digital technologies that I have discussed throughout this book, then, will necessarily be an ongoing, iterative process. We might build democratic spaces that suit the needs of a community at one point in time, only to find them insufficient at a later date. We might realize democratic spaces require additional characteristics to those I have outlined here, or that they require fewer. "The idea of democracy," Dewey reminds us, must be constantly "rediscovered, remade and reorganized."[31] And the "standing danger" is that old ideas "will be acted upon implicitly without

[30] This kind of "opting-out" happened after the moderators of r/TwoXChromosomes (discussed in chapter 4) took the subreddit "default." Dissatisfied with the results, and alienated from the process, many users left the subreddit to form new communities, both on Reddit and elsewhere.

[31] John Dewey, "The Challenge of Democracy to Education," in *The Later Works of John Dewey, Volume 11: 1935–1937*, ed. Jo Ann Boydston (Carbondale: Southern Illinois University Press, 2008), 182.

reconstruction to meet new conditions."[32] As we find ourselves in new environments, with new communities and new problems, we will, of course, need to remake our environments to meet these needs. The conceptual framework of democratic space—boundaries, durability, and flexibility—is but one tool we have to engage in this work.

The question of how to design (digital) democratic environments is not a problem that can be solved by software developers alone, any more than it can be solved by political scientists or architects working in isolation. It is, at its core, a question of values: of how we want to live together in the communities and spaces we share with others, and how we want to address the problems that will necessarily arise from that shared existence. The problem of digital technologies is, in other words, a question of democracy. And it can therefore only be "solved" (a contested and contingent solution, to be sure) through processes that include the participation of citizens themselves—processes in which we remain, crucially, open to new ideas, including new ways to form, sustain, and improve the communities we share. A better internet—and a more democratic society—*is* waiting for us, just as Newitz's article suggests. But we cannot leave its design and construction to others. The work of democratizing digital technologies—of democratizing our shared world—is work for us all.

[32] John Dewey, "Liberalism and Social Action," in *The Later Works of John Dewey, Volume 11: 1935–1937*, ed. Jo Ann Boydston (Carbondale: Southern Illinois University Press, 2008), 37.

References

Achen, Christopher H., and Larry M. Bartels. *Democracy for Realists: Why Elections Do Not Produce Responsive Government*. Princeton, NJ: Princeton University Press, 2016.

Addams, Jane. *Peace and Bread in Time of War*. New York: Macmillan, 1922.

Alfonso, Fernando, III. "Reddit Punishes Pro-Trump Community r/The_donald for Threats, Other 'Rule-Breaking Behavior.'" *Forbes*, June 2019. https://www.forbes.com/sites/fernandoalfonso/2019/06/26/reddit-punishes-pro-trump-community-rthedonald-for-rule-breaking-behavior/.

Allen, Danielle S. *Talking to Strangers: Anxieties of Citizenship since Brown v. Board of Education*. Chicago: University of Chicago Press, 2004.

Allport, G. W. *The Nature of Prejudice*. Cambridge, MA: Perseus Books, 1954.

Altman, Irwin, and Setha M. Low, eds. *Place Attachment*. New York: Plenum Press, 1992.

Angwin, Julia, Surya Mattu, and Terry Parris Jr. "Facebook Doesn't Tell Users Everything It Really Knows about Them." *ProPublica*, December 27, 2016. https://www.propublica.org/article/facebook-doesnt-tell-users-everything-it-really-knows-about-them.

Angwin, Julia, Madeleine Varner, and Ariana Tobin. "Facebook Enabled Advertisers to Reach 'Jew Haters.'" *ProPublica*, September 14, 2017. https://www.propublica.org/article/facebook-enabled-advertisers-to-reach-jew-haters.

Arendt, Hannah. *The Human Condition*. 2nd ed. Chicago: University of Chicago Press, 1998.

Aristotle. *Aristotle's Politics*. Translated by Carnes Lord. 2nd ed. Chicago: University of Chicago Press, 2013.

Aristotle. *Nichomachean Ethics*. Translated by Terence Irwin. 2nd ed. Indianapolis: Hackett Publishing Company, 1999.

Aristotle. *The Eudemian Ethics*. Translated by Anthony Kenny. Oxford: Oxford University Press, 2011.

Aslam, Ali. "Building the Good Life: Architecture and Politics." PhD diss., Duke University, 2010.

Barber, Benjamin. "Malled, Mauled, and Overhauled: Arresting Suburban Sprawl by Transforming Suburban Malls into Usable Civic Space." In *Public Space and Democracy*, edited by Marcel Hénaff and Tracy B. Strong, 201–20. Minneapolis: University of Minnesota Press, 2001.

Barrett, Brian. "What Would Regulating Facebook Look Like?" *WIRED*, March 21, 2018. https://www.wired.com/story/what-would-regulating-facebook-look-like/.

Baym, Nancy K. *Personal Connections in the Digital Age*. 2nd ed. Cambridge, UK: Polity Press, 2016.

Bedingfield, Will. "Reddit Has Banned r/The_Donald. Who It Bans Next Matters More." *WIRED*, July 2020. https://www.wired.co.uk/article/reddit-the-donald-banned.

Bell, Caroline, Cara Fausset, Sarah Farmer, Julie Nguyen, Linda Harley, and W. Bradley Fain. "Examining Social Media Use among Older Adults." In *Proceedings of the 24th ACM Conference on Hypertext and Social Media*, 158–63. Paris: ACM, 2013.

Bell, Karissa. "You Might Want to Rethink What You're 'Liking' on Facebook Now." *Mashable*, February 27, 2017. http://mashable.com/2017/02/27/facebook-reactions-news-feed/#iRAhn2EuAkq5.

Bennett, W. Lance, and Alexandra Segerberg. *The Logic of Connective Action: Digital Media and the Personalization of Contentious Politics*. Cambridge, UK: Cambridge University Press, 2013.

Berkovich, Aaron, Alex Lu, Brian Levine, and Alla Reddy. "Observed Customer Seating and Standing Behavior and Seat Preferences Onboard Subway Cars in New York City." *Transportation Research Record: Journal of the Transportation Research Board* 4, no. 2353 (2013): 33–46.

Bernstein, Joseph. "Alienated, Alone and Angry: What the Digital Revolution Really Did to Us." *BuzzFeed News*, December 17, 2019. https://www.buzzfeednews.com/article/josephbernstein/in-the-2010s-decade-we-became-alienated-by-technology.

Betteridge, Jesse. "Oppression in the Reddit Hivemind: Tracing Patterns of Misogyny in Electronic Public Spaces." Burnaby, BC: Simon Fraser University, 2016.

Bhargava, Rahul, Anna Chung, Neil S. Gaikwad, Alexis Hope, Dennis Jen, Jasmin Rubinovitz, Belén Saldías-Fuentes, and Ethan Zuckerman. "Gobo: A System for Exploring User Control of Invisible Algorithms in Social Media." In *Proceedings of the 2019 Conference on Computer Supported Cooperative Work and Social Computing*, 151–155. Austin, TX: ACM, 2019. https://dl.acm.org/doi/10.1145/3311957.3359452.

Bickford, Susan. "Beyond Friendship: Aristotle on Conflict, Deliberation, and Attention." *Journal of Politics* 58, no. 2 (1996): 398–421.

Bickford, Susan. "Constructing Inequality: City Spaces and the Architecture of Citizenship." *Political Theory* 28, no. 3 (2000): 355–76.

Binns, Amy. "Twitter City and Facebook Village: Teenage Girls' Personas and Experiences Influenced by Choice Architecture in Social Networking Sites." *Journal of Media Practice* 15, no. 2 (2014): 71–91. https://doi.org/10.1080/14682753.2014.960763.

Blakely, Edward J., and Mary Gail Snyder. "Divided We Fall: Gated and Walled Communities in the United States." In *Architecture of Fear*, edited by Nan Ellin, 85–99. Princeton, NJ: Princeton University Press, 1997.

Bleiberg, Joshua, and Darrell M. West. "Have You Pressed the Button?" *Brookings TechTank Blog*, April 27, 2015. https://www.brookings.edu/blog/techtank/2015/04/27/have-you-pressed-the-button/.

Bode, Leticia, and Kajsa E. Dalrymple. "Politics in 140 Characters or Less: Campaign Communication, Network Interaction, and Political Participation on Twitter." *Journal of Political Marketing* 15, no. 4 (2016): 311–32.

Bonaiuto, Marino, Antonio Aiello, Marco Perugini, Mirilia Bonnes, and Anna Paola Ercolani. "Multidimensional Perception of Residential Environment." *Journal of Environmental Psychology* 19 (1999): 331–52. https://doi.org/10.1006/jevp.1999.0138.

Bonnington, Christina. "Why Google Reader Really Got the Axe." *WIRED*, June 6, 2013. https://www.wired.com/2013/06/why-google-reader-got-the-ax/.

Bothwell, Stephanie E., Raymond Gindroz, and Robert E. Lang. "Restoring Community through Traditional Neighborhood Design: A Case Study of Diggs Town Public Housing." *Housing Policy Debate* 9, no. 1 (1998): 89–114.

boyd, danah. "Social Network Sites as Networked Publics: Affordances, Dynamics, and Implications." In *Networked Self: Identity, Community, and Culture on Social Network Sites*, edited by Zizi Papacharissi, 39–58. New York: Routledge, 2010.

boyd, danah m., and Nicole B. Ellison. "Social Network Sites: Definition, History, and Scholarship." *Journal of Computer-Mediated Communication* 13 (2007): 210–30. https://doi.org/10.1111/j.1083-6101.2007.00393.x.

Bradner, Erin, and Gloria Mark. "Why Distance Matters: Effects on Cooperation, Persuasion and Deception." In *Proceedings of the 2002 ACM Conference on Computer Supported Cooperative Work*, 226–35. New Orleans, LA, 2002.

Brignall, Thomas W., III, and Thomas L. Van Valey. "An Online Community as a New Tribalism: The World of Warcraft." In *Proceedings of the 40th Hawaii International Conference on System Sciences*, 179b–179b. Los Alamitos, CA: IEEE, 2007.

Brignull, Harry. "Dark Patterns: Inside the Interfaces Designed to Trick You." *The Verge*, August 29, 2013. https://www.theverge.com/2013/8/29/4640308/dark-patterns-inside-the-interfaces-designed-to-trick-you.

Brock, André. "From the Blackhand Side: Twitter as a Cultural Conversation." *Journal of Broadcasting and Electronic Media* 56, no. 4 (2012): 529–49.

Brown, Barbara, Douglas D. Perkins, and Graham Brown. "Place Attachment in a Revitalizing Neighborhood: Individual and Block Levels of Analysis." *Journal of Environmental Psychology* 23 (2003): 259–71. https://doi.org/10.1016/S0272-4944(02)00117-2.

Bruns, Axel, and Jean Burgess. "Twitter Hashtags: From Ad-Hoc to Calculated Publics." In *Hashtag Publics: The Power and Politics of Discursive Networks*, edited by Nathan Rambukkana, 13–28. New York: Peter Lang Publishing, 2015.

Bryant, Susan, Andrea Forte, and Amy Bruckman. "Becoming Wikipedian: Transformation of Participation in a Collaborative Online Encyclopedia." In *Proceedings of the 2005 International ACM SIGGROUP Conference on Supporting Group Work—GROUP '05*, 1–10. New York: Association for Computing Machinery, 2005. https://doi.org/10.1145/1099203.1099205.

Bucher, Taina, and Anne Helmond. "The Affordances of Social Media Platforms." In *The Sage Handbook of Social Media*, edited by Jean Burgess, Thomas Poell, and Alice Marwick, 233–53. London: Sage Publications, 2018.

Buozis, Michael. "Doxing or Deliberative Democracy? Evidence and Digital Affordances in the Serial Subreddit." *Convergence: The International Journal of Research into New Media Technologies* 25, no. 3 (2019): 357–73.

Burke, Moira, Robert Kraut, and Cameron Marlow. "Social Capital on Facebook: Differentiating Uses and Users." In *Proceedings of the SIGCHI Conference on Human Factors in Computing Systems*, 571–80. Vancouver, BC, 2011.

Burrell, Jenna, Zoe Kahn, Anne Jonas, and Daniel Griffin. "When Users Control the Algorithms: Values Expressed in Practices on the Twitter Platform." In *Proceedings of the 2019 ACM on Human-Computer Interaction*, 1–20. New York: ACM, 2019.

Buyukozturk, Bertan, Shawn Gaulden, and Benjamin Dowd-Arrow. "Contestation on Reddit, Gamergate, and Movement Barriers." *Social Movement Studies* 17, no. 5 (2018): 592–609.

Chadwick, Andrew. *Internet Politics: States, Citizens, and New Communication Technologies*. New York: Oxford University Press, 2006.

Chan, Kathy H. "Growing Beyond Regional Networks." *Facebook*, June 9, 2009. https://www.facebook.com/notes/facebook/growing-beyond-regional-networks/91242982130/.

Chandrasekharan, Eshwar, Mattia Samory, Shagun Jhaver, Hunter Charvat, Amy Bruckman, Cliff Lampe, Jacob Eisenstein, and Eric Gilbert. "The Internet's Hidden Rules: An Empirical Study of Reddit Norm Violations at Micro, Meso, and Macro Scales." In *Proceedings of the 2018 ACM on Human-Computer Interaction-CSCW*, 32:1–25. New York: ACM, 2018.

Cheng, Justin, Cristian Danescu-Niculescu-Mizil, and Jure Leskovec. "How Community Feedback Shapes User Behavior." In *Proceedings of the Eighth International AAAI Conference on Weblogs and Social Media*, 41–50. Ann Arbor, MI, 2014.

Chowdhry, Amit. "Facebook Confirms Emoji 'Reactions' Affects Your News Feed." *Forbes Magazine*, March 2, 2017. https://www.forbes.com/sites/amitchowdhry/2017/03/02/facebook-confirms-emoji-reactions-affects-your-news-feed/.

Chozick, Amy. "This Is the Guy Who's Taking Away the Likes." *New York Times*, January 17, 2020. https://www.nytimes.com/2020/01/17/business/instagram-likes.html.

Chung, Anna Woorim. "Gobo: Your Social Media, Your Rules." *Civic Media Blog*, June 3, 2019. https://civic.mit.edu/index.html%3Fp=2488.html.

Civic Signals. "Building Better Digital Public Spaces." New_Public, n.d. https://newpublic.org/signals.

Clark, Bryan. "Study Reveals Reddit Isn't as Big a Cesspool as You Thought. But It's Still a Cesspool." *The Next Web*, March 20, 2018. https://thenextweb.com/insider/2018/03/20/study-reveals-reddit-isnt-as-big-a-cesspool-as-you-thought-but-its-still-a-cesspool/.

Clark, Meredith. "Black Twitter: Building Connection through Cultural Conversation." In *Hashtag Publics: The Power and Politics of Discursive Networks*, edited by Nathan Rambukkana, 205–17. New York: Peter Lang Publishing, 2015.

Clement, J. "Social Sharing—Statistics & Facts." *Statista*, August 27, 2019. https://www.statista.com/topics/2539/social-sharing/.

Coaston, Jane. "#QAnon, the Scarily Popular Pro-Trump Consipracy Theory, Explained." *Vox*, August 2, 2018. https://www.vox.com/policy-and-politics/2018/8/1/17253444/qanon-trump-conspiracy-theory-reddit.

Cohen, Cathy J., Joseph Kahne, Benjamin Bowyer, Ellen Middaugh, and Jon Rogowski. "Participatory Politics: New Media and Youth Political Action." Oakland, CA, 2012. http://ypp.dmlcentral.net/sites/default/files/publications/Participatory_Politics_New_Media_and_Youth_Political_Action.2012.pdf.

Cole, Jeremy R., Moojan Ghafurian, and David Reitter. "Is Word Adoption a Grassroots Process? An Analysis of Reddit Communities." *Lecture Notes in Computer Science (Including Subseries Lecture Notes in Artificial Intelligence and Lecture Notes in Bioinformatics)* 10354 LNCS (2017): 236–41. https://doi.org/10.1007/978-3-319-60240-0_28.

Congress for the New Urbanism, The. "The Charter of the New Urbanism." https://www.cnu.org/who-we-are/charter-new-urbanism. Accessed October 31, 2016.

Connor, David Patrick, and Richard Tewksbury. "Social Control on Public Buses." *Journal of Theoretical and Philosophical Criminology* 4, no. 1 (2012): 1–13.

Conti, Allie. "Why the Ridiculous 'Paid Protester' Myth Refuses to Die." *Vice*, March 1, 2017. https://www.vice.com/en_us/article/kbkmn9/why-the-ridiculous-paid-protester--myth-refuses-to-die.

Cooper, John M. "Aristotle on the Forms of Friendship." *Review of Metaphysics* 30, no. 4 (1977): 619–48.

Cooper, John M. "Friendship and the Good in Aristotle." *Philosophical Review* 86, no. 3 (1977): 290–315.

Costanza-Chock, Sasha. *Design Justice: Community-Led Practices to Build the Worlds We Need.* Cambridge, MA: MIT Press, 2020.

Dahl, Robert A. "The Concept of Power." *Behavioral Science* 2 (1957): 201–15.

Dahlberg, Lincoln. "Extending the Public Sphere through Cyberspace: The Case of Minnesota E-Democracy." *First Monday* 5, no. 3 (2001). doi:10.5210/fm.v6i3.838.

Dahlberg, Lincoln. "Re-Constructing Digital Democracy: An Outline of Four 'Positions.'" *New Media and Society* 13, no. 6 (2011): 855–72.

Datta, Srayan, and Eytan Adar. "Extracting Inter-Community Conflicts in Reddit." In *Proceedings of the Thirteenth International AAAI Conference on Web and Social Media*, 146–57. Münich, Germany, 2019.

Davies, Rob. "Twitter Loses Ad Revenue despite Gaining 2 Million Users and Trump 'Boost.'" *The Guardian*, February 9, 2017. https://www.theguardian.com/technology/2017/feb/09/twitter-loses-advertising-revenue-rise-users-shares.

Davis, Jenny L. *How Artifacts Afford: The Power and Politics of Everyday Things.* Cambridge, MA: MIT Press, 2020.

Dean, Jodi. "Communicative Capitalism: Circulation and the Foreclosure of Politics." *Cultural Politics* 1, no. 1 (2005): 51–74.

Dean, Jodi. "Communicative Capitalism and Revolutionary Form." *Millennium: Journal of International Studies* 47, no. 3 (2019): 326–40.

Dean, Jodi. *Democracy and Other Neoliberal Fantasies: Communicative Capitalism and Left Politics.* Durham, NC: Duke University Press, 2009.

Deb, Sopan, and Marina Franco. "'Penis Seat' Causes Double Takes on Mexico City Subway." *New York Times*, March 31, 2017. https://www.nytimes.com/2017/03/31/world/americas/penis-seat-mexico-city-harassment.html.

DeCook, Julia. "How Deep Does the Rabbit Hole Go? The 'Wonderland' of r/TheRedPill and Its Ties to White Supremacy." *B2o: An Online Journal* 4, no. 2 (2019). http://www.boundary2.org/2019/11/julia-decook-how-deep-does-the-rabbit-hole-go-the-wonderland-of-r-theredpill-and-its-ties-to-white-supremacy/.

Deseriis, Marco. "Rethinking the Digital Democratic Affordance and Its Impact on Political Representation: Toward a New Framework." *New Media and Society* 23, no. 8 (2021): 2452–73.

Design Justice Network. "About Us," n.d. https://designjustice.org/about-us.

Dewey, John. "'Contrary to Human Nature.'" In *The Later Works of John Dewey, Volume 14: 1939–1941*, edited by Jo Ann Boydston, 258–61. Carbondale: Southern Illinois University Press, 2008.

Dewey, John. "Creative Democracy—The Task before Us." In *John Dewey: The Later Works, Vol. 14, 1939–1941*, edited by Jo Ann Boydston, 224–30. Carbondale: Southern Illinois University Press, 2008.

Dewey, John. "Democracy and Education." In *John Dewey: The Middle Works, Vol. 9, 1899–1924*, edited by Jo Ann Boydston. Carbondale: Southern Illinois University Press, 1916.

Dewey, John. "Democracy and Educational Administration." In *The Later Works of John Dewey, Volume 11: 1935–1937*, edited by Jo Ann Boydston, 217–25. Carbondale: Southern Illinois University Press, 2008.

Dewey, John. "Individuality in Education." In *The Middle Works of John Dewey, Volume 15: 1899–1924*, edited by Jo Ann Boydston, 170–79. Carbondale: Southern Illinois University Press, 2008.

Dewey, John. "Liberalism and Social Action." In *The Later Works of John Dewey, Volume 11: 1935–1937*, edited by Jo Ann Boydston, 1–66. Carbondale: Southern Illinois University Press, 2008.

Dewey, John. "The Bearings of Pragmatism upon Education." In *The Middle Works of John Dewey, Volume 4: 1899–1924*, 178–91. Carbondale: Southern Illinois University Press, 2008.

Dewey, John. "The Challenge of Democracy to Education." In *The Later Works of John Dewey, Volume 11: 1935–1937*, edited by Jo Ann Boydston, 181–90. Carbondale: Southern Illinois University Press, 2008.

Dewey, John. *The Public and Its Problems: An Essay in Political Inquiry*. Chicago: Gateway Books, 1946.

Dewey, John. "The School and Society." In *The Middle Works of John Dewey, Volume 1: 1899–1901*, edited by Jo Ann Boydston, 1–112. Carbondale: Southern Illinois University Press, 2008.

Dewey, John. "The School as a Means of Developing a Social Consciousness and Social Ideals in Children." In *The Middle Works of John Dewey, Volume 15: 1923–1924*, edited by Jo Ann Boydston, 150–57. Carbondale: Southern Illinois University Press, 2008.

Dewey, John. "The School as Social Centre." In *The Middle Works of John Dewey, Volume 2, 1899–1924*, edited by Jo Ann Boydston, 80–94. Carbondale: Southern Illinois University Press, 2008.

Dewey, John, Boyd H. Bode, and William Heard Kilpatrick. "An Active, Flexible Personality." In *The Later Works of John Dewey, Volume 11: 1935–1937*, edited by Jo Ann Boydston, 548–59. Carbondale: Southern Illinois University Press, 2008.

Dignam, Pierce Alexander, and Deana A. Rohlinger. "Misogynistic Men Online: How the Red Pill Helped Elect Trump." *Signs: Journal of Women in Culture and Society* 44, no. 3 (2019): 589–612.

DNLee. "You Should Know: Stephani Page and #BLACKandSTEM." *Scientific American*, July 13, 2014. https://blogs.scientificamerican.com/urban-scientist/you-should-know-stephani-page-and-blackandstem/.

Donath, J., and d. boyd. "Public Displays of Connection." *BT Technology Journal* 22, no. 4 (2004): 71–82.

Donnelly, Patrick G., and Charles E. Kimble. "An Evaluation of the Effects of Neighborhood Mobilization on Community Problems." *Journal of Prevention and Intervention in the Community* 32, no. 1–2 (2006): 61–80.

Dreyfuss, Emily. "Twitter's Chronological Timeline Will Save Us from Ourselves." *WIRED*, September 18, 2018. https://www.wired.com/story/twitter-chronological-timeline-will-save-us/.

Dreyfuss, Emily, and Issie Lapowsky. "Facebook Is Changing News Feed (Again) to Stop Fake News." *WIRED*, April 10, 2019. https://www.wired.com/story/facebook-click-gap-news-feed-changes/.

Drezner, Daniel W. "Who Is Targeting America's Greatest Political Scientists?" *Washington Post*, September 2, 2014. https://www.washingtonpost.com/posteverything/wp/2014/09/02/who-is-targeting-americas-greatest-political-scientists/.

DuBois, David L., and Barton J. Hirsch. "School and Neighborhood Friendship Patterns of Blacks and Whites in Early Adolescence." *Child Development* 61, no. 2 (1990): 524–36.

DubTeeDub. "Open Letter to Steve Huffman and the Board of Directors of Reddit, Inc—If You Believe in Standing Up to Hate and Supporting Black Lives, You Need to Act." *Reddit, r/AgainstHateSubreddits*, June 8, 2020. https://www.reddit.com/r/AgainstHateSubreddits/comments/gyyqem/open_letter_to_steve_huffman_and_the_board_of/.

Dudley, Lauren. "Year in Review: Content Moderation on Social Media Platforms in 2019." *Council on Foreign Relations: Digital and Cyberspace Policy Program*, December 19, 2019. https://www.cfr.org/blog/year-review-content-moderation-social-media-platforms-2019.

Duncan, Hugh D. *Culture and Democracy: The Struggle for Form in Society and Architecture in Chicago and the Middle West during the Life and Times of Louis H. Sullivan*. Totowa, NJ: Bedminster Press, 1965.

Dutton, William H., and K. Guthrie. "An Ecology of Games: The Political Construction of Santa Monica's Public Electronic Network." *Informatisation and the Public Sector* 1 (1991): 279–301.

"Eight Things to Know about Redditgifts." *redditgifts*, n.d. https://www.redditgifts.com/about/.

Ellingsen, Tanja. "Colorful Community or Ethnic Witches' Brew? Multiethnicity and Domestic Conflict during and after the Cold War." *Journal of Conflict Resolution* 44, no. 2 (2000): 228–49.

Ellison, Nicole B., Charles Steinfield, and Cliff Lampe. "Connection Strategies: Social Capital Implications of Facebook-Enabled Communication Practices." *New Media and Society* 13, no. 6 (2010): 873–92. https://doi.org/10.1177/1461444810385389.

Ellison, Nicole B., Charles Steinfield, and Cliff Lampe. "The Benefits of Facebook 'Friends': Social Capital and College Students' Use of Online Social Network Sites." *Journal of Computer-Mediated Communication* 12 (2007): 1143–68.

Ellison, Nicole B., and Jessica Vitak. "Social Network Site Affordances and Their Relationship to Social Capital Processes." In *The Handbook of the Psychology of Communication Technology*, edited by S. Shyam Sundar, 203–27. West Sussex, UK: Wiley Blackwell, 2015. https://doi.org/10.1002/9781118426456.ch9.

Enos, Ryan D. *The Space between Us: Social Geography and Politics*. New York: Cambridge University Press, 2017.

Facebook. "Groups." *Facebook Help Center*, n.d. https://www.facebook.com/help/1629740080681586.

"FAQ." *Reddit, r/TwoXChromosomes*, n.d. https://www.reddit.com/r/TwoXChromosomes/wiki/faq.

Farokhmanesh, Megan. "A Beginner's Guide to Mastodon, the Hot New Open-Source Twitter Clone." *The Verge*, April 1, 2017. https://www.theverge.com/2017/4/7/15183128/mastodon-open-source-twitter-clone-how-to-use.

Farr, James. "Social Capital: A Conceptual History." *Political Theory* 32, no. 1 (February 1, 2004): 6–33. https://doi.org/10.1177/0090591703254978.

Feldman, Roberta M. "Settlement-Identity: Psychological Bonds with Home Places in a Mobile Society." *Environment and Behavior* 22, no. 2 (1990): 183–229.

Feltman, Rachel. "How Redditgifts Is Making Money on Altruism." *Quartz*, July 12, 2013. https://qz.com/103166/how-redditgifts-is-monetizing-altruism/.

Festinger, Leon, Stanley Schachter, and Kurt Back. *Social Pressures in Informal Groups: A Study of Human Factors in Housing*. Stanford, CA: Stanford University Press, 1950.

Fisher, Marc, John Woodrow Cox, and Peter Hermann. "Pizzagate: From Rumor, to Hashtag, to Gunfire in D.C." *Washington Post*, December 6, 2016. https://www.washingtonpost.com/local/pizzagate-from-rumor-to-hashtag-to-gunfire-in-dc/2016/12/06/4c7def50-bbd4-11e6-94ac-3d324840106c_story.html.

Fitzsimmons, Emma G. "A Scourge Is Spreading. M.T.A.'s Cure? Dude, Close Your Legs." *New York Times*, December 20, 2014. https://www.nytimes.com/2014/12/21/nyregion/MTA-targets-manspreading-on-new-york-city-subways.html.

Flores-Saviaga, Claudia, Brian C. Keegan, and Saiph Savage. "Mobilizing the Trump Train: Understanding Collective Action in a Political Trolling Community." In *Proceedings of the 12th International Conference on Web and Social Media (ICWSM 2018), 82–91*. Stanford, CA: AAAI, 2018.

Florini, Sarah. *Beyond Hashtags: Racial Politics and Black Digital Networks*. New York: NYU Press, 2019.

Florini, Sarah. "Tweets, Tweeps, and Signifyin': Communication and Cultural Performance on 'Black Twitter.'" *Television and New Media* 15, no. 3 (2014): 233–37.

Forestal, Jennifer. "The Architecture of Political Spaces: Trolls, Digital Media, and Deweyan Democracy." *American Political Science Review* 111, no. 1 (2017): 149–61.

Forestal, Jennifer. "Constructing Digital Democracies: Facebook, Arendt, and the Politics of Design." *Political Studies* 69, no. 1 (2021): 26–44.

Foster, Sheila R. "Collective Action and the Urban Commons." *Notre Dame Law Review* 87 (2011): 57–134.

Foucault, Michel. *Discipline and Punish: The Birth of the Prison*. 2nd ed. New York: Vintage Books, 1995.

Foucault, Michel. *Power/Knowledge: Selected Interviews and Other Writings 1972–1977*. Edited by Colin Gordon. Translated by Colin Gordon, Leo Marshall, John Mepham, and Kate Soper. New York: Pantheon Books, 1980.

Frank, Jill. *A Democracy of Distinction: Aristotle and the Work of Politics*. Chicago: Chicago University Press, 2005.

Fried, Marc. "Grieving for a Lost Home: Psychological Costs of Relocation." In *Urban Renewal: The Record and the Controversy*, edited by James Q. Wilson, 359–60. Cambridge, MA: MIT Press, 1966.

Friedman, Bill. *Designing Casinos to Dominate the Competition*. Reno, NV: Institute for the Study of Gambling and Commercial Gaming, University of Nevada, 2000.

Fussell, Sidney. "The Endless, Invisible Persuasion Tactics of the Internet." *The Atlantic*, August 2, 2019. https://www.theatlantic.com/technology/archive/2019/08/how-dark-patterns-online-manipulate-shoppers/595360/.

Gallagher, Leigh. "The Cult of the Amtrak Quiet Car." *Fortune*, September 17, 2014. http://fortune.com/2014/09/17/amtrak-quiet-car/.

Galster, George. "On the Nature of Neighborhood." *Urban Studies* 38, no. 12 (2001): 2111–24.

Gibson, James J. *The Ecological Approach to Visual Perception*. Hillsdale, NJ: Lawrence Erlbaum Associates, Inc., 1986.

Gibson, James J. "Notes on Affordances." In *Reasons for Realism: Selected Essays of James J. Gibson*, edited by Edward Reed and Rebecca Jones, 401–18. Hillsdale, NJ: Lawrence Erlbaum Associates, 1982.

Gilbert, Eric. "Widespread Underprovision on Reddit." In *Proceedings of the 2013 Conference on Computer Supported Cooperative Work—CSCW '13*, 803–8. New York: ACM, 2013. https://doi.org/10.1145/2441776.2441866.

Gillespie, Tarleton. "Algorithmically Recognizable: Santorum's Google Problem, and Google's Santorum Problem." *Information, Communication and Society* 20, no. 1 (2017): 63–80.

Gillespie, Tarleton. *Custodians of the Internet: Platforms, Content Moderation, and the Hidden Decisions That Shape Social Media*. New Haven: Yale University Press, 2018.

Gillespie, Tarleton. "The Relevance of Algorithms." In *Media Technologies: Essays on Communication, Materiality, and Society*, edited by Tarleton Gillespie, Pablo J. Boczkowski, and Kirsten A. Foot, 167–94. Cambridge, MA: MIT Press, 2014.

Ginsberg, David, and Moira Burke. "Is Spending Time on Social Media Bad for Us?" *Facebook Newsroom*, December 2017. https://about.fb.com/news/2017/12/hard-questions-is-spending-time-on-social-media-bad-for-us/.

Glaser, April. "How to Use Twitter: Critical Tips for New Users." *WIRED*, May 6, 2016. https://www.wired.com/2016/05/twitter-onboarding-tips-for-new-users/.

glycine. "Comment on 'To the Mods of 2X: A Question.'" *Reddit, r/TwoXChromosomes*, 2014. https://www.reddit.com/r/TwoXChromosomes/comments/25pfj8/to_the_mods_of_2x_a_question/chjl501/.

Goffman, Erving. *Relations in Public: Microstudies of the Public Order*. New York: Basic Books, 1971.

Goldman, Alex. "Being a Feminist on Reddit—The Defaulting of /r/TwoXChromosomes." *WNYC On The Media Blog*, May 19, 2014. https://www.wnyc.org/story/being-feminists-reddit-defaulting-rtwoxchromosomes/.

Goldman, Alex. "Making TwoXChromosomes a Default Subreddit Has Not Gone Over Well with Everyone." *WNYC On the Media Blog*, May 20, 2014. https://www.wnyc.org/story/making-twoxchromosomes-default-subreddit-has-not-gone-over-well-everyone/.

Gould, Roger V. *Insurgent Identities: Class, Community, and Protest in Paris from 1848 to the Commune*. Chicago: University of Chicago Press, 1995.

Graham, Roderick, and Shawn Smith. "The Content of Our #Characters: Black Twitter as Counterpublic." *Sociology of Race and Ethnicity* 2, no. 4 (2016): 433–49.

Granovetter, Mark. "The Strength of Weak Ties." *American Journal of Sociology* 78, no. 6 (1973): 1360–80. https://doi.org/10.1086/225469.

Greenspan, Sam. "Half a House." 99% Invisible, 2016. https://99percentinvisible.org/episode/half-a-house/.

Grimmelmann, James. "Regulation by Software." *Yale Law Journal* 114 (2005): 1719–58.

Gringlas, Sam. "With an Election on the Horizon, Older Adults Get Help Spotting Fake News." *NPR*, February 26, 2020. https://www.npr.org/2020/02/26/809224742/with-an-election-on-the-horizon-older-adults-get-help-spotting-fake-news.

Gui, Xinning, Yubo Kou, Kathleen Pine, Elisa Ladaw, Harold Kim, Eli Suzuki-Gill, and Yunan Chen. "Multidimensional Risk Communication: Public Discourse on Risks during an Emerging Epidemic." In *Proceedings of the 2018 CHI Conference on Human Factors in Computing Systems*, 1–14. New York: ACM Press, 2018.

Gutmann, Amy, and Dennis Thompson. *Democracy and Disagreement*. Cambridge, MA: Harvard University Press, 1996.

Gutmann, Amy, and Dennis Thompson. *The Spirit of Compromise: Why Governing Demands It and Campaigning Undermines It*. Princeton, NJ: Princeton University Press, 2012.

Habib, Hussam, Maaz Bin Musa, Fareed Zaffar, and Rishab Nithyanand. "To Act or React? Investigating Proactive Strategies for Online Community Moderation." *Pre-Print, ArXiv*, 2019. https://arxiv.org/abs/1906.11932.

Halbwachs, Maurice. *On Collective Memory*. Translated by Lewis A. Coser. Chicago: University of Chicago Press, 1992.

Halpern, Daniel, and Jennifer Gibbs. "Social Media as Catalyst for Online Deliberation? Exploring the Affordances of Facebook and YouTube for Political Expression." *Computers in Human Behavior* 29, no. 3 (2013): 1159–68.

Hamilton, William L., Justine Zhang, Cristian Danescu-Niculescu-Mizil, Dan Jurafsky, and Jure Leskovec. "Loyalty in Online Communities." In *Proceedings of the Eleventh International AAAI Conference on Web and Social Media*, 540–43. Montréal, QC, 2017.

Hampton, Keith. "Place-Based and IT Mediated 'Community.'" *Planning Theory and Practice* 3, no. 2 (2002): 228–31.

Hampton, Keith, and Barry Wellman. "Neighboring in Netville: How the Internet Supports Community and Social Capital in a Wired Suburb." *City and Community* 2, no. 4 (2003): 277–311. https://doi.org/10.1046/j.1535-6841.2003.00057.x.

Hare, William. "Education for an Unsettled World: Dewey's Conception of Open-Mindedness." *Journal of Thought* 39, no. 3 (2004): 111–27.

Harris, Joshua, and Sam Haveson. "Fleets: A New Way to Join the Conversation." *Twitter Blog*, November 17, 2020. https://blog.twitter.com/en_us/topics/product/2020/introducing-fleets-new-way-to-join-the-conversation.html.

Harris, Paul B., Carol M. Werner, Barbara B. Brown, and Dave Ingebritsen. "Relocation and Privacy Regulation: A Cross-Cultural Analysis." *Journal of Environmental Psychology* 15 (1995): 311–20.

Hauben, Michael, and Ronda Hauben. *Netizens: On the History and Impact of Usenet and the Internet*. New York: Wiley, 1997.

Hay, Robert Bruce. "Sense of Place in Developmental Context." *Journal of Environmental Psychology* 18, no. 1 (1998): 5–29.

Hénaff, Marcel, and Tracy B. Strong, eds. *Public Space and Democracy*. Minneapolis: University of Minnesota Press, 2001.

Hern, Alex. "Reddit Women Protest at New Front-Page Position." *The Guardian*, May 13, 2014. https://www.theguardian.com/technology/2014/may/13/reddit-women-protest-front-page-subforum-subreddit-position.

Hicks, Matt. "New Groups: Stay Closer to Groups of People in Your Life." *Facebook*, October 6, 2010. https://www.facebook.com/notes/facebook/new-groups-stay-closer-to-groups-of-people-in-your-life/434700832130/.

Hindman, Matthew. *The Internet Trap: How the Digital Economy Builds Monopolies and Undermines Democracy*. Princeton, NJ: Princeton University Press, 2018.

Honan, Mat. "RIP: Google Reader Meets Its Inevitable End." *WIRED*, March 13, 2013. https://www.wired.com/2013/03/r-i-p-google-reader/.

Honig, Bonnie. *Public Things: Democracy in Disrepair*. New York: Fordham University Press, 2017.

Horne, Benjamin D., Sibel Adah, and Sujoy Sikdar. "Identifying the Social Signals That Drive Online Discussions: A Case Study of Reddit Communities." In *Proceedings of the 26th International Conference on Computer Communication and Networks (ICCN)*, 1–9. Vancouver, BC, 2017.

Huang, Jeff, Katherine M. Thornton, and Efthimis N. Efthimiadis. "Conversational Tagging in Twitter." In *Proceedings of the 21st ACM Conference on Hypertext and Hypermedia—HT '10*, 173–8. Toronto, 2010. https://doi.org/10.1145/1810617.1810647.

Huang, Yueng-Hsiang, Michelle M. Robertson, and Kou-I Chang. "The Role of Environmental Control on Environmental Satisfaction, Communication, and Psychological Stress: Effects of Office Ergonomics Training." *Environment and Behavior* 36, no. 5 (2004): 617–37. https://doi.org/10.1177/0013916503262543.

Huckfeldt, R. Robert. "Social Contexts, Social Networks, and Urban Neighborhoods: Environmental Constraints on Friendship Choice." *American Journal of Sociology* 89, no. 3 (1983): 651–69.

Hughes, David John, Moss Rowe, Mark Batey, and Andrew Lee. "A Tale of Two Sites: Twitter vs. Facebook and the Personality Predictors of Social Media Usage." *Computers in Human Behavior* 28, no. 2 (2012): 561–69. https://doi.org/10.1016/j.chb.2011.11.001.

Hunt, Melissa G., Rachel Marx, Courtney Lipson, and Jordyn Young. "No More FOMO: Limiting Social Media Decreases Loneliness and Depression." *Journal of Social and Clinical Psychology* 37, no. 10 (2018): 751–68.

Husain, Nausheen. "Timeline: Legal Fight over Trump's 'Muslim Ban' and the Supreme Court Ruling." *Chicago Tribune*, June 26, 2018. https://www.chicagotribune.com/data/ct-travel-ban-ruling-timeline-htmlstory.html.

Hutchby, Ian. "Technologies, Texts, and Affordances." *Sociology* 35, no. 2 (2001): 441–56.

Jackson, Sarah J., Moya Bailey, and Brooke Foucault Welles. "#GirlsLikeUs: Trans Advocacy and Community Building Online." *New Media and Society* 20, no. 5 (2018): 1868–88. https://doi.org/10.1177/1461444817709276.

Jackson, Sarah J., Moya Bailey, and Brooke Foucault Welles. *#HashtagActivism: Networks of Race and Gender Justice*. Cambridge, MA: MIT Press, 2020.

Jacobs, Jane. *The Death and Life of Great American Cities*. New York: Vintage Books, 1992.

Java, Akshay, Xiaodan Song, Tim Finin, and Belle Tseng. "Why We Twitter: Understanding Microblogging Usage and Communities." In *Proceedings of the 9th WebKDD and 1st SNA-KDD 2007 Workshop on Web Mining and Social Network Analysis*, 56–65. San Jose, CA, 2007. https://doi.org/10.1145/1348549.1348556.

Jenkins, Henry. "'Cultural Acupuncture': Fan Activism and the Harry Potter Alliance." *Transformative Works and Culture* 10 (2012). https://doi.org/10.3983/twc.2012.0305.

Jeong, Sarah. "Mastodon Is Like Twitter without Nazis, So Why Are We Not Using It?" *Vice: Motherboard*, April 4, 2017. https://motherboard.vice.com/en_us/article/783akg/mastodon-is-like-twitter-without-nazis-so-why-are-we-not-using-it.

Jobert, Thibaud. "Story of a Reddit Hug of Death and Lessons Learned." *Medium: CodinGame*, September 27, 2016. https://medium.com/codingame/story-of-a-reddit-hug-of-death-and-lessons-learned-3565bb8a6793.

Joyce, Colin. "Persistent Gropers Force Japan to Introduce Women-Only Carriages." *The Telegraph*, May 15, 2005. https://www.telegraph.co.uk/news/worldnews/asia/japan/1490059/Persistent-gropers-force-Japan-to-introduce-women-only-carriages.html.

Kantrowitz, Alex. "An Algorithmic Feed May Be Twitter's Last Remaining Card to Play." *BuzzFeed News*, June 29, 2015. https://www.buzzfeednews.com/article/alexkantrowitz/an-algorithmic-feed-may-be-twitters-last-remaining-card-to-p.

Karpf, David. *Analytic Activism: Digital Listening and the New Political Strategy*. New York: Oxford University Press, 2016.

Karpf, David. "The Internet and Engaged Citizenship." Cambridge, MA: Commission on the Practice of Democratic Citizenship, 2019.

Karpf, David. *The MoveOn Effect: The Unexpected Transformation of American Political Advocacy*. New York: Oxford University Press, 2012.

Kastrenakes, Jacob. "Reddit Reveals Daily Active User Count for the First Time: 52 Million." *The Verge*, December 2020. https://www.theverge.com/2020/12/1/21754984/reddit-dau-daily-users-revealed.

Kastrenakes, Jacob. "Twitter's User Numbers Are Growing Again." *The Verge*, April 25, 2018. https://www.theverge.com/2018/4/25/17274828/twitter-earning-q1-2018-profit-user-growth.

Kastrenakes, Jacob. "Twitter Lost Users in the US Again, but It Finally Made a Profit." *The Verge*, February 8, 2018. https://www.theverge.com/2018/2/8/16957354/twitter-q4-2017-earnings.

Keller, Megan. "Dem Senator Defends Social Media Platforms Deleting Content: 'Not the Same as Government Censorship.'" *The Hill*, August 7, 2018. http://thehill.com/policy/technology/400740-dem-senator-defends-social-media-deleting-content-not-the-same-as.

Kendall, Mikki. "#SolidarityIsForWhiteWomen: Women of Color's Issue with Digital Feminism." *The Guardian*, August 14, 2013. http://www.theguardian.com/commentisfree/2013/aug/14/solidarityisforwhitewomen-hashtag-feminism.

Kessler, Sarah. "Meet HeartMob: A Tool for Fighting Online Harassment Designed by People Who Have Been Harassed." *Fast Company*, May 14, 2015. https://www.fastcompany.com/3046181/meet-heartmob-a-tool-for-fighting-online-harassment-designed-by-people-who-hav.

KeyserSosa. "An Update on the State of the Reddit/Reddit and Reddit/Reddit-Mobile Repositories." *Reddit, r/Changelog*, September 1, 2017. https://www.reddit.com/r/changelog/comments/6xfyfg/an_update_on_the_state_of_the_redditreddit_and/.

Klinenberg, Eric. "Facebook Isn't Making Us Lonely." *Slate*, April 19, 2012. http://www.slate.com/articles/life/culturebox/2012/04/is_facebook_making_us_lonely_no_the_atlantic_cover_story_is_wrong_.single.html.

Knobloch-Westerwick, Silvia, and Jingbo Meng. "Looking the Other Way: Selective Exposure to Attitude-Consistent and Counterattitudinal Political Information." *Communication Research* 36, no. 3 (2009): 426–48.

Koebler, Jason. "How r/The_donald Became a Melting Pot of Frustration and Hate." *Motherboard*, July 12, 2016. https://motherboard.vice.com/en_us/article/53d5xb/what-is-rthedonald-donald-trump-subreddit.

Kogl, Alexandra. *Strange Places: The Political Potentials and Perils of Everyday Spaces*. Lanham, MD: Lexington Books, 2008.

Kohn, Margaret. *Brave New Neighborhoods: The Privatization of Public Space*. New York: Routledge, 2004.

Kohn, Margaret. *Radical Space: Building the House of the People*. Ithaca, NY: Cornell University Press, 2003.

Korpela, Kalevi M., Matti Ylén, Liisa Tyrväinen, and Harri Silvennoinen. "Stability of Self-Reported Favourite Places and Place Attachment over a 10-Month Period." *Journal of Environmental Psychology* 29, no. 1 (2009): 95–100. https://doi.org/10.1016/j.jenvp.2008.05.008.

Kosnoski, Jason. "Artful Discussion: John Dewey's Classroom as a Model of Deliberative Association." *Political Theory* 33, no. 5 (2005): 654–77.

Kovach, Steve. "Alphabet Had More than $70 Billion in Market Cap Wiped Out, and It Says YouTube Is One of the Problems." *CNBC*, April 30, 2019. https://www.cnbc.com/2019/04/30/youtube-algorithm-changes-negatively-impact-google-ad-revenue.html.

Kramer, Adam D. I., Jamie E. Guillory, and Jeffrey T. Hancock. "Experimental Evidence of Massive-Scale Emotional Contagion through Social Networks." *PNAS* 111, no. 29 (2014): 8788–90.

Kranes, David. "Play Grounds." *Journal of Gambling Studies* 11, no. 1 (1995): 91–102.

Kraut, Robert, Carmen Egido, and Jolene Galegher. "Patterns of Contact and Communication in Scientific Research Collaboration." In *Proceedings of the 1988 ACM Conference on Computer-Supported Cooperative Work*, 1–12. Portland, OR: ACM, 1988.

Kruglanski, Arie W., and Donna M. Webster. "Motivated Closing of the Mind: 'Seizing' and 'Freezing.'" *Psychological Review* 103, no. 2 (1996): 263–83.

Kumparak, Greg. "Reddit Acquires Fan-Made Secret Santa Site, RedditGifts." *TechCrunch*, August 23, 2011. https://techcrunch.com/2011/08/23/reddit-acquires-redditgifts/.

Kunda, Ziva. "The Case for Motivated Reasoning." *Psychological Bulletin* 108, no. 3 (1990): 480–98.

Kwak, Haewoon, Changhyun Lee, Hosung Park, and Sue Moon. "What Is Twitter, a Social Network or a News Media?" In *International World Wide Web Conference Committee*, 591–600. Raleigh, NC, 2010. https://doi.org/10.1145/1772690.1772751.

Lagorio-Chafkin, Christine. "Reddit and the God Emperor of the Internet." *New York Times*, November 19, 2016. https://www.nytimes.com/2016/11/20/opinion/sunday/reddit-and-the-god-emperor-of-the-internet.html.

Lalli, Marco. "Urban-Related Identity: Theory, Measurement, and Empirical Findings." *Journal of Environmental Psychology* 12 (1992): 285–303.

Lampe, Cliff, and Erik Johnston. "Follow the (Slash) Dot: Effects of Feedback on New Members in an Online Community." In *Proceedings of the 2005 International ACM SIGGROUP Conference on Supporting Group Work—GROUP '05*, 11–20. New York: Association for Computing Machinery, 2005. https://doi.org/10.1145/1099203.1099206.

Lampe, Cliff, Paul Zube, Jusil Lee, Chul Hyun Park, and Erik Johnston. "Crowdsourcing Civility: A Natural Experiment Examining the Effects of Distributed Moderation in Online Forums." *Government Information Quarterly* 31, no. 2 (2014): 317–26. https://doi.org/10.1016/j.giq.2013.11.005.

Laniado, David, and Peter Mika. "Making Sense of Twitter." In *9th International Semantic Web Conference, ISWC 2010*, edited by Peter F. Patel-Schneider, Yue Pan, Pascal Hitzler, Peter Mika, Lei Zhang, Jeff Z. Pan, Ian Horrocks, and Birte Glimm, 470–85. Shanghai: Springer, 2010.

Lapowsky, Issie. "15 Moments That Defined Facebook's First 15 Years." *WIRED*, February 4, 2019. https://www.wired.com/story/facebook-15-defining-moments/.

Larsson, Anders Olof, and Hallvard Moe. "Studying Political Microblogging: Twitter Users in the 2010 Swedish Election Campaign." *New Media and Society* 14, no. 5 (2011): 729–47.

Lawrence, Eric, John Sides, and Henry Farrell. "Self-Segregation or Deliberation? Blog Readership, Participation, and Polarization in American Politics." *Perspectives on Politics* 8, no. 1 (2010): 141–57.

Le Corbusier. *The Radiant City: Elements of a Doctrine of Urbanism to be Used as the Basis of Our Machine-Age Civilization*. New York: Orion Press, 1967.

Leavitt, Alex, and Joshua Clark. "Upvoting Hurricane Sandy: Event-Based News Production Processes on a Social News Site." In *Proceedings of the 32nd Annual ACM Conference on*

Human Factors in Computing Systems—CHI '14, 1495–504. New York: Association for Computing Machinery, 2014.

Leavitt, Jacqueline, and Susan Saegert. "The Community-Household: Responding to Housing Abandonment in New York City." *Journal of the American Planning Association* 54, no. 4 (1988): 489–500. https://doi.org/10.1080/01944368808976675.

Lee, So Young, and Jay L. Brand. "Effects of Control over Office Workspace on Perceptions of the Work Environment and Work Outcomes." *Journal of Environmental Psychology* 25, no. 3 (2005): 323–33. https://doi.org/10.1016/j.jenvp.2005.08.001.

Lee, Timothy B. "The Button: The Fascinating Social Experiment Driving Reddit Crazy." *Vox*, April 14, 2015. https://www.vox.com/2015/4/10/8383165/reddit-button-explained.

LeFebvre, Rebecca Kay, and Crystal Armstrong. "Grievance-Based Social Movement Mobilization in the #Ferguson Twitter Storm." *New Media and Society* 20, no. 1 (2018): 8–28.

Lessig, Lawrence. *Code Version 2.0*. New York: Basic Books, 2006.

Levy, Plet. "Christians and Atheists Square Off in Online Battle to Raise Money for Charity." *HuffPost*, December 16, 2010. https://www.huffingtonpost.com/2010/12/16/christian-and-atheist-gro_n_797910.html.

Lewicka, Maria. "Place Attachment: How Far Have We Come in the Last 40 Years?" *Journal of Environmental Psychology* 31, no. 3 (2011): 207–30. https://doi.org/10.1016/j.jenvp.2010.10.001.

Lindgren, Simon, and Randy Lundström. "Pirate Culture and Hacktivist Mobilization: The Cultural and Social Protocols of #WikiLeaks on Twitter." *New Media and Society* 13, no. 6 (2011): 999–1018.

Lippmann, Walter. *The Phantom Public*. New Brunswick, NJ: Transaction Publishers, 1993.

Liu, Miao, Robert W. Gehl, and Diana Zulli. "Rethinking the 'Social' in 'Social Media': Insights into Topology, Abstraction, and Scale on the Mastodon Social Network." *New Media and Society* 22, no. 7 (2020): 1188–205.

Lyons, Kim. "Facebook Bans One of the Largest QAnon Groups for Violating Harassment, Hate Speech Policies." *The Verge*, August 2020. https://www.theverge.com/2020/8/8/21359723/facebook-bans-qanon-twitter-roku-tiktok-reddit.

Machiavelli, Niccolò. *Discourses on Livy*. Translated by Harvey C. Mansfield and Nathan Tarcov. Chicago: Chicago University Press, 1995.

Machkovech, Sam. "Did Reddit's April Fool's Gag Solve the Issue of Online Hate Speech?" *Ars Technica*, April 3, 2017. https://arstechnica.com/gaming/2017/04/in-memoriam-reddits-72-hour-live-graffiti-wall-as-a-social-experiment/.

Mansbridge, Jane J. *Beyond Adversary Democracy*. Chicago: University of Chicago Press, 1983.

Mansbridge, Jane, James Bohman, Simone Chambers, Thomas Christiano, Archon Fung, John Parkinson, Dennis F. Thompson, and Mark E. Warren. "A Systemic Approach to Deliberative Democracy." In *Deliberative Systems: Deliberative Democracy at the Large Scale*, edited by John Parkinson and Jane J. Mansbridge, 1–26. Cambridge, UK: Cambridge University Press, 2012.

Marantz, Andrew. "Reddit and the Struggle to Detoxify the Internet." *New Yorker*, March 19, 2018. https://www.newyorker.com/magazine/2018/03/19/reddit-and-the-struggle-to-detoxify-the-internet.

Marche, Stephen. "Is Facebook Making Us Lonely?" *Atlantic Magazine*, May 2012. http://www.theatlantic.com/magazine/archive/2012/05/is-facebook-making-us-lonely/8930/.

Marcus, Clare Cooper. "Shared Outdoor Space and Community Life." *Places* 15, no. 2 (2003): 32–41.

Martin, Trevor. "Dissecting Trump's Most Rabid Online Following." *FiveThirtyEight*, March 23, 2017. https://fivethirtyeight.com/features/dissecting-trumps-most-rabid-online-following/.

Martineau, Paris. "Facebook's New Content Moderation Tools Put Posts in Context." *WIRED*, July 3, 2019. https://www.wired.com/story/facebooks-new-content-moderation-tools-put-posts-in-context/.

Massey, Douglas S., and Nancy A. Denton. *American Apartheid: Segregation and the Making of the Underclass*. Cambridge, MA: Harvard University Press, 1993.

"The Mastodon Project." *Mastodon*. https://joinmastodon.org/. Accessed July 12, 2018.

Matatyaou, Uri Jacob. "Memory-Space-Politics: Public Memorial and the Problem of Political Judgement." PhD diss., Northwestern University, 2008.

Matias, J. Nathan. "Do Downvote Buttons Cause Unruly Online Behavior?" *CAT Lab*, January 2018 https://civilservant.io/do_downvotes_cause_bad_behavior_jan_2018.html.

Matias, J. Nathan. "Going Dark: Social Factors in Collective Action against Platform Operators in the Reddit Blackout." In *Proceedings of the 2016 CHI Conference on Human Factors in Computing Systems*, 1138–51. New York: ACM, 2016.

Matias, J. Nathan. "Preventing Harassment and Increasing Group Participation through Social Norms in 2,190 Online Science Discussions." *PNAS: Proceedings of the National Academy of Sciences of the United States of America* 116, no. 20 (2019): 9785–89.

Matias, J. Nathan, Reem Al-Kashif, Max Klein, and Eric Pennington. "Volunteers Thanked Thousands of Wikipedia Editors to Learn the Effects of Receiving Thanks." *CAT Lab*, June 2020. https://citizensandtech.org/2020/06/effects-of-saying-thanks-on-wikipedia/.

Matias, J. Nathan, Tyler Simko, and Marianne Reddan. "Study Results: Reducing the Silencing Role of Harassment in Online Feminism Discussions." *CAT Lab*, June 2020. https://citizensandtech.org/2020/06/reducing-harassment-impacts-in-feminism-online/.

Matsakis, Louise. "How to Take Back Your Facebook News Feed." *WIRED*, February 7, 2018. https://www.wired.com/story/take-back-your-facebook-news-feed/.

McLaney, Margaret Anne, and Joseph J. Hurrell Jr. "Control, Stress, and Job Satisfaction in Canadian Nurses." *Work and Stress: An International Journal of Work, Health, and Organisations* 2, no. 3 (1988): 217–24.

Meo, Pasquale de, Emilio Ferrara, Giacomo Fiumara, and Alessandro Provetti. "On Facebook, Most Ties Are Weak." *Communications of the ACM* 57, no. 11 (2014): 78–84.

Metz, Rachel. "Social Networks Are Broken. This Man Wants to Fix Them." *MIT Technology Review*, February 9, 2018. https://www.technologyreview.com/s/610152/social-networks-are-broken-this-man-wants-to-fix-them/.

Milligan, Melinda J. "Interactional Past and Potential: The Social Construction of Place Attachment." *Symbolic Interaction* 21, no. 1 (1998): 1–33. https://doi.org/10.1525/si.1998.21.1.1.

Mills, Richard, and Adam Fish. "A Computational Study of How and Why Reddit.Com Was an Effective Platform in the Campaign Against SOPA." In *Proceedings of the 2015 International Conference on Social Computing and Social Media*, 229–41. Cham: Springer, 2015.

Mitchell, Scott S. D., and Merlyna Lim. "Too Crowded for Crowdsourced Journalism: Reddit, Portability, and Citizen Participation in the Syrian Crisis." *Canadian Journal of Communication* 43 (2018): 399–419.

Mitchell, William J. *City of Bits: Space, Place, and the Infobahn*. Cambridge, MA: MIT Press, 1995.

Montesquieu, Baron de. *The Spirit of the Laws*. Edited by Thomas Nugent. New York: Hafner Press, 1994.

Moore, Charles. *Daniel H. Burnham, Architect, Planner of Cities, Volume 2*. Boston: Houghton Mifflin, 1921.

Mouw, Ted, and Barbara Entwisle. "Residential Segregation and Interracial Friendship in Schools." *American Journal of Sociology* 112, no. 2 (2006): 394–441.

Munroe, Randall. "Reddit's New Comment Sorting System." *Reddit Blog*, October 15, 2009. http://www.redditblog.com/2009/10/reddits-new-comment-sorting-system.html.

Mutz, Diana C. *Hearing the Other Side: Deliberative versus Participatory Democracy*. New York: Cambridge University Press, 2012.

Myers, Seth A., Aneesh Sharma, Pankaj Gupta, and Jimmy Lin. "Information Network or Social Network? The Structure of the Twitter Follow Graph." In *WWW '14 Companion: Proceedings of the 23rd International Conference on World Wide Web*, 493–98. Seoul: ACM, 2014.

Nahemow, Lucille, and M. Powell Lawton. "Similarity and Propinquity in Friendship Formation." *Journal of Personality and Social Psychology* 32, no. 2 (1975): 205–13.

Nardi, Bonnie, and Justin Harris. "Strangers and Friends: Collaborative Play in World of Warcraft." In *CSCW 2006: Proceedings of the ACM Conference on Computer-Supported Cooperative Work*, 149–58. New York: Association for Computing Machinery, 2006.

Natematias. "New Reddit Study: Reducing the Silencing Role of Harassment in r/Feminism." *Reddit, r/Feminism*, June 2020. https://www.reddit.com/r/Feminism/comments/hfmtg5/new_reddit_study_reducing_the_silencing_role_of/.

Natematias. "Study Results: Reducing the Silencing Role of Harassment in r/Feminism." *Reddit, r/TheoryofReddit*, June 2020. https://www.reddit.com/r/TheoryOfReddit/comments/hfo0l7/study_results_reducing_the_silencing_role_of/.

Nathan, Vini. "Residents' Satisfaction with the Sites and Services Approach in Affordable Housing." *Housing and Society* 22, no. 3 (1995): 52–78.

Newcomb, Theodore M. *The Acquaintance Process*. New York: Holt, Rinehart and Winston, 1961.

Newitz, Annalee. "A Better Internet Is Waiting for Us." *New York Times*, November 30, 2019. https://www.nytimes.com/interactive/2019/11/30/opinion/social-media-future.html.

Newman, Oscar. *Creating Defensible Space*. Washington, DC: US Department of Housing and Urban Development, 1996.

Newman, Oscar. *Defensible Space: People and Design in the Violent City*. New York: Macmillan, 1972.

Newton, Casey. "Mastodon.Social Is an Open-Source Twitter Competitor That's Growing like Crazy." *The Verge*, 2017. https://www.theverge.com/2017/4/4/15177856/mastodon-social-network-twitter-clone.

Nicas, Jack. "Alex Jones and Infowars Content Is Removed from Apple, Facebook and YouTube." *New York Times*, August 6, 2018. https://www.nytimes.com/2018/08/06/technology/infowars-alex-jones-apple-facebook-spotify.html.

Nield, David. "Social Media Is Making You Miserable. Here's How to Delete Your Accounts." *Popular Science*, January 20, 2018. https://www.popsci.com/delete-social-media-accounts/.

Noble, Safiya Umoja. *Algorithms of Oppression: How Search Engines Reinforce Racism*. New York: NYU Press, 2018.

Norman, Don. *The Design of Everyday Things*. Rev. and expanded ed. New York: Basic Books, 2013.

Notopoulos, Katie. "RIP Yahoo Answers: It Died as It Lived, Needlessly and Stupidly." *BuzzFeed News*, April 5, 2021. https://www.buzzfeednews.com/article/katienotopoulos/rip-yahoo-answers.

NYPD-32. "The Great r/The_Donald Invasion." *Reddit, r/The_donald*, December 9, 2015. https://www.reddit.com/r/The_Donald/comments/3w0q4n/the_great_rthe_donald_invasion/.

Ochoa Espejo, Paulina. *On Borders: Territories, Legitimacy, and the Rights of Place*. New York: Oxford University Press, 2020.

Ohlheiser, Abby. "Fearing Yet Another Witch Hunt, Reddit Bans 'Pizzagate.'" *Washington Post*, November 24, 2016. https://www.washingtonpost.com/news/the-intersect/wp/2016/11/23/fearing-yet-another-witch-hunt-reddit-bans-pizzagate/.

Ohlheiser, Abby. "Trump's Meme Brigade Took Over Reddit. Now Reddit Is Trying to Stop Them." *Washington Post*, June 17, 2016. https://www.washingtonpost.com/news/the-intersect/wp/2016/06/17/trumps-meme-brigade-took-over-reddit-now-reddit-is-trying-to-stop-them/.

Olson, Mancur, Jr. *The Logic of Collective Action: Public Goods and the Theory of Groups*. Cambridge, MA: Harvard University Press, 1971.

O'Neil, Cathy. *Weapons of Math Destruction: How Big Data Increases Inequality and Threatens Democracy*. New York: Crown Publishers, 2016.

O'Neill, Michael J. "Work Space Adjustability, Storage, and Enclosure as Predictors of Employee Reactions and Performance." *Environment and Behavior* 26, no. 4 (1994): 504–26.

Oremus, Will. "How Twitter Solved One of Its Oldest Problems." *Medium: OneZero*, September 6, 2019. https://onezero.medium.com/how-twitter-solved-one-of-its-oldest-problems-7ca8b3dd0604.

Oremus, Will. "Twitter's New Order: Inside the Changes That Could Save Its Business--and Reshape Civil Discourse." *Slate*, March 5, 2017. http://www.slate.com/articles/technology/cover_story/2017/03/twitter_s_timeline_algorithm_and_its_effect_on_us_explained.html.

Oremus, Will. "Who Controls Your Facebook Feed." *Slate*, January 3, 2016. http://www.slate.com/articles/technology/cover_story/2016/01/how_facebook_s_news_feed_algorithm_works.html.

Orsini, Lauren Rae. "TwoXChromosomes, Reddit's Biggest Female-Focused Community, Turns 3." *The Daily Dot*, July 16, 2012. https://www.dailydot.com/culture/twoxchromosomes-reddit-women-subreddit-anniversary/.

Ostrom, Elinor. *Governing the Commons: The Evolution of Institutions for Collective Action*. Cambridge, UK: Cambridge University Press, 1990.

Ostrom, Elinor, and T. K. Ahn, eds. *Foundations of Social Capital: Foundations of Social Capital*. Northampton, MA: Edward Elgar, 2003.

Owen, Laura Hazard. "One Year In, Facebook's Big Algorithm Change Has Spurred an Angry, Fox News–Dominated—and Very Engaged!—News Feed." *NiemanLab*, March 15, 2019. https://www.niemanlab.org/2019/03/one-year-in-facebooks-big-algorithm-change-has-spurred-an-angry-fox-news-dominated-and-very-engaged-news-feed/.

Pandell, Lexi. "An Oral History of the #Hashtag." *WIRED*, May 19, 2017. https://www.wired.com/2017/05/oral-history-hashtag/.

Pangle, Lorraine Smith. *Aristotle and the Philosophy of Friendship*. Cambridge, UK: Cambridge University Press, 2003.

Pardes, Arielle. "The Inside Story of Reddit's Redesign." *WIRED*, April 2, 2018. https://www.wired.com/story/reddit-redesign/.

Pariser, Eli. *The Filter Bubble: What the Internet Is Hiding from You*. New York: Penguin Press, 2011.

Park, Chang Sup. "Does Twitter Motivate Involvement in Politics? Tweeting, Opinion Leadership, and Political Engagement." *Computers in Human Behavior* 29, no. 4 (2013): 1641–48.

Parkinson, John. *Democracy and Public Space*. Oxford: Oxford University Press, 2012.

Pasquale, Frank. *The Black Box Society: The Secret Algorithms That Control Money and Information*. Cambridge, MA: Harvard University Press, 2015.

Pateman, Carole. *Participation and Democratic Theory*. Cambridge, UK: Cambridge University Press, 1970.

Pateman, Carole. "Participatory Democracy Revisited." *Perspectives on Politics* 10, no. 1 (2012): 7–19. https://doi.org/10.1017/S1537592711004877.

Payton, Michelle A., David C. Fulton, and Dorothy H. Anderson. "Influence of Place Attachment and Trust on Civic Action: A Study at Sherburne National Wildlife Refuge." *Society and Natural Resources* 18, no. 6 (2005): 511–28. https://doi.org/10.1080/08941920590947940.

Peattie, Lisa R. "Some Second Thoughts on Sites-and-Services." *Habitat International* 6, no. 1–2 (1982): 131–39.

Perez, Sarah. "Twitter Officially Expands Its Character Count to 280 Starting Today." *TechCrunch*, November 7, 2017. https://techcrunch.com/2017/11/07/twitter-officially-expands-its-character-count-to-280-starting-today/.

Peters, Jay. "Twitter to Introduce Clubhouse-like Voice Chat Rooms in Testing Later This Year." *The Verge*, November 17, 2020. https://www.theverge.com/2020/11/17/21570150/twitter-spaces-clubhouse-voice-rooms-testing.

Phua, Joe, Seunga Venus Jin, and Jihoon (Jay) Jay. "Uses and Gratifications of Social Networking Sites for Bridging and Bonding Social Capital: A Comparison of Facebook, Twitter, Instagram, and Snapchat." *Computers in Human Behavior* 72 (2017): 115–22. https://doi.org/10.1016/j.chb.2017.02.041.

Porter, Jon. "Twitter Is Making It Easier to Toggle between Latest and Top Tweets." *The Verge*, November 1, 2018. https://www.theverge.com/2018/11/1/18051200/twitter-chronological-timeline-toggle-test.

Postman, Neil. *Amusing Ourselves to Death: Public Discourse in the Age of Show Business*. New York: Penguin Books, 1985.

Pro_creator. "We Have a Racist User Problem and Reddit Won't Take Action." *Reddit, r/Blackladies*, August 25, 2014. https://www.reddit.com/r/blackladies/comments/2ejg1b/we_have_a_racist_user_problem_and_reddit_wont/.

Proferes, Nicholas. "Information Flow Solipsism in an Exploratory Study of Beliefs about Twitter." *Social Media + Society* 3, no. 1 (2017): 1–17. doi:10.1177/2056305117698493.

Proshansky, Harold M., Abbe K. Fabian, and Robert Kaminoff. "Place-Identity: Physical World Socialization of the Self." *Journal of Environmental Psychology* 3 (1983): 57–83.

Purdom, Clayton. "Reddit Gave Its Users Something to Fight Over besides Anime and Cucks." *The AV Club*, April 3, 2017. https://news.avclub.com/reddit-gave-its-users-something-to-fight-over-besides-a-1798259860.

Putnam, Robert D. "Bowling Alone: America's Declining Social Capital." *Journal of Democracy* 6, no. 1 (1995): 65–78.

Putnam, Robert D. *Bowling Alone: The Collapse and Revival of American Community*. New York: Simon & Schuster, 2000.

Putnam, Robert D. *Making Democracy Work: Civic Traditions in Modern Italy*. Princeton, NJ: Princeton University Press, 1993.

Quillian, Lincoln. "Prejudice as a Response to Perceived Group Threat: Population Composition and Anti-Immigrant and Racial Prejudice in Europe." *American Sociological Review* 60, no. 4 (1995): 586–611.

"R/TwoXChromosomes." *Reddit*, n.d. https://www.reddit.com/r/TwoXChromosomes/.

Rakhamimov, Daniel. "The Global Town Square." *Medium*, November 5, 2015. https://medium.com/swlh/twitter-rooms-e6f34e843e9a.

Read, Max. "Twitter Is a Mall, so It's Going to Regulate Itself like a Mall." *New York Magazine*, January 13, 2016. http://nymag.com/selectall/2016/01/twitter-is-a-mall.html.

Recuero, Raquel, Adriana Amaral, and Camila Monteiro. "Fandoms, Trending Topics and Social Capital in Twitter." *AoIR Selected Papers of Internet Research* 13 (2012): 1–14. https://spir.aoir.org/index.php/spir/article/view/7.

Reddit. "How Do I Delete a Community I've Created?" *Reddit Help*, n.d. https://www.https://reddit.zendesk.com/hc/en-us/articles/360043044052-How-do-I-delete-a-community-I-ve-created-.

Reddit. "Some of My Subreddits Keep Disappearing. Why?" *Reddit Help*, n.d. https://www.reddithelp.com/en/categories/using-reddit/frontpage-and-subscriptions/some-my-subreddits-keep-disappearing-why.

"Reddit by the Numbers." *Reddit*, 2018. https://www.redditinc.com.

Rheingold, Howard. *The Virtual Community: Homesteading on the Electronic Frontier*. Cambridge, MA: MIT Press, 2000.

Rhoades, Logan, and Adrian Carrasquillo. "How the Powerful #IfTheyGunnedMeDown Movement Changed the Conversation about Michael Brown's Death." *BuzzFeed News*, August 13, 2014. http://www.buzzfeed.com/mrloganrhoades/how-the-powerful-iftheygunnedmedown-movement-changed-the-con#.usV5n6N40.

Rhodes, Margaret. "Like Twitter but Hate the Trolls? Try Mastodon." *WIRED*, April 13, 2017. https://www.wired.com/2017/04/like-twitter-hate-trolls-try-mastodon.

Ritholtz, Barry. "How Twitter Is Becoming Your First Source of Investment News." *ABC News*, April 20, 2013. https://www.washingtonpost.com/business/how-twitter-is-becoming-your-first-source-of-investment-news/2013/04/19/19211044-a7b3-11e2-a8e2-5b98cb59187f_story.html.

Robertson, Adi. "Sen. Mark Warner Floats Major Tech Company Regulations That Don't Include Breakups." *The Verge*, July 30, 2018. https://www.theverge.com/2018/7/30/17629854/mark-warner-tech-company-legislation-white-paper-privacy-misinformation-competition.

Romano, Aja. "Reddit Just Banned One of Its Most Toxic Forums. But It Won't Touch The_Donald." *Vox*, November 13, 2017. https://www.vox.com/culture/2017/11/13/16624688/reddit-bans-incels-the-donald-controversy.

Roose, Kevin. "Behind the Velvet Ropes of Facebook's Private Groups." *New York Times*, July 16, 2017. https://www.nytimes.com/2017/07/16/business/behind-the-velvet-ropes-of-facebooks-private-groups.html.

Roose, Kevin. "Can Social Media Be Saved?" *New York Times*, March 28, 2018. https://www.nytimes.com/2018/03/28/technology/social-media-privacy.html.

Roose, Kevin. "The Making of a YouTube Radical." *New York Times*, June 8, 2019. https://www.nytimes.com/interactive/2019/06/08/technology/youtube-radical.html.

Roose, Kevin. "This Was the Alt-Right's Favorite Chat App. Then Came Charlottesville." *New York Times*, August 15, 2017. https://www.nytimes.com/2017/08/15/technology/discord-chat-app-alt-right.html.

Rosen, Aliza, and Ikuhiro Ihara. "Giving You More Characters to Express Yourself." *Twitter Blog*, September 26, 2017. https://blog.twitter.com/official/en_us/topics/product/2017/Giving-you-more-characters-to-express-yourself.html.

Rosenberg, Joe. "Interrobang." 99% Invisible, 2018. https://99percentinvisible.org/episode/interrobang/.

Rosenblum, Nancy L. *Good Neighbors: The Democracy of Everyday Life in America*. Princeton, NJ: Princeton University Press, 2016.

Rousseau, Jean-Jacques. *The Social Contract and Other Later Political Writings*. Edited and translated by Victor Gourevitch. Cambridge, UK: Cambridge University Press, 1997.

Rupp, Rebecca. "Surviving the Sneaky Psychology of Supermarkets." *National Geographic*, June 14, 2015. https://www.nationalgeographic.com/people-and-culture/food/the-plate/2015/06/15/surviving-the-sneaky-psychology-of-supermarkets/.

Samory, Mattia, and Tanushree Mitra. "Conspiracies Online: User Discussions in a Conspiracy Community Following Dramatic Events." In *Proceedings of the Twelfth International AAAI Conference on Web and Social Media (ICWSM 2018)*, 340–49. Stanford, CA: AAAI Publications, 2018.

Sampson, Robert J. "Neighborhood and Community: Collective Efficacy and Community Safety." *New Economy* 11 (2004): 106–13.

Sanders, Lynn M. "Against Deliberation." *Political Theory* 25, no. 3 (1997): 347–76.

Saxena, Aparajita. "Reddit Valued at $3 Billion after Raising $300 Million in Latest Funding Round." *Reuters*, February 11, 2019. https://www.reuters.com/article/us-reddit-funding/reddit-valued-at-3-billion-after-raising-300-million-in-latest-funding-round-idUSKCN1Q020W.

Scannell, Leila, and Robert Gifford. "The Relations between Natural and Civic Place Attachment and Pro-Environmental Behavior." *Journal of Environmental Psychology* 30, no. 3 (2010): 289–97. https://doi.org/10.1016/j.jenvp.2010.01.010.

Schattschneider, E. E. *The Semisovereign People: A Realist's View of Democracy in America*. Boston: Wadsworth, 1960.

Schneider, Nathan. "Here's My Plan to Save Twitter: Let's Buy It." *The Guardian*, September 29, 2016. https://www.theguardian.com/commentisfree/2016/sep/29/save-twitter-buy-platform-shared-ownership.

Scott, James C. *Seeing Like a State: How Certain Schemes to Improve the Human Condition Have Failed*. New Haven: Yale University Press, 1998.

Shakya, Holly B., and Nicholas A. Christakis. "Association of Facebook Use with Compromised Well-Being: A Longitudinal Study." *American Journal of Epidemiology* 185, no. 3 (2017): 203–11.

Shane-Simpson, Christina, Adriana Manago, Naomi Gaggi, and Kristen Gillespie-Lynch. "Why Do College Students Prefer Facebook, Twitter, or Instagram? Site Affordances, Tensions between Privacy and Self-Expression, and Implications for Social Capital." *Computers in Human Behavior* 86 (2018): 276–89. https://doi.org/10.1016/j.chb.2018.04.041.

Sherman, David K., and Geoffrey L. Cohen. "The Psychology of Self-Defense: Self-Affirmation Theory." *Advances in Experimental Social Psychology* 38 (2006): 183–242.

Shuffman56. "Reddit Goes Open Source." *Reddit Blog*, June 17, 2008. https://redditblog.com/2008/06/17/reddit-goes-open-source/.

Sifry, Micah L. "Learning from the Civic Tech Graveyard." *Civicist*, October 1, 2018. https://civichall.org/civicist/civic-tech-graveyard/.

Silverman, Craig. "How the Bizarre Conspiracy Theory behind 'Pizzagate' Was Spread." *BuzzFeed News*, November 4, 2016. https://www.buzzfeed.com/craigsilverman/fever-swamp-election.

simbawulf. "Comment on 'Introducing r/Popular.'" *Reddit, r/Announcements*, February 15, 2017. https://www.reddit.com/r/announcements/comments/5u9pl5/introducing_rpopular/ddsczx1/.

simbawulf. "Introducing r/Popular." *Reddit, r/Announcements*, February 15, 2017. https://www.reddit.com/r/announcements/comments/5u9pl5/introducing_rpopular/.

Singer, Abraham A. *The Form of the Firm: A Normative Political Theory of the Corporation*. New York: Oxford University Press, 2018.

Singleton, Sara, and Michael Taylor. "Common Property, Collective Action and Community." *Journal of Theoretical Politics* 4, no. 3 (1992): 309–15.

Skoric, Marko M., Deborah Ying, and Ying Ng. "Bowling Online, Not Alone: Online Social Capital and Political Participation in Singapore." *Journal of Computer-Mediated Communication* 14, no. 2 (2009): 414–33.

Slawson, Nicola. "Faceblock Campaign Urges Users to Boycott Facebook for a Day." *The Guardian*, April 7, 2018. https://www.theguardian.com/technology/2018/apr/07/faceblock-campaign-urges-users-boycott-facebook-for-one-day-protest-cambridge-analytica-scandal.

Smith, Aaron. "Many Facebook Users Don't Understand How the Site's News Feed Works." *Pew Research Center*, September 5, 2018. https://www.pewresearch.org/fact-tank/2018/09/05/many-facebook-users-dont-understand-how-the-sites-news-feed-works/.

Smith, Naomi, and Peter Walters. "Desire Lines and Defensive Architecture in Modern Urban Environments." *Urban Studies* 55, no. 13 (2018): 2980–95.

Song, Hayeon, Anne Zmyslinski-Seeling, Jinyoung Kim, Adam Drent, Angela Victor, Kikuko Omori, and Mike Allen. "Does Facebook Make You Lonely? A Meta Analysis." *Computers in Human Behavior* 36 (2014): 446–52.

Sorgatz, Rex. "Twitter Should Have Groups and Here Is How They Should Work." *Medium*, February 20, 2019. https://medium.com/@rexsorgatz/twitter-groups-hashtags-5932bb54e27c.

Spez. "Let's All Have a Town Hall about r/All." *Reddit, r/Announcements*, June 16, 2016. https://www.reddit.com/r/announcements/comments/4oedco/lets_all_have_a_town_hall_about_rall/.

Stack, Liam. "Facebook Announces New Policy to Ban White Nationalist Content." *New York Times*, March 27, 2019. https://www.nytimes.com/2019/03/27/business/facebook-white-nationalist-supremacist.html.

Statt, Nick. "Facebook Bug Accidentally Shows You How Popular Your Posts Are." *The Verge*, October 15, 2015. https://www.theverge.com/2015/10/14/9535243/facebook-bug-accidentally-shows-user-view-counts.

Statt, Nick. "Twitter's Disappearing Tweets, Called Fleets, Are Now Available for Everyone." *The Verge*, November 17, 2020. https://www.theverge.com/2020/11/17/21570368/twitter-fleets-disapeating-tweets-stories-launch-available-now.

Statz, Pamela. "Facebook Faces Backlash." *WIRED*, September 6, 2006. https://www.wired.com/2006/09/facebook-faces-backlash/.

Steinfield, Charles, Nicole B. Ellison, and Cliff Lampe. "Social Capital, Self-Esteem, and Use of Online Social Network Sites: A Longitudinal Analysis." *Journal of Applied Developmental Psychology* 29, no. 6 (2008): 434–45.

Stroud, Natalie Jomini. "Media Use and Political Predispositions: Revisiting the Concept of Selective Exposure." *Political Behavior* 30, no. 3 (2008): 341–66.

Sullivan, Gail. "How Facebook and Twitter Control What You See about Ferguson." *Washington Post*, August 19, 2014. https://www.washingtonpost.com/news/morning-mix/wp/2014/08/19/how-facebook-and-twitter-control-what-you-see-about-ferguson/.

Sunstein, Cass R. *#Republic: Divided Democracy in the Age of Social Media*. Princeton, NJ: Princeton University Press, 2017.

Taber, Charles S., and Milton Lodge. "Motivated Skepticism in the Evaluation of Political Beliefs." *American Journal of Political Science* 50, no. 3 (2006): 755–69.

Talen, Emily. "The Social Goals of New Urbanism." *Housing Policy Debate* 13, no. 1 (2002): 165–88.

Tambini, Damian. "New Media and Democracy." *New Media and Society* 1, no. 3 (1999): 305–29.

Tan, Chenhao, and Lillian Lee. "All Who Wander: On the Prevalence and Characteristics of Multi-Community Engagement." In *Proceedings of the 24th International Conference on World Wide Web*, 1056–66. Geneva: International World Wide Web Conferences Steering Committee, 2015.

Taplin, Jonathan. *Move Fast and Break Things: How Facebook, Google, and Amazon Cornered Culture and Undermined Democracy*. New York: Back Bay Books, 2018.

Thats_not_marxist. "We Are Working with CivilServant to Better Your Sub Experience." *Reddit, r/Feminism*, April 2018. https://www.reddit.com/r/Feminism/comments/8cozom/we_are_working_with_civilservant_to_better_your/.

Thekinrar. "Mastodon Instances." Accessed July 12, 2018. https://instances.social/list/advanced.

Theocharis, Yannis, Will Lowe, Jan W. van Deth, and Gema García-Albacete. "Using Twitter to Mobilize Protest Action: Online Mobilization Patterns and Action Repertoires in the Occupy Wall Street, Indignados, and Aganaktismenoi Movements." *Information, Communication and Society* 18, no. 2 (2014): 202–20.

Tiffany, Kaitlyn. "Reddit Is Finally Facing Its Legacy of Racism." *The Atlantic*, June 12, 2020. https://www.theatlantic.com/technology/archive/2020/06/reddit-racism-open-letter/612958/.

Tobin, Ariana, and Jeremy B. Merrill. "Facebook Is Letting Job Advertisers Target Only Men." *ProPublica*, September 18, 2018. https://www.propublica.org/article/facebook-is-letting-job-advertisers-target-only-men.

Tocqueville, Alexis de. *Democracy in America*. Edited by J. P. Mayer. Translated by George Lawrence. New York: HarperPerennial Modern Classics, 1969.

Tufekci, Zeynep. *Twitter and Tear Gas: The Power and Fragility of Networked Protest*. New Haven: Yale University Press, 2017.

Tufekci, Zeynep. "We Already Know How to Protect Ourselves from Facebook." *New York Times*, April 9, 2018. https://www.nytimes.com/2018/04/09/opinion/zuckerberg-testify-congress.html.

Tufekci, Zeynep. "Why Zuckerberg's 14-Year Apology Tour Hasn't Fixed Facebook." *WIRED*, April 6, 2018. https://www.wired.com/story/why-zuckerberg-15-year-apology-tour-hasnt-fixed-facebook/.

Tufekci, Zeynep. "YouTube, the Great Radicalizer." *New York Times*, March 10, 2018. https://www.nytimes.com/2018/03/10/opinion/sunday/youtube-politics-radical.html.

Tufekci, Zeynep. "YouTube Has a Video for That." *Scientific American*, April 2019. https://www.scientificamerican.com/article/youtubes-recommendation-algorithm-has-a-dark-side/.

Turkle, Sherry. *Alone Together: Why We Expect More from Technology and Less from Each Other*. New York: Basic Books, 2011.

Turner, John F. C. "Housing as a Verb." In *Freedom to Build: Dweller Control of the Housing Process*, edited by John F. C. Turner and Robert Fichter, 148–75. New York: Macmillan, 1972.

Twenge, Jean M., Thomas E. Joiner, Megan L. Rogers, and Gabrielle N. Martin. "Increases in Depressive Symptoms, Suicide-Related Outcomes, and Suicide Rates Among U.S. Adolescents after 2010 and Links to Increased New Media Screen Time." *Clinical Psychological Science* 6, no. 1 (2018): 3–17.

Twigger-Ross, Clare L., and David L. Uzzell. "Place and Identity Processes." *Journal of Environmental Psychology* 16 (1996): 205–20. https://doi.org/10.1006/jevp.1996.0017.

Twitter. "About Spaces on Twitter," n.d. https://help.twitter.com/en/using-twitter/spaces.

U/[deleted]. "TwoXChromosomes Is on TLDR, the Blog for NPR's Program, on the Media Talking about Becoming a Default Subreddit." *Reddit, r/TwoXChromosomes,* 2014. https://www.reddit.com/r/TwoXChromosomes/comments/25yvyc/twoxchromosomes_is_on_tldr_the_blog_for_nprs/.

Vaidhyanathan, Siva. *Antisocial Media: How Facebook Disconnects Us and Undermines Democracy.* New York: Oxford University Press, 2018.

Van Valkenburgh, Shawn P. "Digesting the Red Pill: Masculinity and Neoliberalism in the Manosphere." *Men and Masculinities* 24, no. 1 (2018): 1–20.

Vanman, Eric J., Rosemary Baker, and Stephanie J. Tobin. "The Burden of Online Friends: The Effects of Giving Up Facebook on Stress and Well-Being." *Journal of Social Psychology* 158, no. 4 (2018): 496–508.

Vargo, Chris J., Lei Guo, and Michelle A. Amazeen. "The Agenda-Setting Power of Fake News: A Big Data Analysis of the Online Media Landscape from 2014 to 2016." *New Media and Society* 20, no. 3 (2018): 2028–49.

Verduyn, Philippe, David Seungjae Lee, Jiyoung Park, Holly Shablack, Ariana Orvell, Joseph Bayer, Oscar Ybarra, John Jonides, and Ethan Kross. "Passive Facebook Usage Undermines Affective Well-Being: Experimental and Longitudinal Evidence." *Journal of Experimental Psychology* 144, no. 2 (2015): 480–88.

Villa, Dana. *Public Freedom*. Princeton, NJ: Princeton University Press, 2008.

Vitak, Jessica, Nicole B. Ellison, and Charles Steinfield. "The Ties That Bond: Re-Examining the Relationship between Facebook Use and Bonding Social Capital." In *Proceedings of the 44th Hawaii International Conference on System Sciences,* 1530–605. Piscataway, NJ: IEEE, 2011.

Vitruvius. *The Ten Books on Architecture*. Translated by Morris Hicky Morgan. Cambridge, MA: Harvard University Press, 1914.

Vrechopoulos, Adam P., Robert M. O'Keefe, Georgios I. Doukidis, and George J. Siomkos. "Virtual Store Layout: An Experimental Comparison in the Context of Grocery Retail." *Journal of Retailing* 80, no. 1 (2004): 13–22.

Wagner, Kurt. "Reddit Raised $200 Million in Funding and Is Now Valued at $1.8 Billion." *Recode,* July 31, 2017. https://www.recode.net/2017/7/31/16037126/reddit-funding-200-million-valuation-steve-huffman-alexis-ohanian.

Waller, Isaac, and Ashton Anderson. "Generalists and Specialists: Using Community Embeddings to Quantify Activity Diversity in Online Platforms." In *Proceedings of the 2019 World Wide Web Conference,* 1954–64. New York: ACM, 2019.

Wamsley, Laurel. "As Facebook Shows Its Flaws, What Might a Better Social Network Look Like?" *NPR: The Two-Way,* May 1, 2018. https://www.npr.org/sections/thetwo-way/2018/05/01/607361849/as-facebook-shows-its-flaws-what-might-a-better-social-network-look-like.

Warren, Mark E., and Jane Mansbridge. "Deliberative Negotiation." In *Negotiating Agreement in Politics,* edited by Jane Mansbridge and Cathie Jo Martin, 86–120. Washington, DC: American Political Science Association, 2013.

Weaver, Russell. "A Cross-Level Exploratory Analysis of 'Neighborhood Effects' on Urban Behavior: An Evolutionary Perspective." *Social Sciences* 4 (2015): 1046–66.

Wellman, Barry, Anabel Quan-Haase, Jeffrey Boase, Wenhong Chen, Keith Hampton, Isabel Díaz, and Kakuko Miyata. "The Social Affordances of the Internet for Networked Individualism." *Journal of Computer-Mediated Communication* 8, no. 3 (2003). https://doi.org/10.1111/j.1083-6101.2003.tb00216.x.

Welser, Howard T., Dan Cosley, Gueorgi Kossinets, Austin Lin, Fedor Dokshin, Geri Gay, and Marc Smith. "Finding Social Roles in Wikipedia." In *Proceedings of the 2011 iConference,* 122–29. Seattle, WA: ACM, 2011. https://doi.org/10.1145/1940761.1940778.

Wilhelm, Alex. "How Reddit Turned One Congressional Candidate's Campaign Upside Down." *The Next Web,* January 16, 2012. https://thenextweb.com/socialmedia/2012/01/17/how-reddit-turned-one-congressional-candidates-campaign-upside-down/.

Williams, Dmitri. "The Impact of Time Online: Social Capital and Cyberbalkanization." *CyberPsychology and Behavior* 8 (2007): 580–84.

WIRED Staff. "Mark Zuckerberg's Letter to Investors: 'The Hacker Way.'" *WIRED*, February 1, 2012. https://www.wired.com/2012/02/zuck-letter/.

Withagen, Rob, Harjo J. de Poel, Duarte Araújo, and Gert-Jan Pepping. "Affordances Can Invite Behavior: Reconsidering the Relationship between Affordances and Agency." *New Ideas in Psychology* 30 (2012): 250–58.

Wonneberger, Anke, Iina R. Hellsten, and Sandra H. J. Jacobs. "Hashtag Activism and the Configuration of Counterpublics: Dutch Animal Welfare Debates on Twitter." *Information, Communication and Society* 24, no. 12 (2021): 1694–711. https://doi.org/10.1080/1369118X.2020.1720770.

Wood, Lisa, Tya Shannon, Max Bulsara, Terri Pikora, Gavin McCormack, and Billie Giles-Corti. "The Anatomy of the Safe and Social Suburb: An Exploratory Study of the Built Environment, Social Capital and Residents' Perceptions of Safety." *Health and Place* 14 (2008): 15–31.

Workman, Hallie. "Formation of Safe Spaces in Gendered Online Communities: Reddit and 'the Front Page of the Internet.'" Ft. Worth: Texas Christian University, 2014.

Wright, Frank Lloyd. *An Organic Architecture: The Architecture of Democracy*. Cambridge, MA: MIT Press, 1970.

Wright, Frank Lloyd. *The Living City*. New York: Horizon Press, 1958.

Wright, Scott. "From 'Third Place' to 'Third Space': Everyday Political Talk in Non-Political Online Spaces." *Javnost—The Public* 19, no. 3 (2012): 5–20.

Yack, Bernard. *The Problems of a Political Animal: Community, Justice, and Conflict in Aristotelian Political Thought*. Berkeley: University of California Press, 1993.

yawkat. "Comment on 'How Does "Hot" vs "Best" vs "controversial" vs "Rising" Work? Is the Algorithm Known, and Does It Depend on Engagement with a Sub, as Opposed to Simply Whether You Are Apart of It or Not?.'" *Reddit, r/TheoryofReddit*, May 17, 2019. https://www.reddit.com/r/TheoryOfReddit/comments/bpmd3x/how_does_hot_vs_best_vscontroversial_vs_rising/envijlj/.

Young, Iris Marion. "Activist Challenges to Deliberative Democracy." *Political Theory* 29, no. 5 (2001): 670–90.

Young, Iris Marion. *Justice and the Politics of Difference*. Princeton, NJ: Princeton University Press, 1990.

Zannettou, Savvas, Tristan Caulfield, Emiliano De Cristofaro, Nicholas Kourtellis, Ilias Leontiadis, Michael Srivianos, Gianluca Stringhini, and Jeremy Blackburn. "The Web Centipede: Understanding How Web Communities Influence Each Other through the Lens of Mainstream and Alternative News Sources." In *Proceedings of the 2017 Internet Measurement Conference*, 405–17. London: ACM Press, 2017.

Zax, David. "#BLACKandSTEM: The Hashtag as Community." *Fast Company*, March 4, 2014. https://www.fastcompany.com/3027122/blackandstem-the-hashtag-as-community.

Zhao, Dingxin. "Ecologies of Social Movements: Student Mobilization during the 1989 Prodemocracy Movement in Beijing." *American Journal of Sociology* 103, no. 6 (1998): 1493–529. https://doi.org/10.1086/231399.

Zignani, Matteo, Sabrina Gaito, and Gian Paolo Rossi. "Follow the 'Mastodon': Structure and Evolution of a Decentralized Online Social Network." In *Proceedings of the Twelfth International AAAI Conference on Web and Social Media (ICWSM 2018)*, 541–50. n.p.: AAAI Publications, 2018.

Zignani, Matteo, Christian Quadri, Sabrina Gaito, Hocine Cherifi, and Gian Paolo Rossi. "The Footprints of a 'Mastodon': How a Decentralized Architecture Influences Online Social Relationships." In *Proceedings of the 2019 IEEE Conference on Computer Communications Workshops*, 472–77. Piscataway NJ: IEEE, 2019.

Zuckerberg, Mark. "A Privacy-Focused Vision for Social Networking." *Facebook*, March 6, 2019. https://www.facebook.com/notes/mark-zuckerberg/a-privacy-focused-vision-for-social-networking/10156700570096634/.

Zuckerberg, Mark. "Bringing the World Closer Together." *Facebook*, June 22, 2017. https://www.facebook.com/zuck/posts/10154944663901634.

Zuckerberg, Mark. "Building Global Community." *Facebook,* February 16, 2017. https://www.facebook.com/notes/mark-zuckerberg/building-global-community/10154544292806634/.

Zuckerman, Ethan. "Facebook Only Cares about Facebook." *The Atlantic,* January 27, 2018. https://www.theatlantic.com/technology/archive/2018/01/facebook-doesnt-care/551684/.

Zuckerman, Ethan. "The Case for a Taxpayer-Supported Version of Facebook." *The Atlantic,* May 7, 2017. https://www.theatlantic.com/technology/archive/2017/05/the-case-for-a-taxpayer-supported-version-of-facebook/524037/.

Zuckerman, Ethan. "The Case for Digital Public Infrastructure." *Knight First Amendment Institute at Columbia University,* January 17, 2020. https://knightcolumbia.org/content/the-case-for-digital-public-infrastructure.

Zuckerman, Ethan. "Who Filters Your News? Why We Built Gobo.Social." *Medium: MIT Media Lab,* November 16, 2017. https://medium.com/mit-media-lab/who-filters-your-news-why-we-built-gobo-social-bfa6748b5944.

Index